SHORTLIST

New York
2007
WHAT'S NEW | WHAT'S ON | WHAT'S NEXT

www.timeout.com/newyork

New York

Contents

New York by Area

Essentials

Published by Time Out Guides Ltd
Universal House
251 Tottenham Court Road
London W1T 7AB
Tel: + 44 (0)20 7813 3000
Fax: + 44 (0)20 7813 6001
Email: guides@timeout.com
www.timeout.com

Editorial/Managing Director Peter Fiennes
Series Editor Ruth Jarvis
Deputy Series Editor Lesley McCave
Business Manager Gareth Garner
Guides Co-ordinator Holly Pick
Accountant Kemi Olufuwa

Time Out Guides is a wholly owned subsidary of Time Out Group Ltd.

© Time Out Group Ltd
Chairman Tony Elliott
Managing Director Mike Hardwick
Financial Director Richard Waterlow
Time Out Magazine Ltd MD David Pepper
Group General Manager/Director Nichola Coulthard
Time Out Communications Ltd MD David Pepper
Production Director Mark Lamond
Group Marketing Director John Luck
Group Art Director John Oakey
Group IT Director Simon Chappell

Time Out and the Time Out logo are trademarks of Time Out Group Ltd.

This edition first published in Great Britain in 2006 by Ebury Publishing

Ebury Publishing is a division of The Random House Group Ltd
Company information can be found on www.randomhouse.co.uk
10 9 8 7 6 5 4 3 2 1

Distributed in USA by Publishers Group West (www.pgw.com)
Distributed in Canada by Publishers Group Canada (www.pgcbooks.ca)
For further distribution details, see www.timeout.com

ISBN To 31 December 2006: 1-904978-77-0. From 1 January 2007: 9781904978770

A CIP catalogue record for this book is available from the British Library

Colour reprographics by Wyndeham Icon, 3 & 4 Maverton Road, London E3 2JE

Printed and bound in Germany by Appl

Papers used by Ebury Publishing are natural, recyclable products made from wood
grown in sustainable forests

New York Shortlist

The **Time Out New York Shortlist 2007** is one of a new series of annual guides that draws on Time Out's background as a magazine publisher to keep you current with everything that's going on in town. As well as New York's classic sights and the best of its eating, drinking and entertainment, the guide picks out the most exciting venues to have opened in the last year, and gives a full calendar of events for September 2006 to December 2007. It also includes features on the important news, trends and openings, all compiled by locally based editors and writers. Whether you're visiting for the first time in your life or just the first time since 2006, you'll find the *Time Out New York Shortlist 2007* contains everything you need to know, in a portable and easy-to-use format. Pick up a copy of *Time Out New York*, the city's definitive weekly listings magazine, and you'll be impeccably informed.

The guide divides Manhattan into Downtown, Midtown and Uptown chapters, each of which contains listings for Sights & museums, Eating & drinking, Shopping, Nightlife and Arts & leisure, along with maps marking all their locations. At the front of the book are chapters rounding up each of these scenes city-wide, and giving a Shortlist of our overall picks in a variety of categories. We also include itineraries for days out, and essentials including transport information and hotels.

Our listings use phone numbers as dialled locally from within the United States. Within New York you need to use the initial 1 and three-digit area code even if you're calling from within that same area code. To call a venue from abroad, use your country's exit code followed by the number given (the initial 1 is the US's country code).

We have given price categories by using one to four dollar signs ($-$$$$), representing budget, moderate, expensive and luxury. Major credit cards are accepted unless otherwise stated. We also indicate when a venue is NEW , and give **Event highlights**.

All our listings are double-checked but businesses do sometimes close or change their hours or prices, so it's a good idea to call a venue before visiting. While every effort has been made to ensure accuracy, the publishers cannot accept responsibility for any errors this guide may contain.

Venues are marked on the maps using symbols numbered according to their order within the chapter and colour-coded by venue type:

❶ Sights & museums
❶ Eating & drinking
❶ Shopping
❶ Nightlife
❶ Arts & leisure

SHORTLIST
Online

The *Time Out New York Shortlist 2007* is as up to date as it is possible for a printed guidebook to be. And to keep it completely current, it has a regularly updated online companion, at **www.timeout.com/newyork**. Here you'll find news of the latest openings and exhibitions, as well as picks from visitors and residents – ideal for planning a trip. Time Out is the city specialist, so you'll also find travel information for more than 100 cities worldwide on our site, at www.timeout.com/travel.

Time Out New York Shortlist 2007

EDITORIAL
Editor Keith Mulvihill
Copy Editors Ruth Jarvis, Lisa Ritchie
Proofreader Patrick Mulkern

STUDIO
Art Director Scott Moore
Art Editor Pinelope Kourmouzoglou
Senior Designer Josephine Spencer
Graphic Designer Henry Elphick
Digital Imaging Dan Conway
Ad Make-up Jenni Prichard
Picture Editor Jael Marschner
Deputy Picture Editor Tracey Kerrigan
Picture Researcher Helen McFarland

ADVERTISING
Sales Director/Sponsorship Mark Phillips
International Sales Manager Ross Canadé
International Sales Executive
  Simon Davies
Advertising Sales Siobhan Shea Rossi
Advertising Assistant Kate Staddon

MARKETING
Marketing Manager Yvonne Poon
Marketing & Publicity Manager, US
  Rosella Albanese
Marketing Designer Anthony Huggins

PRODUCTION
Production Manager Brendan McKeown
Production Co-ordinator Caroline Bradford

CONTRIBUTORS
James Oliver Cury, Brian Gempp, Clare Lambe, Keith Mulvihill, Pablito Nash, Jay Ruttenberg, Steven Smith, Bruce Tantum, Elisabeth Vincentelli.

PHOTOGRAPHY
All photography by Alys Tomlinson, except: pages 2 (bottom left), 25, 29 Paul Kolnik; pages 13, 18, 20, 52, 93, 98, 116, 117, 158 Sarina Finkelstein; pages 16, 17 Talia Simhi; page 30 Rex Features; page 36 courtesy of Rockefeller Centre; page 44 Michael Ficeto/Hearst Corporation; page 119 Nick Himmel; page 131 James Edstrom. The following images were provided by the featured establishments/artists: pages 8, 11, 66, 180.
Cover photograph: Guggenheim Museum. Credit: Imagestate.

MAPS
JS Graphics (john@jsgraphics.co.uk).

Thanks to Elizabeth Barr, Brian Fiske, Chad Frade, Eric Medelsohn, Amy Plitt, Patrick Welch and all the contributors to past editions of the *Time Out New York Guide*.

About Time Out

Founded in 1968, Time Out has expanded from humble London beginnings into the leading resource for those wanting to know what's happening in the world's greatest cities. As well as our influential what's-on weeklies in London, New York and Chicago, we publish more than a dozen other listings magazines in cities as varied as Beijing, Beirut and Mumbai. The magazines established Time Out's trademark style: sharp writing, informed reviewing and bang up-to-date inside knowledge of every scene.

Time Out made the natural leap into travel guides in the 1980s with the City Guide series, which now extends to over 50 destinations around the world. Written and researched by expert local writers and generously illustrated with original photography, the full-size guides cover a larger area than our Shortlist guides and include many more venue reviews, along with additional background features and a full set of maps.

Throughout this rapid growth, the company has remained proudly independent, still owned by Tony Elliott nearly four decades after he started Time Out London as a single fold-out sheet of A5 paper. This independence extends to the editorial content of all our publications, this Shortlist included. No establishment has been featured because it has advertised, and no payment has influenced any of our reviews. And, for our critics, there's definitely no such thing as a free lunch: all restaurants and bars are visited and reviewed anonymously, and Time Out always picks up the bill. For more about the company, see www.timeout.com.

Don't Miss
2007

American Museum of Natural History p12

American Museum of Natural History p12

WHAT'S NEW
Sights & Museums

If there is one truism about this town it's this: New York has to be seen to be believed. Manhattan offers a sparkling array of art, architecture, culture and history – all crammed on to one small stretch of island. We mean it when we say that there are literally *hundreds* of things to see and do – and in 2007 that list will grow even longer.

Sights

More than five years after 9/11, Ground Zero, the former site of the World Trade Center towers, continues to draw hundreds of visitors – especially on sunny weekends. Unfortunately, because of political infighting, the projected 1,776-foot-tall Freedom Tower is slow going and remains a hole in the ground, but the 'Pit', as it was called during the heroic rescue operation after the attack is itself a moving tribute to the 2,749 lives

lost. Still, there is hope: two years after the cornerstone was laid, construction workers have begun to clear away rock and make way for the foundation. Work will soon be under way on another highly anticipated project: Santiago Calatrava's World Trade Center PATH Station. With its wing-shaped rooftop, it will alight like a dove of peace near the 9/11 memorial plaza, while 30 feet below street level, a meditative grotto, *Reflecting Absence*, will comprise two pools that fill the original footprints of the twin towers. Incredibly, it was recently announced that the cost of the World Trade Center memorial and its associated projects – a museum, a welcome centre and an arts centre – could be as high as $1 billion.

On the brighter (and greener) side, a considerably smaller design project has been completed in

Central Park. After an extensive, year-long, $3.5 million renovation of the city's largest and oldest playground, the Heckscher (located in the south-west quadrant of Central Park) is back in action. Of note are the restored space-age climbing structures replete with sprinklers and shallow canals designed in the 1970s by famed playground architect Richard Dattner.

If you've set your sights on loftier pursuits, look no further than the recently reopened Top of the Rock observation deck, perched on Midtown's 30 Rockefeller Center. Completed in 1933, the monumental building is the crown jewel in one of the country's most significant (and copied) urban design projects. One of the most impressive elements of the art deco tower – its stunning observation decks, with unparalleled 360-degree views of Manhattan – was declared off-limits in 1986, when another landmark, the glamorous Rainbow Room on the 65th floor, underwent a renovation and expansion, cutting off access to the roof. Now, 20 years later, the observatory, which occupies the 67th to 70th floors, is waiting to dazzle you.

Museums

Art connoisseurs who have toured Paris, Rome or London may argue about New York's position in the world's rankings, but one thing is beyond dispute: Manhattan's museums offer something for everyone, from old masters at the Frick Collection to mummies at the Metropolitan Museum of Art (which locals simply call the Met).

The big news in 2007 is the return of an old friend, the Morgan Library, which had shut its doors for three years and embarked on its largest growth spurt since 1928. (The Morgan Library was originally

SHORTLIST

Best new
- Morgan Library (p109)
- New Museum of Contemporary Art (p66)

Best for hipsters
- Whitney Museum of American Art (p145)
- Washington Square Park (p89)
- Museum of Modern Art (MoMA) (p123)
- PS 1 Contemporary Art Center (p165)

Best green scene
- Central Park (p136)
- The Cloisters (p157)
- New York Botanical Garden (p161)

Best Americana
- Statue of Liberty (p62)
- Ellis Island Immigration Museum (p62)
- Coney Island (p163)

Best free
- Staten Island Ferry (p62)
- Walk across Brooklyn Bridge (p55)

Best view
- Top of the Rock (p125)
- Empire State Building (p122)
- Circle Line Cruises (p129)

Best Olde NYC
- Lower East Side Tenement Museum (p76)
- Fraunces Tavern Museum (p55)

Best relics
- American Museum of Natural History (p149)
- Metropolitan Museum of Art (p144)

Best super cheap
- TKTS (p116)
- Friedsam Memorial Carousel in Central Park (p137)

coffee from the airport where you left your wallet: £1

(still getting six nonstop hours of sleep: priceless)

©2006 MasterCard International Incorporated

Don't worry. MasterCard Global Service™ is available wherever you travel, in any language you speak. So just call the local toll-free number and we'll rush you a new card most anywhere in the world. For a complete list of toll-free numbers, go to www.mastercard.com.

AUSTRALIA	1800-120-113	ITALY	800-870-866
BRAZIL	0800-891-3294	MEXICO	001-800-307-7309
CANADA	1-800-307-7309	PUERTO RICO	1-800-307-7309
FRANCE	0-800-90-1387	SPAIN	900-97-1231
GERMANY	0800-819-1040	UK	0800-96-4767
HONG KONG	800-966677	USA	1-800-307-7309

From all other countries call collect:
1-636-722-7111

there are some things money can't buy. for peace of mind there's MasterCard®

commissioned by rich man Pierpont Morgan, father of JP, to house his growing collection of rare books, manuscripts and artworks.) The expanded museum, designed by Pritzker Prize-winning architect Renzo Piano, has doubled the amount of exhibition space and added a number of new amenities to the old complex's three buildings. Let's be frank here: the Morgan is not the Met or the Museum of Modern Art (MoMA), but its homey atmosphere, small, easily digestible galleries, unusual artworks (ancient Mesopotamian seals, anyone?) and historical display of Pierpont's personal library make it a rare treat. 'People have long felt it is a very special place in New York, where objects of great quality can be viewed in an intimate setting,' says director of communications Patrick Milliman. 'We haven't changed that with the expansion. Our galleries are still relatively small and intimate, but we have more of them.'

Indeed, the Morgan seems to be making a bid to be taken seriously as a major cultural attraction, not merely the preserve of scholars, or locals who like to wander off the beaten art track. Thanks to the expansion, the museum will now be able to display more of its 350,000 objects than ever before, and the opening shows impressively mine those treasures. You'll be able to drawings by Michelangelo, Rembrandt and Picasso; a first edition of Malory's King Arthur tales from 1485; a copy of *Frankenstein* annotated by Mary Shelley herself; manuscripts by Dickens, Poe, Twain, Steinbeck and Wilde; and sheet-music drafts by the likes of Beethoven and Mozart.

If it's contemporary art you crave, the most highly anticipated opening this year will undoubtedly be the christening of the New Museum of Contemporary Art's stunning new digs on the Lower East Side (p66).

This year business as usual at Manhattan's esteemed cultural institutions includes dozens of exciting new exhibitions. MoMA will feature 'Édouard Manet and *The Execution of Maximilian*' from 5 November 2006 to January 2007 and a retrospective, 'Richard Serra: 40 Years', opens in the summer.

Top of the Rock p9

Museum of Modern Art p11

Covering two million square feet, the Met is the city's largest museum. In 2007 look for crowd-pleasing shows like 'Barcelona and Modernity: Gaudi to Dali' from 7 March to 3 June, and 'Venice and the Islamic World, 828-1797' from 27 March to 8 July. Like many of the well-heeled grandes dames residing in Manhattan, the Met has recently had a facelift – after a four-year cleaning operation, the 105-year old façade on Fifth Avenue sparkles like new. Just across Central Park, another diva, the American Museum of Natural History, is also undergoing a nip and tuck. But don't let the $37 million restoration of the romanesque revival façade facing 77th Street stop you from venturing in to see 'Gold' from November 2006 to 19 August 2007 or 'Mythic Beasts' from May 2007 to January 2008.

Keep in mind that visiting several venues in a single day can be exhausting. Similarly, it's self-defeating to attempt to hit all the major collections during one visit

to an institution as large as the Met or the American Museum of Natural History. So plan, pace yourself, and don't forget to eat: a host of excellent museum cafés and restaurants afford convenient breaks. Delicious refuelling spots include Sarabeth's at the Whitney Museum of American Art (where you can also check out 'Picasso and American Art' from 28 September 2006 to 28 January 2007); the elegant Café Sabarsky at the Neue Galerie; the Jewish Museum's Café Weissman; and a more formal option, the recently opened Modern (p126) at MoMA.

Brace yourself for the local admission prices; they can be steep (tickets to the recently renovated MoMA cost $20 per adult). This is because most of the city's museums are privately funded and receive little or no government support. Even so, many of them, including MoMA, the Whitney and the Guggenheim Museum, offer at least one evening a week when admission fees are either waived or switched to a voluntary donation. Most museums also offer discounts to students and senior citizens with valid IDs. And although the Met suggests a $12 donation for adults, you can pay what you wish any time you visit.

Most New York museums are closed on major US holidays. Nevertheless, some institutions are open on certain Monday holidays, such as Columbus Day and Presidents' Day.

Security remains tight. Guards at all public institutions will ask you to open your purse or backpack for inspection; umbrellas and any large bags must be left (free of charge) in a cloakroom. Most museums are accessible to people with disabilities and furnish free wheelchairs.

Buddha Bar

Eating & Drinking

N ew York City has more than 23,000 restaurants, bars and cafés, so we can include only a sampling of all the great eats it has to offer in this guide. Still, we tried to squeeze in some of the hot new stuff without overlooking some of the tried-and-true establishments that New Yorkers love.

The food chain

In New York, knowing where to dine is a mark of honour. And keeping up with restaurant trends is the local pastime, no matter what budget you have. The problem is: there are too many trends. And they change so damn fast.

For more than a year, giant fancy Japanese restaurants were all the rage; Megu Midtown (p134), Matsuri

and En Japanese Brasserie (p94) were a fraction of the cavernous places that suddenly paired rare sake lists with exotic delicacies beyond the usual kobe beef and blowfish. In the past year, except for the stunning new Buddha Bar (p92), the Asian focus has largely shifted to China. Among the noteworthy additions: a former Mr Chow chef opened Philippe in Midtown (33 E 60th Street, between Park & Madison Avenues, 1-212 644 8885), Stephen Starr opened Buddakan in the Meatpacking District (75 Ninth Avenue, between 15th & 16th Streets, 1-212 989 6699), Lulzim Rexhepi (Citarella, Kittichai) unveiled Xing (p130) in Hell's Kitchen, and organic eaterie Ginger (p146) won the latest *Time*

Out New York Readers' Choice Eat Out award for best new Upper East Sider. Without a doubt, Chinese is no longer just for take out.

While some big splashy new Japanese eateries, like Morimoro and Nobu 57, did get attention – often for their slick design – it was the small sushi sultans whose food stood out most. Naka Naka (p106), Le Miu and Oga attracted legions of fans... or at least as many as could pack into their limited space.

Another odd flip-flop: barbecue joints, which were smokin' hot last year, have fizzled a bit. Three pretty good ones burned out fast: Smoked, RIB and Maroons Smoke Shack. In their place, so it seems, are *churrascarias* from Brazil and Argentina. Leading the pack, Porcao (360 Park Avenue South, at 26th Street, 1-212 252 7080), Industria Argentina (329 Greenwich Street, between Duane & Jay Streets, 1-212 965 8560) and Carne Vale (46 Ave B, between 3rd & 4th Streets) were perhaps the biggest and best. All employ the tried-and-true tricks of the *riodizio* trade: servers wielding skewers of meats wander from table to table slicing their beef, pork and chicken on to the plate of any diner who hasn't yet flipped the yes-no chip from green to red.

In other meat news, steak purists got many more steakhouses, each helmed by former Peter Luger (the famed steakhouse in Brooklyn) employees. Beef eaters can satisfy their carnivorous cravings at one of two new Wolfgang's, or Ben & Jack's Steak House (219 E 44th Street, between Second & Third Avenues, 1-212 682 5678) or Blair Perrone Steakhouse (885 Second Avenue, at 47th Street, 1-212 796 8000). The word is still out on whether the new kids on the block compete with the master original, but early reports bode well.

Best New
- Buddha Bar (p92)
- El Centro (p130)
- Room 4 Dessert (p75)
- Telepan (p153)

Best for fun & games
- Dave & Busters (p116)
- Dive 75 (p153)

Best view
- Bouchon Bakery (p151)
- Top of the Tower (p135)

Best cocktail bar
- Pegu club (p67)
- Loft (p153)
- East Side Company Bar (p77)

Dine with models
- Thor (p78)
- Café Habana (p73)
- Cafeteria (p101)

Best for winos
- VinoVino (p68)
- Uva (p147)

Best for sunny days
- Plunge (p95)
- Central Park Boathouse (p137)
- New Leaf Café (p159)

Best for brunch
- Balthazar (p65)
- Clinton Street Baking Company (p76)
- Jane (p89)

Best dive
- Subway Inn (p146)
- Welcome to the Johnsons (p78)
- Rififi (p85)

Best looking
- The Modern (p126)
- Public (p74)
- Freemans (p77)

Most romantic
- Dévi (p111)
- Strip House (p90)

Megu Midtown p13

It's no surprise that offshoots thrive. New Yorkers know what they like and follow talented chefs to their new digs. The latest batch? Josh DeChellis (of Sumile fame) opened the Italian Jovia (p146), Marc Meyer (Five Points) unveiled organic-obsessed Cookshop (156 Tenth Avenue, at 20th Street, 1-212 924 4440), Kurt Guttenbruner (Wallse) opened Austrian Thor (p78) and Geoffrey Zacharian (Town) gave us the very high-end Country (box p112). John DeLafamina added the Orchard (162 Orchard Street, at Stanton, 1-212 353 3570) to the Lower East Side after scoring successes with Peasant and Apizz, and Zak Palacchio fathered Fatty Crab (643 Hudson Street, between Gansevoort & Horatio Streets, 1-212 352 3590), specialising in Malaysian street food, around the corner from more upscale 5 Ninth in the Meatpacking District.

Herban living

Every year, vegetarians get a handful of cool new dining destinations. Thomas Keller, for example, introduced a vegetarian tasting menu when he opened the otherwise meat-full Per Se. Even newer, and less expensive, is Blossom (187 Ninth Avenue, between 21st and 22nd Streets), which offers one big surprise: all the eggless pastas and mock meats actually taste pretty good. For vegans, it's a candlelit godsend.

That said, old reliables continue to draw regulars: the A-list includes Angelica Kitchen (300 E 12th Street, between First & Second Avenues, 1-212 228 2909), Pure Food and Wine (54 Irving Place, between 17th & 18th Streets, 1-212 477 1010) and Counter (105 First Avenue, between 6th & 7th Streets, 1-212 982 5870), which gets many of its herbs from a rooftop garden.

That's the spirit!

New York has thousands of bars but most of them fall under one of five categories: wine bar, cocktail lounge, alehouse, sports bar or dive. The city lost two respected wine and beer destinations in the last year – Rhone and the Blind Tiger Ale House, respectively – but gained scores of other watering holes. Oenophiles rave about Tarallucci e Vino (15 E 18th Street, between Broadway & Fifth Avenue, 1-212 228 5400), Epistrophy (200 Mott Street, at Spring Street, 1-212 966 0904), Aroma (p83) and Uva (p147), which recently won a *Time Out New York* Eat Out Award for best new wine bar. The place offers not-too-pricey wines (35 by the glass) and food in a rustic brick-walled room with flickering ruby-red tealights.

Hopheads and other beer lovers should make it a point to go to

Stout, a new 16,000-square-foot beer theme park (133 W 33rd Street, between Sixth & Seventh Avenues) with more than 100 beers on the list. Downtown, at the Hop Devil Grill in the East Village (129 St Marks Place, at Avenue A, 1-212 533 4467), two guys who run David Copperfield's (another brew-centric destination) serve 24 beers on tap and 100 by the bottle. In keeping with the tavern theme, the brothers also offer pub fare like shepherd's pie and bangers and mash.

The cocktail world may have seen the most exciting new openings: Pegu Club (p67), Loft (p153), East Side Company Bar (p77), Blue Owl, and Salon (505 West Street, at Jane Street, 1-212 929 4303) all boast top-notch mixologists using fresh seasonal ingredients in drinks that run the gamut from obscure classics to creative originals. Many of these places are hard to find – on purpose. Call it speakeasy chic. At Blue Owl (196 Second Avenue, at 12th Street), for example, instead of looking for a traditional sign, you have to hunt for the blue neon owl and then descend a staircase to get to the subterranean spot. At East Side Bar, you have to search for a wooden door with tiny plaque that has the bar name on it. And so on.

And another thing

The hardest part about eating out in New York is the sheer choice; it's downright dizzying, even for locals. Snagging reservations can be tough (especially at weekends). Super-trendy spots can be fully booked weeks in advance, but luckily, the majority require only a few days' notice or less. Most restaurants fill up between 7pm and 9pm. If you don't mind eating early (5pm) or late (after 9.30pm), your chances of getting into a popular place will improve greatly.

Alternatively, you can try to snag a hard-to-land rezzo by calling at 5pm on the day you want to dine and hope for a last-minute cancellation. Dress codes are rarely enforced any more, but some ultra-fancy eateries require men to don a jacket and tie. If in doubt, call and ask. And remember: you can never really overdress in this town.

Huff and puff

A strict citywide smoking ban has changed the way smokers carouse: some go to bars and restaurants that allow smoking, but these are few and far between. The only legal indoor places to smoke are either venues that largely cater to cigar smokers (and actually sell cigars and cigarettes) or spaces that have created areas specifically for smokers – and that somehow pass legal muster. Try Circa Tabac (32 Watts Street, between Sixth Avenue and Thompson Street, 1-212 941 1781) or Club Macanudo (26 E 63rd Street between Madison and Park Avenues, 1-212 752 8200).

Naka Naka p15

Ben Sherman

WHAT'S NEW
Shopping

Clotheshorses of the world, we feel your pain! It sucks to come home empty-handed after you've mustered up the energy to brave NYC's overwhelming shopping scene. The challenge at hand is narrowing down your options. To help you get the most from your sprees, we've included many of the latest and greatest places to nab new fashions. Here's how to navigate the complicated retail landscape like a pro, whether your taste leans towards classic Fifth Avenue glam or downtown chic.

Wear yourself out

Every season a new crop of shops explodes on the scene. Long gone are the days when you could take in the high-end designer shops along Madison Avenue and, later, pop down to Soho for funkier boutiques and feel like you've seen it all.

In the past year or so, far-flung neighbourhoods have got their own piece of the high life. In Harlem, for example, the glamorous new N (p160) reigns supreme for chic designer labels above 100th Street.

Nolita and the Meatpacking District are now counted among the city's fashion foundations. In the latter, look for what are fast becoming the new classic shops including Jeffrey, Girlshop and Scoop – and don't miss Tracy Reese's glorious new flagship (for all, see p97).

Many serious shoppers still agree that the most cutting-edge young labels are found in the Lower East Side, along Ludlow Street. The West Village's Bleecker Street has become a hot property seemingly overnight, with the likes of Intermix, Cynthia Rowley, two Ralph Lauren stores (one for men and one for women) and no fewer than three Marc Jacobs stores.

However, if you are looking to be wowed in a *Lifestyles of the*

Rich and Famous kind of way, Fifth Avenue (between 42nd and 59th Streets) is hard to beat.

In the know

Shopping events such as Barneys' (p147) ever-popular twice-yearly warehouse sales and designers' frequent sample sales are excellent sources for reduced-price clothing by fashion's biggest names. To find out who's selling where during any given week, consult the Check Out section of *Time Out New York*. Top Button (www.topbutton.com) and the SSS Sample Sales hotline (1-212 947 8748, www.clothingline.com) are also great discount resources. Sales are usually held in the designers' shops or in rented loft spaces. Typically, loft sales are not equipped with changing rooms, so bring a courageous spirit with you (and plenty of cold, hard cash!) and remember to wear appropriate undergarments. To gen up on the latest stores and hotspots that are making waves on New York's design scene, visit the *Time Out New York* website (www.timeout ny.com), click on Check Out and scan the archives.

Pressed for time? Head to one of New York's shopping malls… yes, we said shopping mall. We won't get the best deal or the uniqueness of a boutique, but the Shops at Columbus Circle (Time Warner Center, 10 Columbus Circle, at 59th Street), and the myriad stores in Trump Tower (Fifth Avenue, at 56th Street), Grand Central Terminal (p133) and South Street Seaport's cobblestoned Pier 17 (Fulton Street, at the East River) are convenient options.

Thursday is the universal – though unofficial – shop-after-work night; most stores remain open until at least 7pm. In general, the shops Downtown stay open an hour or so later than those Uptown.

SHORTLIST

Best New
- Ben Sherman (p68)
- Annie O (p78)

Best New Yorker
- Barney's (p147)
- Henri Bendel (p126)
- Patricia Field (p86)

Best antiques
- The Garage (p107)
- Hell's Kitchen Flea Market (p132)

Best yummy treats
- Billy's Bakery (p107)
- Magnolia Bakery (p97)

Best housewares
- ABC Carpet & Home (p113)
- Conran Shop (p148)

Best for kids
- Toys 'R' Us (p117)
- Kidding Around (p107)

Best vintage
- Marmalade (p79)
- Local Clothing (p86)
- Foley & Corinna (p79)

Best sneakers
- Classic Kicks (p75)
- Adidas (p68)

Best jewels
- Tiffany & Co (p129)
- Doyle & Doyle (p79)

Best chocolate
- Haven (p95)
- La Maison du Chocolat (p148)

Best urban
- Phat Farm (p69)
- Triple Five Soul (p70)

Best bodycare
- John Masters Organics (p69)
- Kiehl's (p86)

Best bargains
- Century 21 (p64)
- Find Outlet (p75)

Mo Pitkin's House of Satisfaction p23

WHAT'S NEW
Nightlife

When the sun goes down Manhattan really fires up. So for those of you who want to experience a sleepless night here, grab a triple espresso and peruse our round-up of life after dark.

Greetings from clubland

Here we go again. 'RAIDING COPS SHUT SEVEN CLUBS', shouts one headline; 'CLUBS FEEL STING OF POLICE RAIDS', runs another. No, they're not lifted from the dark days of New York clubbing – the Giuliani '90s – when deputy mayor Rudy Washington branded nightspots as 'little buckets of blood', and city-ordered club closings were rife. Sadly, these headlines are recent. While Mayor Michael Bloomberg may not be as open in his distaste for clubbing

as his predecessor was, the current administration's war on nightlife continues as strongly as ever. Of course, the bizarre anti-dancing cabaret law, which severely limits where you can cut a rug in Gotham, is still on the books, thanks to a recent state court decision, which upheld its constitutionality. Add to that the surging real-estate market, which has raised club rents to the point where many venues are afraid to take a chance on any music more challenging than Top 40 hip-hop and dance pop, and it would seem that the city has the makings of an anaemic nightlife.

Still, this is New York City, and the tradition that wends its way through the Loft, Studio 54, Paradise Garage, Pyramid (p87), Sound Factory and Twilo dies hard. Although it's unlikely that we'll ever see a return to the scene's glory days, when it could lay claim to being one of the world's most vibrant, there's still plenty of fun to be had in clubland if you know where to look. For starters, Element (see box p84), in an old bank on the Lower East Side, is the newest club that's revving up the city's heartbeat. Underground-house and techno heads can turn to venues such as Sullivan Room (p91) and Cielo (p99); even megaclubs like Avalon, Crobar (both p107) and the recently opened Pacha (p133) have been scheduling dubstep or electro-disco nights on occasion.

And there are always NYC's semi-hidden weapons. The Meatpacking District's APT (p99) regularly scores some of the world's best spinners to play at what's essentially a nothing more fancy than a bar with a sound system, albeit a really killer sound system. There's the rollicking rock & roll circus Motherfucker (www.motherfucker.com), a roving party which is regularly touted by the press as the world's best party – and they might be right. PS 1's Warm Up (p165), a weekly summertime soirée held in the courtyard of a Queens museum, attracts thousands of kids who like nothing better than to boogie down to some pretty twisted DJs. And if you're really lucky, you might even hear about an illegal warehouse party hidden away in the outer boroughs – though you'd better hope the cops don't hear about it too.

Doin' it live

The New York rock club scene can resemble a Whac-a-Mole carnival game: each time one venue gets beaten into the ground by the powers-that-be (soaring rents, noise police, fickle audiences), a new

S H O R T L I S T

Best new
- Mo Pitkin's House of Satisfaction (p87)
- Nokia Theatre Times Square (p118)
- Element (p84)
- Pacha (p133)

Best for rockers
- Continental (p86)
- Ace of Clubs (p86)

Best for cabaret
- Don't Tell Mama (p118)
- Danny's Skylight Room (p118)
- Joe's Pub (p87)

Best for jazz
- Birdland (p118)
- Village Vanguard (p91)
- Smoke (p154)

Best for laughs
- Laugh Lounge nyc (p80)

Best for hipsters
- Cake Shop (p80)
- Rothko (p81)
- Nublu (p87)

Best for megastar DJs
- APT (p99)
- Cielo (p99)
- Spirit (p107)

Best for indie bands
- Arlene's Grocery (p80)
- Bowery Ballroom (p80)
- Delancey (p80)
- Mercury Lounge (p81)

Best neo-burlesque
- Slipper Room (p82)

Best world music
- S.O.B's (p70)
- Zinc Bar (p91)
- Copacabana (p132)

Best for gay
- Element (Saturday nights) (p80)
- Pyramid (Friday nights) (p87)

Cielo p21

room pops right up to take its place. This has proven especially true in recent years, as the city has simultaneously experienced a swelling real-estate market and a profitable rock renaissance. For a music fan, it becomes difficult to mourn the loss of fallen venues when there are so many fine new spots, from modest cabarets to cavernous theatres. And while some old standbys have encountered problems – most famously the slowly dying punk landmark CBGB – no other city offers a concertgoer so many options of what to hear and where to hear it.

For larger seated shows, the iconic theatres uptown cannot be beat. The palatial art deco totem Radio City Music Hall, Harlem's decaying benchmark the Apollo Theater (p160), and Carnegie Hall (plus its recently hatched subterranean baby, Zankel Hall, p120) lend historic import to even tedious performances. The sole mammoth upstart is Nokia Theatre Times Square (p118), which hosts a range of popular touring acts. The club begs for character – it has a cookie-cutter aura that would befit a suburban mega-mall – but finds redemption in its creature comforts, with impressive sound and sightlines and (gasp!) edible food.

The rock scene's heart rests downtown. On one Lower East Side block alone lie three teeming smaller venues: Pianos (p81), Living Room and Cake Shop (both p80), a recent addition which has a café and record store on the top floor and a sweaty space for bands in the basement. For medium-size acts, Bowery Ballroom (p80) remains Manhattan's hub. In recent years, its owners (who also handle the smaller Mercury Lounge) have taken advantage of rock's resurgence by booking shows in the larger Webster Hall as well as

Hiro Ballroom, a new space beneath Chelsea's Maritime Hotel that has a flamboyant atmosphere redolent of *Kill Bill*. An equally decadent, albeit scruffier young venue is Nublu (p87) – a tiny East Village room that has launched a scene populated by smart dance bands like the Brazilian Girls and Kudu, spawning a record label and outpost in Brazil. One thing this rollicking club lacks is a sign: it's identified only by the glow of a blue light.

Less glamorous (and perhaps less intimidating) is the recently opened Mo Pitkin's House of Satisfaction (p87), a snug cabaret on the top floor of an East Village Jewish-Latino restaurant. Like the food – which audience members can gobble while watching a show – the space is eclectic and quirky. Music ranges from jazz to folk and from klezmer to rock; there are comedy shows, variety shows, performances featuring celebrities and performances featuring local crazies. In a nutshell, the modest space lives and breathes New York City – and it's still in diapers.

Life is a cabaret

With most of the city's venues operating at full steam, the cabaret scene is hardly looking fragile. Manhattan's three fanciest (and priciest) cabarets – Café Carlyle, Feinstein's at the Regency and the Oak Room at the Algonquin Hotel – are throwbacks to a more elegant, Fred-and-Ginger era of New York nightlife. This is the New York of Woody Allen movies, where well-heeled daters can take in dinner and a show in one swanky package. (Allen himself often plays clarinet in a jazz band at the Carlyle on Monday nights.)

Luckily, there are some terrific venues where prices are much more affordable and the nights very often memorable. Danny's Skylight Room (p118), lodged inside a midtown restaurant, is a solid, neutral-toned boîte presenting singers ranging from novices to seasoned pros, including 1950s jazz-vocal icons Blossom Dearie and Annie Ross. Across the street at Don't Tell Mama (p118), you never know what you're going to get at this eclectic box of chocolates. (But hey, the box is cheap.) Entry-level talents share the space with such local favourites as Judy Garland impersonator Tommy Femia.

Yuck it up

Whether you prefer a standard joke told through a microphone or avant-garde antics, you'll find what your funny bone craves in the city's many clubs, bars and theatres dedicated to an endless parade of punchlines. Hit Laugh Lounge nyc (p80) for a dose of the downtown crowd or check out Gotham Comedy Club (32 W 22nd Street) to hear late-night talk-show circuit comics. Step into the Upright Citizens Brigade Theater (307 W 26th Street) for top-notch improvised and sketch shows by the city's riskier young comedians.

Gay life

The city's gay nightlife is still largely centred in Downtown's Chelsea and the East Village. Midtown's Hell's Kitchen however is slowly but surely establishing itself as a nighttime destination. The new arrival there, Vlada Lounge (p130), offers a chilled, laid-back setting for sipping cocktails. The big question on everyone's mind, however, is whether or not the latest Saturday night soirée, Bank, at the shiny new club, Element (p80), will steal the crown from the Roxy, the long reigning gay boys' dance party. Still, if you're in the mood to shake it in a big time space with a deafening sound system, many of the large clubs like Pacha, Avalon and Crobar all have gay nights.

The best source for all things gay is *HX* magazine, available at most eateries, bars and shops along Chelsea's Eight Avenue, the city's queerest enclave.

Spirit p21

The Producers p27

Arts & Leisure

Culture club

Here in NYC, the Arts (with a capital A) aren't a yes or no proposition; cultural offerings for every taste abound all over town. Whether you are on a tight budget or have money to burn, we guarantee that you'll find more than enough to keep you applauding (OK, wiseguy, and occasionally booing). So, read on – and explore the city's many opportunities to see theatre, film, classical music and dance.

Theatre

For most visitors and many New Yorkers, theatre = musicals = Broadway. And it's true that if you want high production values and sheer entertainment, the Great White Way is your first stop. All right, so you may have to pay upward of $100 for a good seat, but chances are the show will be worth it. Perennial favourites include productions as diverse as *Wicked* (p121), *Avenue Q* (p120) and *The 25th Annual Putnam County Spelling Bee*; the London import *Mary Poppins*, coming in autumn 2006, is likely to join them. Revivals expected to start long runs in autumn 2006 are *A Chorus Line* and *Les Miserables*, while choreographer Twyla Tharp's new *The Times They Are A-Changin'* (based on Bob Dylan songs) should hit town at around the same time.

You can also find straight plays on Broadway, often lit by awesome star wattage: following recent stage turns by Julia Roberts, Denzel Washington and Kathleen Turner, Julianne Moore is scheduled to appear in David Hare's *The Vertical Hour* in November '06.

Yet Broadway is not the be all and end all of theatre in New York. As fun as high-budget productions are, sometimes you need a bit more intimacy. Some can be found very near Broadway, actually, by the western end of 42nd St, where authors like Wallace Shawn and John Guare and actors such as Lily Taylor and Ethan Hawke regularly ply their wares. Check out what's playing at Playwrights Horizons, Second Stage and Signature for quality in a fairly classic mode.

If you need something a little more challenging, a little more iconoclastic, head downtown: the historic centre for avant-garde and experimental theatre is the East Village. At Performance Space 122 (p88), edgy companies from around the world share the spotlight with local favourites – keep an eye out for shows by companies such as Radiohole, Elevator Repair Company, and the National Theater of the United States of America. A few blocks away, New York Theatre Workshop (p88) specialises in elegant productions of works by demanding playwrights such as Eugene O'Neill, Caryl Churchill and Tony Kushner. In August and September the Fringe and Howl! festivals (see Events Calendar, p31) take over Village venues. Some of the action has recently moved even further south to Tribeca, with the excellent, multidisciplinary Flea Theater (p71) on White Street and the quirky Collective: Unconscious group (279 Church Street, at White Street, 1-212 254 5277, www.weird.org).

DON'T MISS: 2007

S H O R T L I S T

Best new show
- *Mary Poppins* (p121)

Best long-running shows
- *Avenue Q* (p120)
- *Wicked* (p121)
- *The Producers* (p121)

Best concert halls
- Carnegie Hall (p120)
- Lincoln Center (p154)
- Merkin Concert Hall (p155)

Best small theatres
- Manhattan Theatre Club (p121)
- Performance Space 122 (p88)
- Flea Theater (p71)
- The Kitchen (p108)

Best movie houses
- Film Forum (p99)
- Landmark's Sunshine Cinema (p82)
- Angelika Film Center (p91)

Best for eclectic shows
- Stomp (p88)
- Blue Man Group (p87)
- Bowery Poetry Club (p87)

Best for athletes
- Chelsea Piers (p108)

Best outdoor culture
- Shakespeare in the Park (p37)
- Midsummer Night Swing (p37)

Best all-round space
- Symphony Space (p156)

Best for dance
- The Joyce (p108)
- Merce Cunningham Studio (p99)
- City Center (p120)

Best spectator sports
- US Open (p165)
- A Yankees game (p163)

Best for cheap tickets
- TKTS (p116)

Time Out
Travel Guides

USA

Available at all good bookshops and at timeout.com/shop

Guides

Film

Let's face it: going to see a new Hollywood movie in New York can be a trial, especially when your $10 ticket buys you the privilege of sitting next to teenagers noisily eating nachos. Thankfully, there's a civilised world away from the multiplexes. Art and foreign films can be found at a variety of venues; one of the best is the Landmark's Sunshine (p82) on the Lower East Side and the Lincoln Plaza Cinemas (across from Lincoln Center) on the Upper West Side. On its three (smallish) screens, Film Forum (p99) programmes a wide range of revivals and new indie features, while Anthology Film Archives specialises in experimental programming. Uptown, the Museum of Modern Art (p123) and the Lincoln Center Film Society's Walter Reade Theater (p155) offer well-curated film series and impeccable screening conditions to alert cinephiles.

Since New York is a city in love with movies, it holds a myriad of small film festivals and two major ones. In April the Tribeca Film Festival (see box p39) takes over many venues around town, while the New York Film Festival is at Lincoln Center in the autumn. If these feel too overwhelming, there's New Directors/New Films in March, or the Human Rights Watch International Film Festival in June, or the Margaret Mead Film and Video Festival in November… the list goes on and on.

Classical music

Whether you're a connoisseur or a curious beginner, New York offers a wealth of classical options, from free concerts in churches or parks to astronomically priced seats at the Met, from Mozart to the hippest contemporary avant-composers.

The epicentre of the city's classical realm is Lincoln Center (p154), which is in the middle of a major overhaul 50 years after its

DON'T MISS: 2007

New York City Ballet p30

birth. Alice Tully Hall closes in spring 2007 for 18 months of renovations, but you can still find high-quality fare on the famed uptown campus. The Metropolitan Opera starts its 40th season in September 2006 with Anthony Minghella's acclaimed staging of Puccini's *Madama Butterfly*. This will be followed by such high-profile offerings as the premiere of Tan Dun's *The First Emperor* in December '06; Deborah Voigt's appearance in Richard Strauss's *Die Ägyptische Helena* in March '07; and choreographer Mark Morris's staging of Gluck's *Orfeo ed Euridice* in May '07.

Those looking for more daring productions or less-known works should simply walk over to the New York State Theater, where City Opera offers a multimedia take on Erich Wolfgang Korngold's *Die Tote Stadt* starting in September '06 and a production of Handel's obscure *Flavio* in April '07.

If the Met and City Opera feel too cavernous, try the scrappy, much-loved Dicapo Opera (184 E 76th Street, between Lexington & Third Avenues, 1-212 288 9438), where you can hear a mix of old favourites (Puccini's *Manon Lescaut*) and provocative new works (Tobias Picker's *Thérèse Raquin*) in February '07) in a 204-seat theatre on the Upper East Side. Merkin Concert Hall (p155) and Columbia University's Miller Theater, both on the Upper West Side, also stage new works by contemporary composers.

Dance

Home to some of the world's foremost dance companies (New York City Ballet, Alvin Ailey, Merce Cunningham, Trisha Brown) and cutting-edge choreographers (Sarah Michelson, Liv-Ann Young, Miguel Guttierez, Eiko & Koma), NYC continually demonstrates the endless ways the human body can get its move on. For classical and neoclassical fare, it's hard to beat American Ballet Theatre (at the Metropolitan Opera every spring) and New York City Ballet (at the New York State Theater in winter and spring), while modern-dance lovers should check out listings for Dance Theater Workshop (219 W 19th Street, between Seventh & Eighth Avenues, 1-212 924 0077), Danspace Project (131 E 10th Street, at Second Avenue, 1-212 674 8191), the Kitchen (p108) and Movement Research at Judson Church (55 Washington Square South, at Thompson Street, 1-212 539 2611). The latter is the home of the famed Judson Dance Theater, which revolutionised dance in the 1960s and continues to offer free showcases of new artists.

Roger Federer at the US Open p27

Calendar

Central Park SummerStage p37

Dates highlighted in **bold** are public holidays.

September 2006

4 Labor Day

8-16 **Howl!**
East Village
www.howlfestival.com
A grab bag of art events, films, performance art, readings and more.

10 **Broadway on Broadway**
Times Square
www.broadwayonbroadway.com
Stars perform in Times Square.

14-7 Jan 2007 **Cézanne to Picasso: Ambroise Vollard, Patron of the Avant-Garde**
Metropolitan Museum of Art, Upper East Side
www.metmuseum.org

14-24 **Feast of San Gennaro**
Little Italy
www.sangennaro.org
Massive Italian-American street fair.

26-28 Feb 2007 **Witness to History: The Face in Medieval Sculpture**
Metropolitan Museum of Art, Upper East Side
www.metmuseum.org

28-28 Jan 2007 **Picasso and American Art**
Whitney Museum of American Art, Upper East Side
www.whitney.org

October 2006

Ongoing Cézanne to Picasso: Ambroise Vollard, Patron of the Avant-Garde

Ongoing Witness to History: The Face in Medieval Sculpture

Ongoing Picasso and American Art

Early-mid **New York Film Festival**
Lincoln Center, Upper West Side
www.filmlinc.com
Annual cinematic showcase.

9 Columbus Day

7-8 Open House New York
Various locations
www.ohny.org
Architectural sites normally off-limits
open their doors.

31 Village Halloween Parade
Greenwich Village
www.halloween-nyc.com
Check out the amazing costumes or
show off your own.

**31-4 Nov CMJ Music Marathon
& FilmFest**
Various locations
www.cmj.com
Showcase for new musical acts and
music-related films.

November 2006

Ongoing Cézanne to Picasso:
Ambroise Vollard, Patron of the
Avant-Garde

Ongoing Witness to History: The
Face in Medieval Sculpture

Ongoing Picasso and American Art

Ongoing CMJ Music Marathon &
FilmFest

**1-2 Jan Radio City Christmas
Spectacular**
Radio City Music Hall, Midtown
www.radiocity.com
The Rockettes' holiday show.

Early-19 Aug 2007 **Gold**
American Museum of Natural
History, Upper West Side
www.amnh.org

5 New York City Marathon
Various locations
www.nycmarathon.org
35,000 runners hotfoot it through all
five boroughs.

5-29 Jan 2007 **Édouard Manet
and *The Execution of Maximilian***
Museum of Modern Art (MoMA),
Midtown
www.moma.org

11 Veterans' Day

**22-23 Macy's Thanksgiving Eve
Balloon Blowup & Thanksgiving
Day Parade**
Various locations

www.macys.com
The stars of this annual parade are
the gigantic, inflated balloons.

23 Thanksgiving Day

Late-early Jan ***The Nutcracker***
Lincoln Center, Upper West Side
www.nycballet.com

Late **Christmas Tree-Lighting
Ceremony**
Rockefeller Center, Midtown
www.rockefellercenter.com
Brave the crowds to marvel at the
twinkling giant evergreen.

December 2006

Ongoing Cézanne to Picasso:
Ambroise Vollard, Patron of the
Avant-Garde

Ongoing Witness to History:
The Face in Medieval Sculpture

Ongoing Picasso and American Art

Ongoing Gold

Ongoing Édouard Manet and
The Execution of Maximilian

Ongoing *The Nutcracker*

Mid **The National Chorale
Messiah Sing-In**
Lincoln Center, Upper West Side
www.nationalchorale.org

25 Christmas Day

31 New Year's Eve Ball Drop
Times Square
www.timessquarebid.org
See the giant illuminated ball descend.

31 New Year's Eve Fireworks
Central Park
www.centralparknyc.org
The fireworks explode at midnight.

31 New Year's Eve Midnight Run
Central Park
www.nyrrc.org
Start the new year as you mean to go
on – with a four-mile jog.

January 2007

Ongoing Cézanne to Picasso:
Ambroise Vollard, Patron of the
Avant-Garde

Ongoing Witness to History: The Face in Medieval Sculpture

Ongoing Picasso and American Art

Ongoing Gold

Ongoing Édouard Manet and *The Execution of Maximilian*

Ongoing *The Nutcracker*

1 New Year's Day

1 New Year's Day Marathon Poetry Reading
East Village
www.poetryproject.com
Big-name bohemians step up to the mic in this free, all-day spoken-word spectacle.

15 Martin Luther King, Jr Day

Mid-late **Winter Antiques Show**
Midtown East
www.winterantiquesshow.com
One of the world's most prestigious antiques shows.

Late **Winter Restaurant Week**
Various locations
www.nycvisit.com
An opportunity to sample gourmet food at low prices in the last two weeks of January (weekdays only).

February 2007

Ongoing Witness to History: The Face in Medieval Sculpture

Ongoing **Gold**

7-6 May 2007 **Lorna Simpson**
Whitney Museum of American Art, Upper East Side
www.whitney.org

18 Chinese New Year
Chinatown
www.explorechinatown.com
Festivals and fun during the two weeks of the Lunar New Year.

19 Presidents' Day

22-26 **The Art Show**
Seventh Regiment Armory, Upper East Side
www.artdealers.org
Serious collectors and casual art fans peruse this vast fair.

22-26 **The Armory Show**
Piers 90 & 92, Midtown West
www.thearmoryshow.com
A huge contemporary-art mart.

March 2007

Ongoing Gold

Ongoing Lorna Simpson

4-11 June 2007 **Comic Abstraction: Image Breaking, Image Making**
Museum of Modern Art (MoMA), Midtown
www.moma.org

7-3 June 2007 **Barcelona and Modernity: Gaudí to Dalí**
Metropolitan Museum of Art, Upper East Side
www.metmuseum.org

17 Saint Patrick's Day Parade
Fifth Avenue
www.saintpatricksdayparade.com
Manhattan's massive march of green-clad merrymakers.

27-8 July 2007 **Venice and the Islamic World, 828-1797**
Metropolitan Museum of Art, Upper East Side
www.metmuseum.org

Late **Ringling Bros and Barnum & Bailey Circus Animal Parade**
Midtown
www.ringling.com
Elephants, horses and zebras march through Manhattan.

April 2007

Ongoing Gold

Ongoing Lorna Simpson

Ongoing Barcelona and Modernity: Gaudí to Dalí

Ongoing Venice and the Islamic World, 828-1797

6-15 **New York International Auto Show**
Jacob Javitz Convention Center, Midtown West
www.autoshowny.com
More than 1,000 autos and futuristic concept cars on display.

smart funny sexy authoritative trusted in-the-know comprehensive sharp entertaining quick playful witty timely weird sexy stylish spirited cutting-edge dependable honest weird straightforward tried entertaining outspoken frank reliable quirky dependable honest tried and true witty daring devoted genius dependable newsworthy dynamic frank profound zealous thorough plucky quick daring one hundred percent new york acute genius modern plucky nimble cheeky energetic inclusive exhaustive sharp sexy earnest inspired enthusiastic accurate acute gung-ho smart funny sexy authoritative weird trusted in-the-know qa newsworthy sharp entertaining uninhibited timely stylish spirited savvy cutting-edge playful blunt unceremonious outspoken reliable quirky dependable honest weird straightforward tried and true gregarious selective witty daring devoted newsworthy dependent one hundred found zealous cheeky est inspired hart funny know comprehensive quick uninhibited cutting-edge unceremonious spoken reliable quirky honest weird straightforward tried and true gregarious selective witty daring devoted newsworthy dynamic sexy enthusiastic accurate gung-ho. and so much more...

Midsummer Night Swing p37

8 **Easter Parade**
Fifth Ave
Admire the myriad creative Easter bonnets on show.

Late **New York Antiquarian Book Fair**
Upper East Side
www.sanfordsmith.com
Book dealers showcase all manner of rare and antique tomes over three days.

Late **Tribeca Film Festival**
Tribeca
www.tribecafilmfestival.org
Two-week Robert De Niro-organised festival of independent films.

May 2007

Ongoing **Gold**
Ongoing **Lorna Simpson**
Ongoing **Barcelona and Modernity: Gaudí to Dalí**
Ongoing **Venice and the Islamic World, 828-1797**

Early-Jan 2008 **Mythic Beasts**
American Museum of Natural History, Upper West Side
www.amnh.org

5 **Global Marijuana March**
Downtown
www.globalmarijuanamarch.com
Meet and greet local stoners and learn about marijuana-related issues.

8 **Bike New York: The Great Five Boro Bike Tour**
www.bikenewyork.org
Thousands of cyclists take part in a 42-mile (68km) Tour de New York.

23-29 **Fleet Week**
Midtown West
www.intrepidmuseum.org
New York's streets swell with sailors.

25-27 **Lower East Side Festival of the Arts**
Lower East Side
www.theaterforthenewcity.net
Theatre, poetry readings, films and family-friendly programming.

Happy holidays

Sometimes regular old department stores and boutiques just won't cut it when it comes to buying holiday gifts. That's where the city's holiday bazaars come in. These sprawling temporary shops are filled with offbeat toys, handmade crafts, and more soap and candles than you ever thought existed. But don't forget to check out the big shops' spectacular window displays...

Holiday Market at Union Square

The goods Lots of candles and soap, plus toys, ties, clocks and nativity sets. Most items are reasonably priced, though some jewellery and imported goods can be quite expensive.

The vibe The competition for customers is fierce, so vendors are aggressive. Frustration can run high when a group stops in front of a booth, easily causing a bottleneck in the narrow walkways with few escape routes.

Grand Central Terminal Holiday Fair

The goods You'll find lots of jewellery incorporating silver and/or turquoise at this indoor fair, as well as booths housing unusual (and pricey) gifts from the likes of Our Name is Mud, the Czechoslovak-American Marionette Theatre and the American Folk Art Museum. But the biggest draw is a huge selection of Christmas-tree ornaments.

The vibe There are musicians playing over-the-top Christmas tunes, but the crowd is low-key.

Holiday Market at Columbus Circle

The goods This one's from the same people who put on the Union Square Market, but it seems to have more diverse merchandise. The air still hangs thick with the scent of soap and candles though.

The vibe Lots of determined, no-nonsense shopping.

Window wonderland

Come the holidays, these stores compete for our attention – and our cash – by tarting themselves up with over-the-top spectacles of lights and Yuletide fanfare:
Barneys New York (p147) 25 Nov-5 Jan; **Bergdorf Goodman** (p126) 25 Nov-5Jan; **Bloomingdale's** (p135) 25 Nov-1 Jan; **Henri Bendel** (p126) 25 Nov-5 Jan; **Macy's** (p115) 25 Nov-5 Jan; **Saks Fifth Avenue** (p129) 25 Nov-31 Dec.

28 Memorial Day

Late-Aug 2007 **Bryant Park Free Summer Season**
Midtown
www.bryantpark.org
Alfresco movies on Monday nights, Broadway-musical numbers and more.

Late **Ninth Avenue International Food Festival**
Midtown West
www.hellskitchennyc.com

Late-Sept **Washington Square Outdoor Art Exhibit**
Washington Square Park, Greenwich Village
One-of-a-kind arts and crafts.

June 2007

Ongoing Gold

Ongoing Barcelona and Modernity: Gaudí to Dalí

Ongoing Venice and the Islamic World, 828-1797

Ongoing Mythic Beasts

Ongoing Bryant Park Free Summer Season

Ongoing Washington Square Outdoor Art Exhibit

Early-Aug **Met in the Parks**
Central Park
www.metopera.org
The Metropolitan Opera stages free performances.

Early-Aug **Central Park SummerStage**
Central Park
www.summerstage.org
Rockers, symphonies, authors and dance companies take over the stage.

Early-Aug **Shakespeare in the Park**
Delacorte Theater, Central Park
www.publictheater.org
Celebrities pull on their tights and take a whack at the Bard.

Early **SOFA New York**
Upper East Side
www.sofaexpo.com
Giant show of Sculptural Objects and Functional Art.

10 **National Puerto Rican Day Parade**
Fifth Avenue
www.nationalpuertoricandayparade.org
Celebrate the city's largest Hispanic community.

12 **Museum Mile Festival**
Various locations, Fifth Avenue
www.museummilefestival.org
Nine major museums are free of charge to the public.

17 **Broadway Bares**
Roseland Ballroom, Midtown
www.broadwaycares.org
This fund-raiser features Broadway's hottest bodies *sans* costumes.

Mid **JVC Jazz Festival**
Various locations
www.festivalproductions.net
This jazz bash is an NYC institution.

24 **Gay & Lesbian Pride March**
Greenwich Village
www.hopinc.org
Downtown is a sea of rainbow flags.

Late **Mermaid Parade**
Coney Island, Brooklyn
www.coneyisland.com
Decked-out mermaids share the parade route with elaborate, kitschy floats.

Late-July **Midsummer Night Swing**
Lincoln Center Plaza, Upper West Side
www.lincolncenter.org
Dance under the stars to salsa, Cajun, swing and other music.

July 2007

Ongoing Gold

Ongoing Venice and the Islamic World, 828-1797

Ongoing Mythic Beasts

Ongoing Bryant Park Free Summer Season

Ongoing Washington Square Outdoor Art Exhibit

Ongoing Met in the Parks

Ongoing Central Park SummerStage

Ongoing Shakespeare in the Park

timeout.com

Over 50 of the world's greatest
cities reviewed in one site.

4 Independence Day

4 Nathan's Famous July 4 Hot Dog Eating Contest
Coney Island, Brooklyn
www.nathansfamous.com

4 Macy's Fireworks Display
East River
www.macys.com
World-famous annual display.

Mid **New York Philharmonic Concerts in the Parks**
Central Park and various locations
www.newyorkphilharmonic.org
Classical-music programme in many of the city's larger parks.

Late **Mostly Mozart Festival**
Lincoln Center, Upper West Side
www.lincolncenter.org
Four weeks of works by Mozart and his contemporaries.

Late **Summer Restaurant Week**
Various locations
www.nycvisit.com
An opportunity to sample gourmet food at low prices in the last two weeks of July (weekdays only).

August 2007

Ongoing Gold

Ongoing Mythic Beasts

Ongoing Washington Square Outdoor Art Exhibit

Ongoing Met in the Parks

Ongoing Central Park SummerStage

Ongoing Shakespeare in the Park

Ongoing Mostly Mozart

Early **Central Park Zoo Chillout Weekend**
Central Park
www.wcs.org
Freeze-fest features penguin and polar-bear talent shows, games and more.

Early-Sept **Lincoln Center Out of Doors Festival**
Lincoln Center, Upper West Side
www.lincolncenter.org
Month-long free family-friendly festival of classic and contemporary works.

Reel player

Tribeca Film Festival 2007 will put stars in your eyes.

The Tribeca Film Festival celebrated its fifth anniversary last year by more than doubling the number of seats available to film fans. 'It keeps growing and changing because of its own impetus,' says Jane Rosenthal, who co-founded the fest with Robert De Niro. Their aim was to revitalise the shattered Tribeca neighbourhood after the World Trade Center attacks. 'It was a way for us to embrace our community,' says Rosenthal.

The annual event, which mixes A-list attendees and red-carpet premieres with street fairs and puppet shows, is beloved by residents and film folk alike. 'I was skeptical at first,' says Tribeca-based producer Jason Kliot, 'but they've won me over.'

From the beginning, ad hoc cinemas were set up anywhere and everywhere – including the local high school – but, frustratingly, every show would sell out immediately. Now that the fest has grown twice as big, extending to cinemas uptown while keeping the same number of seats in the original neighbourhood, snagging tickets to one of the 174 feature films from 40 different countries should be a lot easier in 2007. But be warned: screenings may still sell out fast because Tribeca residents and American Express card holders get first pick. And remember, if you do wind up sitting next to a celebrity, act like a New Yorker – and ignore them.
■ www.tribecafilmfestival.com

Early-mid **New York International Fringe Festival**
Various locations, Downtown
www.fringenyc.org
Wacky, weird and sometimes great. Hundreds of performances in 16 days.

Harlem Week
Harlem
www.harlemdiscover.com
Massive August street fair serving up live music, art and food.

September 2007

Ongoing Mythic Beasts

3 Labor Day

Early **Broadway on Broadway**
Times Square
www.broadwayonbroadway.com
Stars perform in Times Square.

Mid **Feast of San Gennaro**
Little Italy
www.sangennaro.org
Massive Italian-American street fair.

Mid **Howl!**
East Village
www.howlfestival.com
Art events, films, readings and more.

October 2007

Ongoing Mythic Beasts

Early-mid **New York Film Festival**
Lincoln Center, Upper West Side
www.filmlinc.com

Early **Open House New York**
Various locations
www.ohny.org
Architectural sites normally off-limits open their doors.

8 Columbus Day

31 **Village Halloween Parade**
Greenwich Village
www.halloween-nyc.com

Late **CMJ Music Marathon & FilmFest**
Various locations
www.cmj.com
Showcase for new musical acts and music-related films.

November 2007

Ongoing Mythic Beasts

Early **Radio City Christmas Spectacular**
Radio City Music Hall, Midtown
www.radiocity.com
The Rockettes' holiday show.

Early **New York City Marathon**
Various locations
www.nycmarathon.org

11 Veterans' Day

21-22 **Macy's Thanksgiving Eve Balloon Blowup & Thanksgiving Day Parade**
Various locations
www.macys.com
The stars of this annual parade are the gigantic, inflated balloons.

22 Thanksgiving Day

Late **The Nutcracker**
Lincoln Center, Upper West Side
www.nycballet.com

Late **Christmas Tree-Lighting Ceremony**
Rockefeller Center, Midtown
www.rockefellercenter.com
Marvel at the giant evergreen.

December 2007

Ongoing Mythic Beasts

Mid **The National Chorale Messiah Sing-In**
Lincoln Center, Upper West Side
www.nationalchorale.org

25 Christmas Day

31 **New Year's Eve Ball Drop**
Times Square
www.timessquarebid.org
See the giant illuminated ball descend.

31 **New Year's Eve Fireworks**
Central Park
www.centralparknyc.org
The fireworks explode at midnight.

31 **New Year's Eve Midnight Run**
Central Park
www.nyrrc.org
Start the new year as you mean to go on – with a four-mile jog.

Itineraries

Empire State Building p46

Almighty Towers

Manhattan offers something for every architectural taste, from City Hall's neo-classical rotunda of 1811 to the impressive international style slab of Chase Manhattan Plaza (1960) with its fountain landscaped by Isamu Noguchi and its tree-like sculpture by Jean Dubuffet.

Above all, New York is a city of skyscrapers, so the logical starting point for a tour is the **Skyscraper Museum** in the Financial District (39 Battery Place, 1-212 968 1961, www.skyscraper.org, noon-6pm Wed-Sun). If you want to complete your tour in one day, it's best to arrive as soon as it opens. Here you can view a timeline of the world's tallest buildings, many of them in Manhattan, as well as fascinating architectural artefacts like the original model of the World Trade Towers from 1971 and variations of what the Freedom Tower may look like.

Afterwards, it's time to visit one of the most powerfully moving sites in recent history: **Ground Zero** (p55) where the mighty Twin Towers once stood. Head out the door, make a left and follow Battery Place across West Street and along the northern edge of Battery Park. Turn left up Greenwich Street, and at Moore Street (look for the Blarney Stone pub) walk along Trinity Place to make a brief stop at **Trinity Church**. In stark contrast to the skyscrapers that surround it, Trinity – the third church to stand on this spot – remains frozen in Gothic revival style, but it was the island's tallest structure when it was completed in 1846. The churchyard, which dates back to 1697, is one of New York's oldest cemeteries. Alexander Hamilton (the nation's first secretary of the treasury – check out his mug on the $10 bill) is buried here.

Hearst Magazine Building p46

From the church, continue up Trinity Place for two more blocks and cross over Liberty Street. That big gaping hole to your left is Ground Zero. Take a while to view the enlarged photos and read the plaques. Construction of the 1,776-foot-tall Freedom Tower and the planned memorial, *Reflecting Absence* (p8), is extremely slow-going, but happily, crews for both projects have begun working.

From the tragedy of Ground Zero, it's onwards and upwards to the very spot where the race to the heavens began. Walk along Church Street (the continuation of Trinity Place) past Vessey Street and then left on to Barclay Street. On the corner at 233 Broadway, is the **Woolworth Building**. Note the flamboyant Gothic terracotta cladding designed by Cass Gilbert in 1913. The 55-storey, 793-foot 'Cathedral of Commerce' was the world's tallest structure for 16 years until it was topped by the Chrysler Building.

The Woolworth Building overlooks City Hall Park, which is where you are now headed. Walk through the park and aim for the foot of the **Brooklyn Bridge** (p55). Alas, our sojourn is about buildings, not bridges – but we wouldn't mind one bit if you made a detour here; it takes about an hour to walk out to the middle of the bridge and back, allowing plenty of time to gaze upon the East River and marvel at the web of steel cables. Back to the itinerary: once you've passed through the park (bordered to the east by Park Row) look for a subway entrance to your left. Board the Uptown 4 or 5 train to Grand Central-42nd Street. On the subway journey, consider this: it took ten years of unflagging effort for Jacqueline Kennedy Onassis to save **Grand Central Terminal** (p133), the nation's most

famous train station. After the glorious (original) Pennsylvania Station was demolished in 1964, developers unveiled plans to wreck Grand Central and erect an office tower in its place. Jackie O would have none of it and rallied politicians and celebrities to her cause. In 1978 her Committee won a Supreme Court decision affirming landmark status for the beloved beaux arts building. When you exit the subway, head upstairs and take in the thrilling main concourse. Curiously, the constellations on the ceiling are drawn in reverse, as if you were staring down from space.

Now you must be simply famished. Head back downstairs to one of Manhattan's most famous eateries, the Oyster Bar and Restaurant, for a late lunch. Before heading inside, linger a moment under the low ceramic arches, dubbed the 'whispering gallery'. Instruct a friend to stand in an opposite, diagonal corner from you and whisper sweet nothings to each other – they'll sound as clear as if you were face to face.

Revitalised, you're ready for the next stop on our journey: **Columbus Circle**. Either hop back on the subway (S to Times Square, transfer to the Uptown 1 train and get off at 59th Street-Columbus Circle) or, preferably, you can hoof it there in about 40 minutes. Exit Grand Central on 42nd Street and head west. At Fifth Avenue, you'll pass by another beaux arts treasure from the city's grand metropolitan era, the sumptuous white-marble **New York Public Library** (p125). Built on a former Revolutionary War battleground, the library now sits on the greensward known as Bryant Park. When you get to Broadway, make a right and head north into Times Square. Imposing, sentinel-like skyscrapers mark the

southern entry to the electric carnival here; the **Condé Nast Building** (4 Times Square) and the **Reuters Building** (No.3), both by Fox & Fowle, complement Kohn Pedersen Fox's postmodern **5 Times Square** and the recent addition of David Childs' **Times Square Tower** (No.7).

March among the pedestrian-packed sidewalks of Broadway until you spot Chris gazing out from his perch in the center of Columbus Circle at 59th Street. The newly renovated traffic circle with its ring of fountains and recessed benches is the perfect place to contemplate a new set of twin towers, the **Time Warner Center** (p151), also designed by David Childs. To the south, **2 Columbus Circle**, a 1964 edifice of perforated white marble curves, is currently undergoing a highly controversial facelift. The work of disaffected modernist Edward Durell Stone, who helped design the original Museum of Modern Art, the building failed to achieve landmark status last year.

Skyscraper Museum p43

The latest development in New York's skyscraper evolution is green design, meant to minimise the impact of construction on the environment. Lord Norman Foster's extraordinary **Hearst Magazine Building** (959 Eighth Avenue, at W 57th Street) is a shining example. Look south-west and you can't miss it; it's the one that resembles a giant greenhouse.

At this point you have two options. The first is to end the day at the Time Warner Center and enjoy the staggering view from a leather chair in the **Mandarin Oriental Hotel**'s Lobby Lounge, perched 35 floors in the air. The drink prices here are equally staggering, but the Fifth Avenue and Central Park South skylines, glittering through the walls of windows, make the few extra bucks worth the splurge. Alternatively, you can hail a cab and top off a day of skyscraper gazing with unparalleled panoramic views at the newly reopened **Top of the Rock** observation deck at Rockefeller Center (p125). From this vantage point, look out for William Van Alen's silver-hooded **Chrysler Building**. The acme of art deco design, it was part of a madcap three-way race to become the world's tallest building just before the Depression. The competitors were the now forgotten 40 Wall Street and the **Empire State Building** (p122). Van Alen waited for 40 Wall Street to top out at 927 feet before unveiling his secret weapon – a spire assembled inside the Chrysler's dome and raised from within to bring the height to 1,048 feet. At 102 storeys and 1,250 feet, the Empire State Building surpassed it only 11 months later.

Now that you're done, one last landmark awaits: grab a cocktail in the **Rainbow Room** on the 65th floor and let your spirits soar.

Union Square Greenmarket p48

Step to It

You can cruise aboard a boat round the circumference of Manhattan or surf the streets on top of a double-decker tour bus. Heck, you can even hire a pedicab and let the poor, sweating soul on the bike pull you along from sight to sight. But not one of these options will allow you to experience the city like good old-fashioned pedestrianism can. Here's an easy walk that passes by some of the city's vintage treasures and offers a chance to reverse the clock and see how folks lived last century.

The journey back in time begins on the south-west corner of Fifth Avenue and East 34th Street in the shadow of Manhattan's 75-year-old, 102-storey silver ambassador: the **Empire State Building** (p122).

Built in the Depression (drawing design inspiration from a common pencil), this art deco masterpiece represents the ultimate marriage of Manhattan sophistication with technological dominance – not to mention serving as the notorious rendezvous for a certain female beauty with a rather large ape.

Saunter west on 34th Street and it'll only take you a city block to arrive at **Herald Square**, home for over 100 years to another icon of Manhattan's urban streetscape, **Macy's** department store (p115).

Turn south down Sixth Avenue and stroll past the handbag, T-shirt and hat wholesalers. When you reach 25th Street you'll be in the heart of Manhattan's antiquarian soul – the flea market and collectibles district. Turn right (west) along 25th Street (peek in one of the many collectible co-operative shops along the way) until you get to the indoor **Garage** flea markets (p107), on bi-level floors of a gigantic parking garage to your left. Here you can spend hours hunting among junk and jewels, trash and treasure, posh and porn. When you're done browsing, head back east on 25th Street. If the weather is decent, don't miss the outdoor weekend flea market in a parking lot on 25th Street between Sixth Avenue and Broadway.

One block's walk further west will get you to Broadway, where you'll be staring into the shady copse of **Madison Square Park**. A public space in the city since 1686, this park (later named after President James Madison) is in the centre of Manhattan's vibrant Flatiron District. It once housed the Statue of Liberty's arm while funds were secured for the rest of her. Enjoy canine antics at the dog run, then head out the south-west exit to get a close look at the district's namesake, the **Flatiron Building**

Union Square Greenmarket

(p109), named for its resemblance to a... oh, you'll figure it out.

Make your way south down Broadway. A cache of shops housed in 19th-century, mansard-roofed buildings awaits you, notable among them the crown jewel of housewares: **ABC Carpet & Home** (p113)

If you're a glutton for period authenticity, shop for food the way they did in Manhattan's early days at the **Union Square Greenmarket** (p113), a few more blocks south. A showcase of produce from over 200 farmers, it's the spot to load up on flowers, fruit and veg, handicrafts, even wine and handmade pretzels, from the tri-state area.

Exit the park's south side at University Place, then head west on 14th Street. When you get to Fifth Avenue, turn left and walk south until you get to an indisputable gem of Manhattan history, the unofficial capitol of Greenwich Village: **Washington Square Park** (p89). Through its famed arch you'll find the epicentre of the city's bohemian life. The park has a colourful past, to say the least, having served as a potter's field for yellow fever victims, public gallows (the hanging tree still stands), a beatnik meeting place in the 1950s and, more recently, a skateboarders' paradise.

At the southern end of the park you'll find yourself on 4th Street. Stroll east and make a social call at 29 E 4th Street, the **Merchant's House Museum** (1-212 777 1089, www.merchantshouse.com), the city's only preserved family home from the 19th century. Built in 1832, the house is a virtual portal into domestic life of the time and the perfect way to wrap up a day of nostalgia, time travel and treasure hunting in a city that once sold for $24 in beads and blankets.

Washington Square Park

Overnight Sensations

Sure, you've heard it a million times: New York is the City That Never Sleeps. Prove it, you say? Not a problem. But before we make you sorry you doubted us, might we recommend a revitalising nap? Just be sure you're ready to go by 10pm. All set? Good.

Since it's ill-advised to start a night of revelry on an empty stomach, your first stop will be Manhattan's block-long Koreatown, along 32nd Street between Broadway and Fifth Avenue – a paradise for nocturnal carnivores. At **Kang Suh** (1250 Broadway, at 32nd Street, 1-212 564 6845), one of the strip's several 24-hour barbecue joints, you'll be cooking with gas – literally. A personal table-side grill allows each diner to play chef with fresh

vegetables, shrimp, chicken or *chumooluck* (prime rib steak).

Now that your tank is full, chug across the street and check out **Chorus** (Third Floor, 25 W 32nd Street, 1-212 967 2244). At this super mod karaoke club, you can serenade the crowd until 5am, or, if you're not quite ready for *American Idol*, quit while you're ahead and head to the fifth floor for some after-hours bodywork. At **Juvenex Spa** (1-646 733 1330), aestheticians are standing by to pummel and pamper your sleep-deprived body 24 hours a day, seven days a week. A women's spa by day, this oasis welcomes couples after 9.30pm. An hour-long 'energy balancing' therapeutic massage or luxurious seaweed facial will calm and soothe the most committed

Empire Diner

delicacies are prepared here around the clock with flavours like onions, poppy seeds and garlic. Pick up a baker's dozen, head back out on to Broadway and hail a cab to the new **Apple Store** (767 Fifth Avenue, between 58th and 59th Streets, 1-212 336 1440). The gleaming glass cube is open 24/7 – purchase a new iPod or just email friends back home for free.

With the night nearly half over, you'll need a pick-me-up. Cab it down to Chelsea to the chrome comfort of the **Empire Diner** (210 Tenth Avenue, between 22nd and 23rd Streets, 1-212 243 2736), an art deco-style joint that's been serving blue-plate specials since 1976. While the staff's deadpan efficiency and lack of effusiveness have been mistaken for crankiness on occasion, cut them some slack – they've been up all night. Everything on the menu is a real treat – just be sure to order plenty of coffee.

For your final destination, you have a choice. If you still have energy (and $20 burning a hole in your pocket) get yourself to **Club Shelter** in Soho (150 Varick Street). Join the mult-culti crowd and dance the morning away at this infamous Saturday-night party that goes until noon on Sunday.

If you'd rather take in more of the city, get a cab to Manhattan's southern end at South Ferry (adjacent to Battery Park). Here you can catch a free ride on the Staten Island Ferry (p62) every hour on the half-hour. If you don't mind windblown hair, stand at the helm for the full effect of city lights gleaming on the Hudson. And as the sun rises, take in the dazzling view of the lower Manhattan skyline and Lady Liberty. Congratulations, you didn't waste a perfectly good night in New York sleeping.

night owl. Just don't get too calm: the night is still young.

Outside, hail a cab (heading towards uptown) on Broadway. Tell the driver to take you to 344 Amsterdam Avenue, between 76th & 77th Streets, and get ready to break some balls. Welcome to **Amsterdam Billiard Club** (1-212 496 8180), where an hour of pool will only set you back $8.50 per person; just make sure you allow enough time before the place closes (4am weekends; 3am weekdays). Polished wood and brass surround the handsome young professionals who gather here to shoot at the 31 tables and mingle. Sip international beers and keep your eyes peeled for celebrity drop-ins like Jerry Seinfeld.

As you exit the pool hall, hang a left and then another left on 77th Street. When you get to Broadway, turn right and follow your nose a few blocks to 80th Street. That yeasty scent emanates from H&H Bagels (p154) on the south-west corner. The boiled-and-baked

New York by Area

Battery Park

Downtown

Lower Manhattan has undergone a demographic sea change. For most of its life, the area has been populated by a down-to-earth crowd, from the immigrants who packed their families into Lower East Side tenements more than a century ago to the Greenwich Village beatniks. Nowadays, Downtown is home to some of the priciest real estate on the planet, as formerly grungy neighbourhoods such as the Meatpacking District and the East Village become ritzified, and the value of a loft in Soho or Tribeca continues to skyrocket. Still, downtowners adore their meandering streets, their historical touchstones, their newly revitalised waterfront, their underground fashion and music scenes – and even their minuscule apartments. A day or two of exploring is all it takes to understand why.

Financial District

The southern tip of Manhattan is generally known as the Financial District because, in the days before telecommunications, banking institutions established their headquarters here to be near the city's active port. Down here, Atlantic Ocean breezes remind you that millions of people once travelled to the city on creaking, overcrowded sailing ships. You can trace the final stretch of their journey past the golden torch of the **Statue of Liberty**, through the immigration and quarantine centres of **Ellis Island** and, finally, to the statue-dotted **Battery Park promenade**. Nearby, is the boarding place for the famous **Staten Island Ferry**.

While this area is bisected vertically by the ever-bustling Broadway, it's that east-west thoroughfare **Wall Street** that is synonymous with the world's greatest den of capitalism.

Over on the eastern shore of lower Manhattan is the **South Street Seaport**, which was redeveloped in the mid 1980s and is now lined with reclaimed and renovated buildings that have been converted into shops, restaurants, bars and a museum. Check out the fine views of the **Brooklyn Bridge**.

Sights & museums

African Burial Ground

Duane Street, between Broadway & Centre Streets, behind 290 Broadway (www.africanburialground.com). Subway: W, R, N, Q to Canal Street; J, M, Z to Brooklyn Bridge-City Hall. **Open** 9am-4pm Mon-Fri. **Admission** free. **Map** p56 C2 ❶

A major archaeological discovery, the African Burial Ground is a small remnant of a five-and-a-half-acre cemetery where between 10,000 and 20,000 African men, women and children were buried long ago. The cemetery, which closed in 1794, was unearthed during construction of a federal office building in 1991 and designated a National Historic Landmark.

Brooklyn Bridge

Subway: A, C to High Street; J, M, Z to Chambers Street; 4, 5, 6 to Brooklyn Bridge-City Hall. **Map** p57 D3 ❷

The stunning views and awe-inspiring web of steel cables will take your breath away. As you walk, bike or Rollerblade along its wide wood-planked promenade, keep an eye out for plaques detailing the story of the bridge's construction.

City Hall

City Hall Park, from Vesey to Chambers Streets, between Broadway & Park Row (1-212 788 3000/www.nyc.gov). Subway: J, M, Z to Chambers Street; 2, 3 to Park Place; 4, 5, 6 to Brooklyn Bridge-City Hall. **Map** p56 C2 ❸

For group tours only; call two weeks in advance.

Ground Zero

Subway: 1, 2, 3 to Chambers Street; R, W to Cortlandt Street. **Map** p56 B3 ❹

The streets around Ground Zero, the former site of the World Trade Center, have been drawing crowds since the terrorist attacks of 2001. People come in droves to pay their respects to the nearly 2,800 people who lost their lives on 9/11. The area is currently surrounded by a high fence on which pictures of the devastation are hung alongside historical photos of the area.

Federal Reserve Bank

33 Liberty Street, between Nassau & William Streets (1-212 720 6130/www.newyorkfed.org). Subway: 2, 3, 4, 5 to Wall Street. **Open** 9.30-11.30am, 1.30-2.30pm Mon-Fri. **Tours** every hour on the half hour. Tours must be arranged at least one week in advance; tickets are sent by mail. **Admission** free. **Map** p56 C3 ❺

A block north on Liberty Street is an imposing structure built in the Florentine style. It holds the nation's largest store of gold – just over 9,000 tons – in a vault five storeys below street level, an exhibit about which is open to the public (advance reservations required).

Fraunces Tavern Museum

54 Pearl Street, at Broad Street (1-212 425 1778/www.frauncestavern museum.org). Subway: J, M, Z to Broad Street; 4, 5 to Bowling Green. **Open** noon-5pm Tue-Fri; 10am-5pm Sat. **Admission** $4; free-$3 reductions. No credit cards. **Map** p56 C4 ❻

This 18th-century tavern was George Washington's watering hole and the site of his famous farewell to the troops

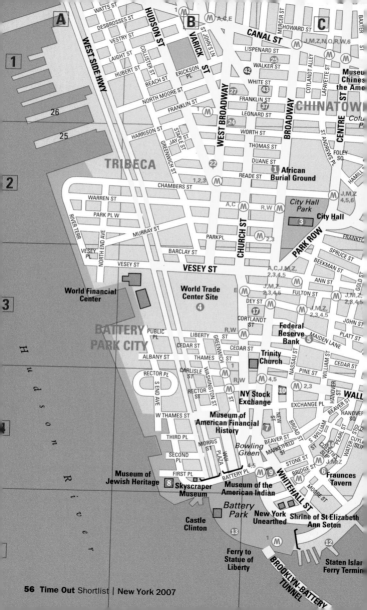

WATTS ST
DESBROSSES ST
A
HUDSON ST
VESTRY ST
LAIGHT ST
HUBERT ST
COLLISTER ST
ERICKSON PL
BEACH ST
NORTH MOORE ST
FRANKLIN ST
HARRISON ST
STAPLE ST
GREENWICH ST

B
VARICK ST
ST JOHN'S LN
WEST BROADWAY
42
27
M
24
22

C
A,C,E
HOWARD ST
CANAL ST
MERCER ST
BAXTER ST
J.M.Z,N,Q,R,W,6
LISPENARD ST
WALKER ST
25
WHITE ST
FRANKLIN ST
43
37
LEONARD ST
WORTH ST
THOMAS ST
DUANE ST
READE ST

Museu
Chines
the Ame
CHINATOWN
BROADWAY
CENTRE
COTLANDT ALLEY
LAFAYETTE ST
ELIZABETH ST
ST ANDREWS PL
FOLEY
SQ
Colu
P

TRIBECA

WARREN ST
PARK PL W
MURRAY ST
VESEY PL
RIVER TERR
NORTH END AVE
CHAMBERS ST
1,2,3
M

African
Burial Ground
HAMILL
City Hall
Park
M
J.M.Z,
4,5,6
City Hall
3

A.C
M
R,W
PARK ROW
FRANKF
SPRUCE ST
BEEKMAN ST
ANN ST
FULTON ST
J.M.Z,
2,3,4,5

2,3
M

WORLD FINANCIAL
CENTER

WORLD TRADE
CENTER SITE
4

VESEY ST

CHURCH ST
MURRAY ST
PARKPL
BARCLAY ST
VESEY ST

BATTERY
PARK CITY
PUBLIC
PL
LIBERTY
CEDAR ST
ALBANY ST
CARLISLE
ST
RECTOR PL
S END AVE
W THAMES ST
THIRD PL
MORRIS
ST
SECOND
PL
FIRST PL
BATTERY PL
Museum of
Jewish Heritage
8
Skyscraper
Museum
Castle
Clinton
13
Ferry to
Statue of
Liberty

GREENWICH ST
WASHINGTON ST
THAMES ST
CEDAR ST
RECTOR ST
ST

A,C,J,M,Z,
2,3,4,5
J.M.Z,
2,3,4,5
DEY ST
17
CORTLANDT
ST
J.M.Z,
2,3,4,5
M

E
M
R,W
Federal
Reserve
Bank
6
MAIDEN LANE
PLATT ST
JOHN ST

Trinity
Church
M
R,W
4,5
PINE ST
NASSAU ST
WILLIAM ST
CEDAR ST
2,3
10
M
HANOVER
WALL
NY Stock
Exchange
EXCHANGE PL
Museum of
American Financial
History
NEW ST
BROAD ST
7
BEAVER ST
HANOVER
SQ
OLD
S WILLIAM ST
PEARL ST
WATER ST
Bowling
Green
MARKETFIELD
ST
STONE ST
BRIDGE ST
J.M.Z
9
4,5
M
WHITEHALL ST
MOORE ST
Fraunces
Tavern
Museum of the
American Indian
New York
Unearthed
Shrine of St Elizabeth
Ann Seton
Battery
Park
M
12
Staten Islar
Ferry Termin
BROOKLYN-BATTERY
TUNNEL

H
u
d
s
o
n

R
i
v
e
r

THE BOWERY

D

CHRYSTIE ST
FORSYTH ST
ELDRIDGE ST
ALLEN ST
ORCHARD ST
LUDLOW ST
ESSEX ST

E **EAST BROADWAY**

F

East River Park

HENRY ST
MADISON ST
MONTGOMERY ST
GOUVERNEUR ST
WATER ST

1

Seward Park
Ⓜ

Eldridge St. Synagogue 61

JEFFERSON ST
CLINTON ST
CHERRY ST

51
Confucius Plaza

50
PELL ST
YARD ST
DIVISION ST

HENRY ST
MARKET ST
RUTGERS ST
MADISON ST
PIKE ST

Rutgers Park

PARK ROW

MONROE ST
CATHERINE ST
OLIVER ST

First Shearith Israel Graveyard

ST JAMES PL
WATER ST
SOUTH ST

MANHATTAN BRIDGE

2

ROOSEVELT DR

WAGNER PL

D

DOVER ST 15
PECK SLIP
WATER ST
BEEKMAN ST
FULTON ST

FRANKLIN

2 **BROOKLYN BRIDGE**

3

South Street Seaport 19

18

11
South St Seaport Museum 16

17

16

15

DEPEYSTER ST 14

New York City Police Museum 13

ERNEUR LN 11

9

BROOKLYN

0 ——— 200 m
0 ——— 200 yds

© Copyright Time Out Group 2006

1 Sights & museums
1 Eating & drinking
1 Shopping
1 Nightlife
1 Arts & leisure

Museum at FIT

A | **B** | **C**

W 26TH ST

NINTH AVE

SIXTH AVE

Dia: Chelsea

1

W 23RD ST

W 22ND ST

M C,E · M 1 · M F,V · M N,R,W

Madison Square

BROADWAY

New Museum of Contemporary Art

CHELSEA

EIGHTH AVE

SEVENTH AVE

Flatiron Building

FLATIRON

General Theological Seminary of the Episcopal Church

W 20TH ST

W 18TH ST

Theodore Roosevelt Birthplace

PARK AVE SOUTH

Joyce Theater

M 1

TENTH AVE

W 16TH ST

Union Square

FIFTH AVE

2

158, 161, 166

160, 164

W 14TH ST · A,C,E,L · M 1,2,3 · M F,V,L · L,N,Q,R,W, 4,5,6

144 · 143,145,152,154 · W 13TH ST · 136

157,165 · 162 · HORATIO · 153 · W 12TH ST

163 · JANE ST · 147 · GREENWICH AVE · W 11TH ST · UNIVERSITY PL

LITTLE W 12TH ST · W 10TH ST

GANSEVOORT ST · W 9TH ST

MEATPACKING DISTRICT · 140 · WAVERLY PL · SIXTH AVE · W 8TH ST · E 8TH ST

156 · 159 · W 4TH ST · 138

BETHUNE ST · HUDSON ST · BLEECKER ST · WAVERLY PL · 129 · **GREENWICH**

168 · BANK ST · 132 · WASHINGTON PL · **Washington Square** · WASH SQ EAST · GREENE ST

W 11TH ST · GREENWICH ST · 137 131 · WASH SQ WEST · 128 · WASH SQ EAST

3 · 50 · PERRY ST · 148 · GROVE ST · JONES ST · 151 · **New Unive**

46 · CHARLES ST · 146 · BARROW ST · CORNELIA · AIA Center for Architecture · 135 · 139 · **VILLAGE**

45 · W 10TH ST · BEDFORD ST · COMMERCE ST · LEROY ST · CARMINE ST · 133 · LA GUARDIA PL · 130 141

CHRISTOPHER ST · BARROW ST · 150 · 142

MORTON ST · 149 · ST LUKE'S PL · DOWNING ST · 41 · W HOUSTON ST · B,D,F,V

42 · LEROY ST · CLARKSON ST · 167 · MACDOUGAL ST · SULLIVAN ST · PRINCE ST · 26 · BROADWAY · 36 · N,R,W

40 · W HOUSTON ST · 155 · VARICK ST · KING ST · 9E · 42 · WOOSTER ST · 28 · SPRING ST · 30

4 · 34 · CHARLTON ST · VANDAM ST · SPRING ST · 28 · THOMPSON ST · 34 · GREENE ST · MERCER ST

WASHINGTON ST · GREENWICH ST · DOMINICK ST · 44 · **SOHO** · BROOME ST

HOLLAND TUNNEL · **New York City Fire Museum** · WATTS ST · DESBROSSES ST · GRAND ST · HOWARD

CANAL ST · HUDSON ST · WATTS ST · VESTRY ST · **CANAL ST** · A,C,E · **CANAL ST**

26 · 0 · 300 m · LAIGHT ST · 25 · LISPENARD ST · J,M,Z, Q,R,W,6

0 · 300 yds · HUBERT ST · BEACH ST · ERICKSON ST · WALKER ST · 43 · WHITE ST

© Copyright Time Out Group 2006 · NORTH MOORE ST · 27 · FRANKLIN ST · **CHINA**

FRANKLIN ST · LEONARD ST

HARRISON ST · WORTH ST

THOMAS ST

JAY ST · **TRIBECA**

WEST SIDE HWY · WEST BROADWAY · VARICK ST · HUDSON ST

This is a map of the Lower East Side, East Village, and Gramercy Park areas of Manhattan, New York.

Legend:
- ➊ Sights & museums
- ➊ Eating & drinking
- ➊ Shopping
- ➊ Nightlife
- ➊ Arts & leisure

Map labels include:
- THIRD AVE
- E 26TH ST
- E 24TH ST
- E 23RD ST
- GRAMERCY PARK
- Peter Cooper Village
- E 20TH ST
- Manhattan Marina
- FRANKLIN D ROOSEVELT DR
- ASSER LEVY PL
- SECOND AVE
- FIRST AVE
- E 18TH ST
- E 16TH ST
- E 15TH ST
- Stuyvesant Town
- Stuyvesant Square
- RUTHERFORD PL
- NATHAN D PERLMAN PL
- E 14TH ST
- E 13TH ST
- E 12TH ST
- E 11TH ST
- E 10TH ST
- E 9TH ST
- E 8TH ST
- E 7TH ST
- E 6TH ST
- E 5TH ST
- E 4TH ST
- E 3RD ST
- E 2ND ST
- SZOLD PL
- AVENUE A
- AVENUE B
- AVENUE C
- AVENUE D
- St. Mark's Church in-the-Bowery
- STUYVESANT ST
- ST MARKS PLACE
- Tompkins Square
- EAST VILLAGE
- FOURTH AVE
- GREAT JONES ST
- BOND ST
- BLEECKER ST
- E HOUSTON ST
- STANTON ST
- RIVINGTON ST
- NORFOLK ST
- CLINTON ST
- SUFFOLK ST
- ATTORNEY ST
- RIDGE ST
- PITT ST
- COLUMBIA ST
- FREEMAN ALLEY
- MULBERRY ST
- MOTT ST
- ELIZABETH ST
- KENMARE ST
- DELANCEY ST NORTH
- DELANCEY ST SOUTH
- WILLIAMSBURG BRIDGE
- LEWIS ST
- BIALYSTOKER PL
- ABRAHAM E KAZAN ST
- Lower East Side Tenement Museum
- LOWER EAST SIDE
- BROOME ST
- GRAND ST
- ORCHARD ST
- ALLEN ST
- ELDRIDGE ST
- FORSYTH ST
- CHRYSTIE ST
- LUDLOW ST
- ESSEX ST
- THE BOWERY
- LITTLE ITALY
- BAXTER ST
- CENTRE ST
- HESTER ST
- Museum of Chinese in the Americas
- Eldridge St. Synagogue
- Seward Park
- EAST BROADWAY
- HENRY ST
- MADISON ST
- GOUVERNEUR ST
- MONTGOMERY ST
- JEFFERSON ST
- RUTGERS ST
- JACKSON ST
- CHERRY ST
- WATER ST
- D ROOSEVELT DR
- PIKE ST
- MARKET ST
- MONROE ST
- Confucius Plaza
- Columbus Park
- BAYARD ST
- PELL ST
- MOSCO ST
- DIVISION ST
- PARK ROW
- FRANKLIN
- East River Park
- CHINATOWN

Numbered markers: 70, 69, 112, 106, 111, 124, 108, 100, 116, 113, 109, 126, 120, 117, 125, 101, 103, 107, 105, 102, 123, 99, 110, 98, 118, 119, 104, 122, 114, 6, 70, 59, 60, 48, 62, 85, 83, 67, 91, 88, 81, 94, 79, 72, 64, 95, 84, 92, 90, 89, 80, 78, 73, 74, 71, 96, 82, 49, 86, 65, 56, 45, 51, 46, 61, 50

at the Revolution's close. During the mid to late 1780s, the building housed the fledgling nation's departments of war, foreign affairs and treasury. In 1904, Fraunces became a repository for artefacts collected by the Sons of the Revolution in the State of New York. Ongoing exhibits include 'George Washington: Down the Stream of Life'. The tavern and restaurant serve hearty fare, Monday to Saturday.

Museum of American Financial History

28 Broadway, between Beaver Street & Exchange Place (1-212 908 4110/www. financialhistory.org). Subway: 1 to Rector Street. **Open** 10am-4pm Tue-Sat. **Admission** $2. **Map** p56 C4 ❼
The permanent collection, which traces the development of Wall Street and America's financial markets, includes ticker tape from the morning of the big crash of 29 October 1929, an 1867 stock ticker and the earliest known photograph of Wall Street.

Museum of Jewish Heritage

Robert F Wagner Jr Park, 36 Battery Place, at First Place (1-646 437 4200/ www.mjhnyc.org). Subway: 1 to South Ferry; 4, 5 to Bowling Green. **Open** 10am-5.45pm Mon-Tue, Thur, Sun; 10am-8pm Wed; 10am-3pm Fri, eve of Jewish holidays (until 5pm in the summer). **Admission** $10; free-$7 reductions; free 4-8pm Wed. **Map** p56 B4 ❽
Opened in 1997 and expanded in 2003, this museum offers one of the most moving cultural experiences in the city. Detailing the horrific attacks on (and inherent joys of) Jewish life during the past century, the collection consists of 24 documentary films, 2,000 photographs and 800 cultural artefacts, many donated by Holocaust survivors and their families.

National Museum of the American Indian

George Gustav Heye Center, Alexander Hamilton Custom House, 1 Bowling Green, between State & Whitehall

Poetry in motion

Poets House, the city's premier public resource centre for spoken and written verse, will be moving from its location in Soho's trendy shopping district to the more pedestrian-friendly Battery Park City in late 2007.

'With respect to collections of contemporary American poetry, Poets House has few rivals,' says executive director Lee Briccetti. 'The new space will allow for our collection to grow in one of the most beautiful spots anywhere.' The collection features every poetry book published in the US.

The new location offers an expansive view of the Hudson River and Statue of Liberty, iterating the organisation's belief in poetry's democratic, life-affirming value. The 10,000-square-foot space occupies the ground and second floors of One River Terrace, a 32-storey building designed by Polshek Partnership. Featuring a double-height glass curtain entry and an ornamental book-wall and staircase, the interior is fully visible from the park. Inside you'll find poetry written on the walls and other unlikely places, encouraging visitors to make physical contact with language. An expanded children's area will offer workshop space to encourage a generation raised on digital media to continue the tradition. 'We're creating an atmosphere of friendship and affection for anyone who loves poetry,' says Briccetti.
■ www.poetshouse.org

Fraunces Tavern p55

public, but the street outside offers an endless pageant of brokers, traders and their minions.

South Street Seaport Museum

Visitors' Center, 12 Fulton Street, at South Street (1-212 748 8600/www. southstseaport.org). Subway: A, C to Broadway-Nassau Street; J, M, Z, 2, 3, 4, 5 to Fulton Street. **Open** *Apr-Oct* 10am-6pm Tue-Sun. *Nov-Mar* 10am-6pm Fri-Sun. **Admission** $8; free-$6 reductions. **Map** p57 D3 ⑪

Occupying 11 blocks along the East River, the museum is an amalgam of galleries, historic ships, 19th-century buildings and a visitors' centre. Wander around the rebuilt streets and pop in to see an exhibition on marine life and history before climbing aboard the four-masted 1911 *Peking*. The seaport is generally thick with tourists, but it's still a lively place to spend an afternoon, especially for families with children, who are likely to enjoy the atmosphere and intriguing seafaring memorabilia.

Staten Island Ferry

Battery Park, South Street, at Whitehall Street (1-718 727 2508/www.si ferry.com). Subway: 1 to South Ferry; 4, 5 to Bowling Green. **Open** 24hrs daily. **Tickets** free. **Map** p56 C5 ⑫

During this commuter barge's 25-minute crossing, you'll get stunning panoramas of lower Manhattan and the Statue of Liberty. Boats depart South Ferry at Battery Park.

Statue of Liberty & Ellis Island Immigration Museum

Statue of Liberty (1-212 363 3200/www.nps.gov/stli). Travel: R, W to Whitehall Street; 1 to South Ferry; 4, 5 to Bowling Green; then take the Statue of Liberty ferry (1-212 269 5755), departing every 25 minutes from gangway 4 or 5 in southernmost Battery Park. **Open** Ferry runs 8.30am-3.30pm daily. Purchase tickets at Castle Clinton in Battery Park. **Admission** $10; free-$8 reductions. **Map** p56 B5 ⑬

Streets (1-212 514 3700/www.nmai. si.edu). Subway: R, W to Whitehall Street; 1 to South Ferry; 4, 5 to Bowling Green. **Open** 10am-5pm Mon-Wed, Fri-Sun; 10am-8pm Thur. **Admission** free. **Map** p56 C4 ⑨

This branch of the Smithsonian Institution displays its collection around the grand rotunda of the 1907 Custom House, at the bottom of Broadway (which, many moons ago, began as an Indian trail). The life and culture of Native Americans are presented in rotating exhibitions – from intricately woven fibre Pomo baskets to beaded buckskin shirts – along with contemporary artwork.

New York Stock Exchange

11 Wall Street, between Broad & New Streets. Subway: 2, 3, 4, 5 to Wall Street. **Map** p56 C4 ⑩

The nerve centre of the US economy is the New York Stock Exchange. For security reasons, the Exchange is no longer open to the

Ground Zero p.55

Frédéric-Auguste Bartholdi's *Liberty
Enlightening the World*, a gift from the
people of France, was unveiled in 1886.
After security concerns placed the statue off-limits for nearly three years, its
pedestal finally reopened for guided
tours in summer 2004 (you still can't
climb up to the crown, and backpacks
and luggage are not permitted on the
island). Still, there's ample room to
absorb the 1883 Emma Lazarus poem
that includes the renowned lines 'Give
me your tired, your poor/Your huddled
masses yearning to breathe free.' On the
way back to Manhattan, the ferry will
stop at the popular Immigration
Museum, on Ellis Island, through
which more than 12 million entered the
country between 1892 and 1954. The $6
audio tour is informative and inspiring.

Eating & drinking

Adrienne's Pizza Bar
54 Stone Street, between Mill Street
& Coenties Alley (1-212 248 3838).
Subway: A, C, E to Canal Street.

Open 11am-11pm Mon-Thur; 11am-
midnight Fri; 10.30am-midnight Sat,
Sun. $$. **Italian**. Map p56 C4 ⑭
A bright, modern pizzeria on a quaint,
cobbled pedestrian street. You can get
your pizza by the slice or thin-crust pie,
and wolf it down at the standing-room
bar, or more properly in the sit-down
dining area. Dinner guests will find an
extended menu of small plates and
entrées, and plenty of outdoor seating.

Bridge Cafe
279 Water Street, at Dover Street
(1-212 227 3344). Subway: A, C to
Broadway-Nassau Street; J, M, Z, 2, 3,
4, 5 to Fulton Street. Open Sun, Mon
11.45am-10pm; Tue-Thur 11.45am-
11pm; Fri 11.45am-midnight; Sat 5pm-
midnight. $$. **American creative**.
Map p57 D3 ⑮
This 1794 building did time as a 'dis-
orderly house' long ago – and its
romantic tin-ceilinged dining room can
still inspire some old-fashioned hanky-
panky.You and your hot date can slip
into this hideaway, in the shadow of

NEW YORK BY AREA

South Street Seaport p55

the Brooklyn Bridge, and dine on pine-nut-crusted chicken with artichoke-caper-lemon confit or soft-shell crabs with spicy potatoes.

Heartland Brewery

93 South Street at Fulton Street (1-646 572-2742). Subway: A, C to Broadway-Nassau Street; 2, 3, 4, 5 to Fulton Street. **Open** 11am-10pm daily. **Bar**. **Map** p56 D3 ⑯

All of the microbrews served at Heartland come from a Fort Greene brewery, so there's always a little touch of Brooklyn here.

Shopping

Century 21

22 Cortlandt Street, between Broadway & Church Street (1-212 227 9092/ www.c21stores.com). Subway: R, W to Cortlandt Street. **Open** 7.45am-8pm Mon-Wed, Fri; 7.45am-8.30pm Thur; 10am-8pm Sat; 11am-7pm Sun. **Map** p56 C3 ⑰

Directly east of Ground Zero, bargain hunters can sift through the stock at this enormous discount-designer-duds

vault. The score is rare but intoxicating; savings are usually between 25% and 75% off regular retail prices.

Tribeca & Soho

Tribeca throbs with energy, but a few pockets appear abandoned – the cobblestones crumbling and dirty, the cast-iron buildings chipped and unpainted. Don't be fooled; derelict areas like these are transformed with deluxe makeovers seemingly overnight. Fine small-scale cast-iron architecture still stands along White Street and the parallel thoroughfares.

Soho, New York's glamorous downtown shopping destination, was once earmarked for destruction, but, thankfully, its signature cast-iron warehouses were saved by the many artists who inhabited them. Chain stores have moved in among the boutiques and bistros, drawing a shopping-mall-at-Christmas-time crush every weekend.

NEW YORK BY AREA

PIER 16

LINE MUSEUM ENTRY CIRCLE

NEW YORK BY AREA

the Brooklyn Bridge, and dine on pine-nut-crusted chicken with artichoke-caper-lemon confit or soft-shell crabs with spicy potatoes.

Boarding the Staten Island Ferry p62

Sights & museums

New York City Fire Museum

*278 Spring Street, between Hudson &
Varick Streets (1-212 691 1303/www.
nycfiremuseum.org). Subway: C, E to
Spring Street; 1 to Houston Street.*
Open 10am-5pm Tue-Sat; 10am-4pm
Sun. **Admission** suggested donation
$5; $1-$2 reductions. **Map** p58 B4 ⑱
An active firehouse from 1904 to 1959,
this museum is filled with gadgetry
and pageantry, from late 18th-century
hand-pumped fire engines to present-
day equipment. The museum also
houses a permanent exhibit commem-
orating firefighters' heroism after the
attack on the World Trade Center.

Eating & drinking

Antique Garage

*41 Mercer Street, between Broome
& Grand Streets (1-212 219 1019).
Subway: J, M, N, Q, R, W, Z, 6 to Canal
Street.* **Open** noon-midnight daily. **$**.
Mediterranean. Map p58 C4 ⑲

Formerly an auto-repair shop, the
Antique Garage has good acoustics
and ample Turkish carpeting to control
the volume of its garrulous crowd,
which comes for the live music as well
as the food. Other assets: faded paintings and peeling mirrors on the walls,
heirloom plates and antique chandeliers – all of which are for sale. The
kitchen manages to live up to the decor
with decent portions of borek (feta-
stuffed filo), creamy houmous, and
seared tuna doused in red-pepper purée.

Balthazar

*80 Spring Street, between Broadway
& Crosby Street (1-212 965 1414).
Subway: N, R, W to Prince Street; 6 to
Spring Street.* **Open** 7.30-11.30am,
noon-5pm, 6pm-1am Mon-Wed; 7.30-
11.30am, noon-5pm, 6pm-1.30am Thur;
7.30-11.30am, noon-5pm, 6pm-2am Fri;
10am-4pm, 6pm-2am Sat; 10am-4pm,
5.30pm- midnight Sun. **$$**. **French
bistro**. Map p58 C4 ⑳
Now heading for its tenth birthday,
this authentic French brasserie is still
a scene – especially for the Saturday

NEW YORK BY AREA

New Museum of Contemporary Art

Staying current with a new location.

The New Museum's relocation to a permanent site at 235 Bowery on the Lower East Side embodies its mission statement, 'New Art, New Ideas'. Its latest address also confirms its other primary calling, to cut 'clear, smart and bold' moves within the field of contemporary art.

'We're all very, very excited to bring a dynamic New Museum back into Manhattan's cultural trust,' says chief curator Richard Flood. The 65,000-square-foot facility, scheduled to open in autumn 2007, is primarily dedicated to contemporary art, with emphases on emerging media and surveys of important but 'under-recognised' artists. Recent years have showcased the work of Ana Mendieta, Tom Friedman and Andrea Zittel. For a museum with this much cultural capital, relocating to the (former) skids of the Bowery is a pioneering step, but Flood sees the new space dovetailing with the museum's legacy as the city's most innovative 'laboratory for change in terms of contemporary art practice'. Sited on a former parking lot wedged between Stanton and Rivington Streets in a neighbourhood known more for its restaurant supply wholesalers and flop houses than high-end conceptual art, the building reflects the New Museum's spirit.

The seven-storey structure, encased in rippling silver metal, was designed by the Tokyo-based firm Sejima and Nishizawa/SANAA. The interior challenges the conventional museum space, featuring unusual light sources and hidden pockets where art will be tucked for visitors to discover. Other features include a black box auditorium accommodating 180 people and offering downtown art goers a much-needed venue for an array of public programs.

■ www.newmuseum.org

and Sunday brunch, when the room is packed with media executives, rail-thin lookers and trendy boys in chic hoodies. A three-tiered seafood platter (a house special) casts the most impressive shadow of any appetiser in town. Frisée aux lardons is exemplary, as is roasted chicken on mashed potatoes for two, and skate with brown butter and capers.

Blue Ribbon

97 Sullivan Street, between Prince & Spring Street (1-212 274 0404). Subway: C, E to Spring Street. **Open** 4pm-4am Tue-Sun. **$$. American creative**. Map p58 C4 ㉑
Since 1992, this Soho fixture has continuously attracted global foodies and off-the-clock chefs from the neighbourhood, who come for the pristine raw bar, excellent blue-cheese burgers and beef marrow with oxtail marmalade. As it's open until 4am, the restaurant lures the fabulous for a late-night nosh – which usually means oysters and champagne.

Bouley Bakery & Market

130 West Broadway, at Duane Street (1-212 608 5829). Subway: A, C, 1, 2, 3 to Chambers Street. **Open** Bakery 7.30am-7.30pm daily. Restaurant 6-11pm Tue-Sat. **$-$$. French**. Map p56 B2 ㉒
Chef David Bouley's new bakery has pastries, breads, sandwiches, salads and pizza on the ground floor; a cellar full of fresh seafood, meats and cheeses; and on the first floor, a dining room with a sushi bar and cocktails. Sidewalk seats appear in warm weather.

Fanelli's Café

94 Prince Street, at Mercer Street (1-212 226 9412). Subway: N, R, W to Prince Street. **Open** 10am-2.30am Mon-Thur; 10am-3am Fri, Sat; 11am-12.30am Sun. **$. American**. Map p58 C4 ㉓
Deemed the second-oldest restaurant in New York, Fanelli's has stood at this cobblestoned intersection since 1847, and local artists and worldly tourists pour into the lively landmark for perfectly charred beef patties on toasted onion rolls. The long bar, prints of boxing legends and check tablecloths add to the charm.

Landmarc

179 West Broadway, between Leonard & Worth Streets (1-212 343 3883). Subway: 1 to Franklin Street. **Open** noon-2am Mon-Fri; 11am-2am Sat, Sun. **$$$. French**. Map p56 B1/p58 C5 ㉔
Chef Marc Murphy has a great kids' menu – which buys the grown-ups time to savour the good stuff: tender braised lamb shanks, steaks grilled in an open hearth, mussels steamed with chorizo and onions. An enticing bottles-only wine list is also served in half-bottle portions.

M1-5

52 Walker Street, between Broadway & Church Street (1-212 965 1701). Subway: J, M, Z, N, Q, R, W, 6 to Canal Street. **Open** Daily 4pm-4am. **Bar**. Map p56 C1/p58 C5 ㉕
The name of the huge, red-walled hangout refers to Tribeca's zoning ordinance, which permits trendy restaurants to coexist with warehouses. The mixed-use label also applies to M1-5's crowd: suited brokers shoot pool next to aging garage-bandmates and youthful indie screenwriters. No velvet rope, no fancy cocktails, just a full, well-stocked bar.

Pegu Club

NEW *77 W Houston Street, between West Broadway & Wooster Street (1-212 473 7348). Subway: 6 to Bleecker Street; B, D, F, V to Broadway-Lafayette Street.* **Open** 5pm-2am Sun-Wed; Thur-Sat 5pm-4am. **Bar**. Map p58 C4 ㉖
Located on an unassuming Soho block, This bar is both hidden and welcoming. Upstairs, what greets cocktail connoisseurs is an elegant space with a long maple bar and a faint air of nostalgic colonial glamour. Owner-mixologist Audrey Saunders stubbornly discourages trendy vodkas – gin is the basis for most of the menu.

Adidas

VinoVino

211 West Broadway, between Franklin & White Streets (1-212 925 8510). Subway: 1 to Franklin Street. **Open** 5-11pm Tue, Wed; 5pm-1am Thu, Fri; 1pm-1am Sat; 1-8pm Sun. **Wine Bar**. **Map** p56 B1/p58 C5 ㉗

VinoVino is a narrow, 2,200-square-foot space in Tribeca that's one part wine shop and one part enoteca. Husband-and-wife team Jay and Ashley Donayre didn't want shoppers to feel intimidated by their stock of artisanal and rare vintages, so sippers can try wines by the glass at the bar before buying a bottle in the store.

Shopping

A Bathing Ape

91 Greene Street, between Prince & Spring Streets (1-212 925 0222). Subway: N, R, W to Prince Street. **Open** noon-7pm Mon-Sat; noon-6pm Sun. **Map** p58 C4 ㉘

The cult streetwear label created by Japanese designer Nigo planted its first US flagship in Soho. Nigo, who has collaborated with Adidas and NERD frontman Pharrell Williams, among others, devotes most of his shop to BAPE threads, while an upstairs shoe salon housing BAPEsta kicks has made the city's sneaker-hungry masses go ape.

Adidas

610 Broadway, at Houston Street (1-212 529 0081). Subway: N, R, W to Prince Street. **Open** 10am-8pm Mon-Sat; 11am-7pm Sun. **Map** p58 C4 ㉙

Inside this 29,500sq ft Soho space – decorated with giant images of athletes – you'll find every imaginable garment associated with the brand, including sportster threads by Stella McCartney.

Ben Sherman

NEW *96 Spring Street, at Mercer Street (1-212 680 0160/www.bensherman usa.com). Subway: C, E to Spring Street; N, R, W to Prince Street.* **Open** 10am-9pm Mon-Sat; 11am-7pm Sun. **Map** p58 C4 ㉚

Bringing a touch of London's Carnaby Street to Soho, Ben Sherman, the eponymous streetwear brand born of the original swinging '60s mod god, has dropped its first US flagship. As a salute to its English roots, the coed emporium is peppered with mannequins and an antique settee covered in a Union Jack pattern.

Dean & DeLuca

560 Broadway, at Prince Street (1-212 431 1691/www.deananddeluca.com). Subway: N, R, W to Prince Street. **Open** 10am-8pm Mon-Sat; 10am-7pm Sun. **Map** p58 C4 ③

Dean & DeLuca's flagship store (one of only two that offer more than just a fancy coffee bar) provides the most sophisticated (and pricey) selection of speciality food items in the city.

INA

101 Thompson Street, between Prince & Spring Streets (1-212 941 4757). Subway: C, E to Spring Street. **Open** noon-7pm Mon-Thur, Sun; noon-8pm Fri, Sat. **Map** p58 C4 ②

INA has reigned over the downtown consignment scene for more than a decade. The Soho location features drastically reduced couture pieces, while the Nolita shop, on Prince Street, carries trendier clothing.

John Masters Organics

77 Sullivan Street, between Spring & Broome Streets (1-212 343 9590/ www.johnmasters.com). Subway: C, E to Spring Street; N, R, W to Prince Street. **Open** 11am-7pm Mon-Sat. **Map** p58 C4 ③

Organic doesn't get more orgasmic than it is in John Masters' chic apothecary line. Blood orange and vanilla body wash and lavender and avocado intensive conditioner are just two of the good-enough-to-eat products that you can get to go.

Le Corset by Selima

80 Thompson Street, between Broome & Spring Streets (1-212 334 4936). Subway: C, E to Spring Street. **Open** 11am-7pm Mon-Fri; noon-8pm Sat; noon-7pm Sun. **Map** p58 C4 ③

John Masters Organics

In addition to Selima Salaun's slinky lingerie and loungewear, this boudoir-like boutique stocks antique camisoles and vintage silk kimonos. Victorian- and Edwardian-inspired corsets can be custom made for a perfect fit.

Marc Jacobs

163 Mercer Street, between Houston & Prince Streets (1-212 343 1490/ www.marcjacobs.com). Subway: B, D, F, V to Broadway-Lafayette Street; N, R, W to Prince Street; 6 to Bleecker Street. **Open** 11am-7pm Mon-Sat; noon-6pm Sun. **Map** p58 C4 ③

Men and women get fashion parity at Jacobs' Soho boutique. A separate-but-equal policy rules on the designer's Bleecker Street strip (Nos.403-405 & 385), where a trio of stores – men's, women's and accessories – keeps the West Village well outfitted.

Phat Farm

129 Prince Street, between West Broadway & Wooster Street (1-212 533 7428/www.phatfarmstore.com).

NEW YORK BY AREA

Subway: C, E to Spring Street; N, R, W to Prince Street. **Open** 11am-7pm Mon-Sat; noon-6pm Sun. **Map** p58 C4 ⑯

Find Def Jam impresario Russell Simmons's classy, conservative take on hip-hop couture: phunky-phresh baggy clothing for guys, and for gals, the curvy Baby Phat line.

Rogan

NEW *91 Franklin Street, between Broadway & Church Street (1-646 827 7554). Subway: A, C, E to Canal Street.* **Open** 11am-7pm daily. **Map** p56 C1/p58 C5 ⑰

Ever wonder what makes enigmatic fashion wunderkind Rogan Gregory tick? A twirl through Tribeca's new Rogan flagship reveals that the designer behind culty labels Rogan, EDUN, Loomstate and A Litl Betr has an appreciation for rugged materials, as evidenced by the store's exposed brick, driftwood 'sculptures' and raw concrete floors.

Stüssy

140 Wooster Street, between Houston & Prince Streets (1-212 995 8787). Subway: N, R, W to Prince Street. **Open** noon-7pm Mon-Thur; 11am-7pm Fri, Sat; noon-6pm Sun. **Map** p58 C4 ⑱

Tricky isn't the only one who wants to be dressed up in Stüssy. Come here for the collection of skate- and surfwear that made Sean Stüssy famous, as well as utilitarian bags from Japanese label Headporter.

Supreme

274 Lafayette Street, between Prince & Houston Streets (1-212 966 7799). Subway: B, D, F, V to Broadway-Lafayette Street; N, R, W to Prince Street; 6 to Spring Street. **Open** 11.30am-7pm Mon-Sat; noon-6pm Sun. **Map** p59 D4 ⑲

Filled mostly with East Coast brands such as Chocolate, Independent and Zoo York, this skatewear store also stocks its own line. Look out for pieces by Burton and DC Shoe – favourite labels of skaters such as Colin McKay and Danny Way.

Triple Five Soul

290 Lafayette Street, between Houston & Prince Streets (1-212 431 2404/ www.triple5soul.com). Subway: B, D, F, V to Broadway-Lafayette Street; N, R, W to Prince Street; 6 to Bleecker Street. **Open** 11am-7pm Mon-Thur, Sun; 11am-7.30pm Fri, Sat. **Map** p59 D4 ⑳

Although the label is no longer exclusive to New York, the city can still boast the brand's sole stores. Find the very necessary hooded sweatshirts and T-shirts stamped with the Triple Five logo at this Soho spot.

Nightlife

S.O.B.'s

204 Varick Street, at Houston Street (1-212 243 4940/www.sobs.com). Subway: 1 to Houston Street. **Open** times vary, call or check website. **Map** p58 B4 ㊶

The titular sounds of Brazil are just some of many global genres that keep this Tribeca spot hopping. Hip hop, soul, reggae and Latin beats figure into the mix, with MIA, Seu Jorge, Leela James and Yellowman each appearing of late. Careful at the bar – drinks are outrageously priced. But the sharp-looking clientele doesn't seem to mind.

Studios

Tribeca Grand Hotel, 2 Sixth Avenue, between Walker & White Streets (1-212 519 6677/www.tribecagrand. com). Subway: A, C, E to Canal Street; 1 to Franklin Street. **Open** 9pm-2am daily. **Map** p56 B1/p58 C5 ㊷

When the Tribeca Grand first started showcasing DJs and live music in its downstairs, club-like sanctum, it unexpectedly became one of the city's top spots for underground beats – thanks mostly to its of-the-moment electroclash and nu-rock. Things have calmed down since then, but the place still rocks at the Saturday night Fixed affair, where groundbreaking DJs and live acts – folks like Glasgow's Optimo and crazed bleep-funk duo Mu – sometimes hold court. It's best to call before visiting as the room is also used for private functions.

Arts & leisure

Flea Theater

41 White Street, between Broadway & Church Street (1-212 226 2407/ www.theflea.org). Subway: A, C, E, J, M, N, Q, R, W, Z, 1, 6 to Canal Street. **Map** p56 C1/p58 C5 ㊸
Founded in 1997, Jim Simpson's cosy, well-appointed venue has presented both avant-garde experimentation (the work of Mac Wellman) and politically provocative satires (mostly by AR Gurney).

HERE

145 Sixth Avenue, at Broome Street (1-212 647 0202/Smarttix 1-212 868 4444/www.here.org). Subway: C, E to Spring Street. **Map** p58 C4 ㊹
Containing three intimate performance spaces, an art gallery and a chic café, this lovely Tribeca arts complex, dedicated to non-profit arts enterprise, has hosted a number of exciting companies. It was the launching pad for such well-known shows as Eve Ensler's *Vagina Monologues*.

Chinatown, Little Italy & Nolita

You won't hear much English along the crowded streets of **Chinatown**, lined by fish-, fruit- and vegetable-stocked stands. This is the largest Chinese community outside Asia. **Canal Street**, a bargain hunter's paradise, is infamous for its (illegal) knockoff designer handbags, perfumes and other goods among the numerous cheap gift shops.

Little Italy, which once ran from Canal to Houston Streets between Lafayette Street and the Bowery, hardly resembles the insular community famously portrayed in Martin Scorsese's *Mean Streets*. Italian families have fled Mott Street and gone to the suburbs, Chinatown has crept north, and rising rents have forced mom-and-pop businesses to surrender to the stylish boutiques of **Nolita** – North of Little Italy (a misnomer, since it technically lies within Little Italy).

Chi-chi restaurants and boutiques have taken over Nolita. Elizabeth, Mott and Mulberry Streets, between Houston and Spring Streets in particular, are now the source of everything from perfectly cut jeans to hand-blown glass.

Sights & museums

Eastern States Buddhist Temple of America

64 Mott Street, between Bayard & Canal Streets (1-212 966 6229). Subway: J, M, N, Q, R, W, Z, 6 to Canal Street. **Open** 9am-6pm daily. **Map** p57 D1/p59 D5 ㊺

Museum of Chinese in the Americas

Second Floor, 70 Mulberry Street, at Bayard Street (1-212 619 4785/www. moca-nyc.org). Subway: J, M, N, Q, R, W, Z, 6 to Canal Street. **Open** noon-6pm Tue-Thur, Sat, Sun; noon-7pm Fri. **Admission** suggested donation $3; free-$1 reductions; free Friday. No credit cards. **Map** p57 D1/p59 D5 ㊻
In the heart of downtown Manhattan's Chinatown, a century-old former schoolhouse holds a two-room museum focused on Chinese-American history and the Chinese immigrant experience. Call for details about walking tours of the neighbourhood.

Eating & drinking

Barmarché

14 Spring Street, at Elizabeth Street (1-212 219 9542). Subway: N, R, W to Prince Street; 6 to Spring Street. **Open** 11am-11pm Mon, Sun; 11pm-midnight Tue-Thur; 10am-1am Fri, Sat. **$$**. **American**. **Map** p59 D4 ㊼
Peer inside this bright, white-on-white brasserie, and you'll be tempted to come in and join the party: the dining room is often filled with lively groups,

Chinatown p71

and the kitchen keeps them happy and well fed. The menu is American in the melting-pot sense, covering all the greatest-hits, no-nonsense dishes from around the world: home-made fettuccine with pesto; thick gazpacho with guacamole; tuna tartare with grated Asian pear and citrus ponzu; croques-monsieur; and a juicy, made-in-the-USA burger.

Café Habana

17 Prince Street, at Elizabeth Street (1-212 625 2001). Subway: N, R, W to Prince Street; 6 to Spring Street. **Open** 9am-midnight daily. **$. Cuban. Map** p59 D4 ⓭

Hipsters storm this café day and night for its addictive grilled corn doused in butter and rolled in grated cheese and chilli powder. Other staples include crisp beer-battered catfish tortas with spicy mayo, and juicy marinated skirt steak with yellow rice and black beans. This year the owners opened a second location in Greenpoint, Brooklyn.

Congee Village

100 Allen Street, between Broome & Delancey Streets (1-212 941 1818). Subway: F to Delancey Street; J, M, Z to Delancey-Essex Streets. **Open** 10.30am-2am daily. **$. Chinese. Map** p59 E4 ⓭

If you've never indulged in the starchy comfort of congee, this is a good place to start. The rice porridge in a clay pot over a slow fire is best early in the day; pick a chunky version such as the treasure-laden seafood or sliced fish. Crab is impeccably fresh, as is the well-seasoned whole fish served over glistening Chinese broccoli. It may seem incongruous, but the Congee has a great pina colada – and it will only cost you $3 during the weekday happy hour (4-7pm).

Doyers Vietnamese Restaurant

11 Doyers Street, between Bowery & Pell Street (1-212 513 1521). Subway: J, M, N, Q, R, W, Z, 6 to Canal Street. **Open** 11am-10pm Mon-Thur, Sun; 11am-11pm Fri, Sat. **$. Vietnamese. Map** p57 D1/p59 D5 ⓾

The search to find this restaurant is part of the fun: it's tucked away in a basement on a zigzagging Chinatown alley. The 33 appetisers include balls of grilled minced shrimp wrapped around sugarcane sticks and a delicious Vietnamese crêpe filled with shrimp and pork. Hot pot soups, served on a tabletop stove, are made with an exceptional fish-broth base. For maximum enjoyment, come with a six-pack of Singha beer in tow (the restaurant is BYOB only).

Golden Bridge

50 Bowery, between Bayard & Canal Streets (1-212 227 8831). Subway: B, D to Grand Street; J, M, N, Q, R, W, Z, 6 to Canal Street. **Open** 9am-11pm daily. **$. Chinese. Map** p57 D1/p59 D5 ⓯

Dim sum devotees often pick Flushing, Queens, over Manhattan, but they should reconsider with this serious Cantonese venue above a Popeye's on the Bowery. An armada of carts offers fresh and flavourful standards like clams in black bean sauce and pillowy steamed pork buns, plus unusual items such as egg tarts with a soft taro crust. Look for the elusive cart bearing a mysterious wooden bucket; it's filled with an irresistible, lightly sweetened tofu.

Lombardi's

32 Spring Street, between Mott & Mulberry Streets (1-212 941 7994). Subway: 6 to Spring Street. **Open** 11.30am-11pm Mon-Thur; 11.30am-midnight Fri, Sat; 11.30am-10pm Sun. **$. Italian.** No credit cards. **Map** p59 D4 ⓬

Established in 1905, Lombardi's is the city's oldest pizzeria and offers pizza at its best: made in a coal-fired oven and with a chewy, thin crust. The pepperoni is fantastic, as are the killer meatballs in tomato sauce. The setting is classic pizza-parlour – wooden booths, red-and-white checked tablecloths.

Lovely Day

196 Elizabeth Street, between Prince & Spring Streets (1-212 925 3310). Subway: J, M, Z to Bowery; 6 to Spring

Greenwich Village p89

Street. **Open** noon-11pm Mon-Thur; noon-midnight Fri; 11am-midnight Sat; 11am-11pm Sun. **$. Pan Asian**. **Map** p59 D4 53

At Lovely Day tamarind appears in the shrimp summer roll's dressing, and again in the dressing for the flank steak served with rice and vegetables. But the spice isn't the only asset here: coconut curry noodles and pineapple fried rice are equally good. Slide into a booth and take your cue from the scents wafting from the tiny kitchen. Or come for brunch, which features crisp banana rolls.

Porcupine

20 Prince Street, between Elizabeth & Mott Streets (1-212 966 8886). Subway: N, R, W to Prince Street; 6 to Spring Street. **Open** 11am-11pm Mon-Fri; 11am-11.30pm Sat, Sun. **$$**. **French bistro**. **Map** p59 D4 54

Jacques Ouari prepares audacious seasonal dishes from local artisanal ingredients. For lunch, you can try hearty sandwiches like a croque-madame with fried egg and vinegar radishes, or grilled leg of lamb with prune-hyssop butter and rocket. Dinners are meaty too: suckling pig with apple and celeriac, for example, or mustard-braised veal with lemon pickles. Non-meat dishes could include Taylor Bay scallop and blackfish stew with almond milk and acorn squash.

Public

210 Elizabeth Street, between Prince & Spring Streets (1-212 343 7011). Subway: N, R, W to Prince Street; 6 to Spring Street. **Open** 6-11.30pm Mon-Fri; 6-12.30pm Sat; 6-10.30pm Sun. **$$**. **Eclectic**. **Map** p59 D4 55

This gorgeous industrial space is high on concept – machine-age glass lamps, pre-war office doors and a library card catalogue make sly references to public spaces. Chef Brad Farmerie, from London's acclaimed Providores, has created the menu in tandem with Providores colleagues Anna Hansen and Peter Gordon. Look for a Kiwi influence in dishes such as grilled kangaroo on coriander falafel and New Zealand venison with pomegranates and truffles. The desserts are equally eclectic.

Room 4 Dessert

NEW *7 Cleveland Place, between Kenmare & Spring Streets (1-212 941 5405). Subway: 6 to Spring Street; F, V to Broadway-Lafayette Street.* **Open:** 6pm-midnight Mon-Thur; 6pm-1am Fri, Sat. **$.** **Dessert.** **Map** p59 D4 🟤
Yes, you could plan to stop by this dessert-only restaurant *after* you've had a meal somewhere else, but you'd be full, and your taste buds wouldn't be optimally receptive to Will Goldfarb's spectrum of flavours. Instead, why not have dessert for dinner once in your life? Goldfarb and his team of treat makers operate what feels like a science lab for sweet teeth.

Shopping

Classic Kicks

298 Elizabeth Street, between Houston & Bleecker Streets (1-212 979 9514). Subway: B, D, F, V to Broadway-Lafayette Street; 6 to Bleecker Street. **Open** noon-7pm Mon-Sat. **Map** p59 D3 🟤
One of the more female-friendly sneaker shops, Classic Kicks stocks mainstream and rare styles of Converse, Lacoste, Puma and Vans, to name but a few, for both boys and girls, along with a decent selection of clothes.

Find Outlet

229 Mott Street, between Prince & Spring Streets (1-212 226 5167). Subway: N, R, W to Prince Street; 6 to Spring Street. **Open** noon-7pm daily. **Map** p59 D4 🟤
Skip the sample sales and head to Find Outlet instead. High-fashion samples and overstock are at drastically reduced prices (50% off, on average), so you can dress like a fashion editor on an editorial assistant's budget.

The Market NYC

268 Mulberry Street, between Houston & Prince Streets (www.themarket nyc.com). Subway: B, D, F, V to *Broadway-Lafayette Street; N, R, W to Prince Street; 6 to Bleecker Street.* **Open** 11am-7pm Sat, Sun. No credit cards. **Map** p59 D4 🟤
Yes, it's housed in the gymnasium of a church's youth centre, but it's no small shakes. Every Saturday, contemporary fashion and accessory designers hawk their (usually unique) wares here. Open weekends only.

Rebecca Taylor

260 Mott Street, between Houston & Prince Streets (1-212 966 0406/www. rebeccataylor.com). Subway: B, D, F, V to Broadway-Lafayette Street; N, R, W to Prince Street; 6 to Bleecker Street. **Open** 11am-7pm daily. **Map** p59 D4 🟤
This New Zealand designer's shop is adorned with murals of fairy worlds and butterflies – arguably the source of inspiration for her whimsical, kittenish dresses and jackets.

Lower East Side

The **Lower East Side** was shaped by New York's immigrants, millions upon millions of whom poured into the city from the late 19th century onwards. The resulting patchwork of dense communities is great for dining and exploration. In the 1980s a new breed of immigrant began moving in: young artists and musicians attracted by low rents. Bars, boutiques and music venues sprang up on and around Ludlow Street, creating an annexe to the East Village.

Sights & museums

Eldridge Street Synagogue

12 Eldridge Street, between Canal & Division Streets (1-212 219 0888/ www.eldridgestreet.org). Subway: F to East Broadway. **Tours** 11am-4pm Tue, Wed, Thur, Sun and by appointment. Guided tours on the hour 11am-3pm. **Admission** $5; $1-$3 reductions. **Map** p57 D1/p59 E5 🟤

NEW YORK BY AREA

Rebecca Taylor p75

Lower East Side Tenement Museum

90 Orchard Street, at Broome Street (1-212 431 0233/www.tenement.org). Subway: F to Delancey Street; J, M, Z to Delancey-Essex Streets. **Open** Visitors' Center 11am-5.30pm Mon; 11am-6pm Tue-Fri; 10.45am-5.30pm Sat, Sun. **Admission** $12; $10 reductions. **Map** p59 E4 ⑫

Housed in an 1863 tenement building along with a gallery, shop and video room, this fascinating museum is accessible only by guided tour. The tours, which regularly sell out (definitely book ahead), explain the daily life of typical tenement-dwelling immigrant families. (See the website for 360-degree views of the museum's interior.) From April to December, the museum also leads walking tours of the Lower East Side.

Eating & drinking

Brown

61 Hester Street, at Ludlow Streets (1-212 477 2427). Subway: F to East Broadway. **Open** 9am-11pm Tue-Sat; 9am-6pm Sun. **$**. **Café**. **Map** p59 E5 ⑬

Owner Alejandro Alcocer opened this small café to compensate for the lack of a decent cup of joe in the hood. Not only can you get a mean latte here, but now you can also choose from more than 20 entrées based on organic ingredients. Daily specials, scribbled on the front-door glass, usually include a soup, a frittata and a cheese-and-fruit plate. Alcocer recently started serving beer and wine and a dinner menu.

Clinton Street Baking Company

4 Clinton Street, between Houston & Stanton Streets (1 646 602 6263). Subway: F to Delancey Street; J, M, Z to Delancey-Essex Streets. **Open** 8am-11pm Mon-Fri; 10am-4pm, 6-11pm Sat; 10am-4pm Sun. **$**. **Café**. **Map** p59 E4 ⑭

The warm buttermilk biscuits here are reason enough to face the brunchtime crowds; if you want to avoid the onslaught, however, the homely Lower East Side spot is just as reliable at lunch and dinner, when locals drop in for fish tacos, grilled pizzas and a daily $10 beer-and-burger special. Pssst – to better your odds for getting a table at brunch (the best in town), show up between 9 and 10am, when coffee and pastries are served before the rest of the kitchen opens.

East Side
Company Bar

49 Essex Street, between Broome & Grand Streets (1-212 614 7408). Subway: F to Delancey Street; J, M, Z to Delancey-Essex Streets. **Open** 7pm-4am daily. **Bar**. No credit cards. Map p59 E4 🚳
This snug space has a '40s vibe (leather booths, classic cocktails), as well as a few welcome touches, such as a raw bar and slashed prices.

Freemans

2 Freeman Alley, off Rivington Street, between Bowery & Chrystie Street (1-212 420 0012). Subway: F, V to Lower East Side-Second Avenue; J, M, Z to Bowery. **Open** 5pm-11.30pm Mon-Fri; 11am-3.30pm, 6pm-midnight Sat, Sun. **$$$**. **American**. Map p59 D4 🚳
Once you find this secret restaurant you'll feel as though you've stepped into a ski lodge on a mountaintop in Aspen. Those in the know feast on affordable dishes like juicy trout, warm artichoke dip, rich wild-boar terrine, and perfect batches of mac and cheese, all served under the gaze of mounted animal heads. Brunch, when the sun streams through the front windows, is rather more tranquil.

Katz's Delicatessen

205 E Houston Street, at Ludlow Street (1-212 254 2246). Subway: F, V to Lower East Side-Second Avenue. **Open**: 8am-10pm Sun-Tue; 8am-11pm Wed, Thu; 8am-3am Fri, Sat. **$**. **American Deli**. Map p59 E4 🚳
This capacious, no-frills deli draws queues for its pastrami – some of the best you'll find in New York (FYI, Meg Ryan's famous 'orgasm' scene in *When Harry Met Sally...* was filmed here).

La Esquina

NEW *106 Kenmare Street, between Cleveland Place & Lafayette Street (646-613-7100). Subway: 6 to Spring Street.* **Open** 6pm-midnight daily. **$$**. **Mexican**. Map p59 D4 🚳
Many first-time diners here stand on the corner of Lafayette and Kenmare Streets staring at the deli sign, wondering if they wrote down the wrong address. After watching dozens of people walk through a door marked employees only, it becomes clear that a restaurant does lurk within. Dishes like spicy sirloin with poblano chillies, Mayan shrimp coated in a chipotle glaze and grilled fish with avocado salsa somehow taste better served amid exposed brick, wrought iron and wax-dripping candelabras.

Schiller's Liquor Bar

131 Rivington Street, at Norfolk Street (1-212 260 4555). Subway: F to Delancey Street; J, M, Z to Delancey-Essex Streets. **Open** 11am-4am Mon-Fri; 10am-4am Sat, Sun. **$**. **Eclectic**. Map p59 E4 🚳
A playful all-day bohemian hangout attracting a variety show of a clientele, from suits to drag queens and artfully tousled locals. No dish, except steak, costs more than $16. The menu is a mix of French bistro (steak-frites), British pub (Welsh rarebit) and Louisiana lunch counter (oyster po'boys). Finding your way around the wine list is a cinch – it's a mere six bottles long, designated 'cheap', 'decent' or 'good'.

6's & 8's

205 Chrystie Street, at Stanton Street (1-212 477 6688). Subway: F, V to Lower East Side-Second Avenue. **Open** 9am-4am Tue-Thu; 6pm-4am Fri, Sat. **Bar**. Map p59 D4 🚳
Black-tinted windows reflect the understated cool of this two-level Vegas-style rock club. Leather banquettes, vintage chandeliers, red-panelled walls and classic punk and Zep-era hits make swilling hard liquor seem appropriate. In the basement, you can bet funny money at blackjack or craps tables, or try your luck at the slot machines.

NEW YORK BY AREA

Suba

109 Ludlow Street, between Delancey & Rivington Streets (1-212 982 5714). Subway: F to Delancey Street; J, M, Z to Delancey-Essex Streets. **Open** 6pm-2am Mon-Thur; 6pm-4am Fri-Sat; 6pm-midnight Sun. **$$$**. **Latin American**. **Map** p59 E4 🄐

Acclaimed chef Alex Ureña fuses traditional Spanish dishes with modern techniques. Duck breast with white-peach coulis and cinnamon sauce is undeniably sexy, especially when it's followed by the sultry dark-chocolate almond cake or a lime-pie cocktail.

Tides

102 Norfolk Street, at Delancey Street (1-212 254 8855). Subway: F, J, M, Z to Delancey-Essex Streets. **Open** 11am-3pm, 6-11pm Mon-Fri; 10am-2pm, 5-10pm Sat, Sun. **$$$**. **Seafood**. **Map** p59 E4 🄑

A sleek new seafood restaurant in an intimate Lower East Side space, with custom-designed booths, chairs and tables made from different bamboos. Chef Judy Seto knows her seafood beyond the fish-fry tradition: she pairs mussels with fennel and cream broth and serves grilled shrimp with wild mushroom and chestnut spaetzle. Whole lobster, seared scallops and a lobster roll for every season are available for purists.

Thor

NEW *107 Rivington Street, between Essex & Ludlow Streets (1-212 796 8040). Subway: F to Delancey Street.* **Open** 7am-midnight Mon-Wed; 7am-1am Thur-Fri; 11am-1am Sat; 11am-midnight Sun. **$$$**. **Austrian**. **Map** p59 E4 🄒

A nice lobby and a solid rib eye don't cut it any more at the city's top hotels. These days, restaurateurs are hiring celebrity chefs and cutting-edge designers and praying that the food tastes as good as the dining room looks. At Thor, the marriage was an instant success: crowds packed the Lower East Side hotspot to savour one of downtown's most fashionable scenes and delicious meals. There's no Nordic connection – its name is an acronym for the Hotel on Rivington.

Welcome to the Johnsons

123 Rivington Street, between Essex & Norfolk Streets (1-212 420 9911). Subway: F to Delancey Street; J, M, Z to Delancey-Essex Streets. **Open** 3pm-4am Mon-Fri; 1pm-4am Sat, Sun. **Bar**. No Credit cards. **Map** p59 E4 🄓

There's almost nothing that identifies this ironic white-trash haven as a bar. A well-worn pool table, avocado-coloured fridge, table-format *Pac-Man* and plastic-covered couches contribute to the retro feel. The so-called decor also includes a pictorial homage to Pabst Blue Ribbon, and like everything else, the prices ($1.50 a can at happy hour) are stuck in the '70s.

Shopping

Alife Rivington Club

158 Rivington Street, between Clinton & Suffolk Streets (1-212 375 8128). Subway: F to Delancey Street; J, M, Z to Delancey-Essex Streets. **Open** noon-7pm daily. **Map** p59 E4 🄔

'Sneakers' equal 'religion' in this tiny, out-of-the-way shop, which is arguably the city's main hub for hard-to-get shoes. The store, like its wares, has a rather exclusive vibe: there's no sign, no street number, no indication the joint even exists from the outside. Look closely and ring the bell to check out the rotating selection of 60 or so styles.

Annie O

NEW *105 Rivington Street, between Essex & Ludlow Streets (1-212 475 3490). Subway: F to Delancey Street.* **Open** 1-11pm Tue-Sat; noon-6pm Sun. **Map** p59 E4 🄖

Party like a rock star? Now you can shop like one too at Annie O, a music-themed boutique tucked in the Hotel on Rivington. Shop curator Annie Ohayon – a former music publicist for acts such as Pearl Jam and Smashing Pumpkins – handpicks goods spiked with a naughty, rock 'n' roll sensibility.

Doyle & Doyle

189 Orchard Street, between E Houston & Stanton Streets (1-212 677 9991/www.doyledoyle.com). Subway: F, V to Lower East Side-Second Avenue. **Open** 1-7pm Tue, Wed, Fri; 1-8pm Thur; noon-7pm Sat, Sun. **Map** p59 D4 ⑦

Whether your taste is more art deco or nouveau, Victorian or Edwardian, gemologist sisters Pam and Elizabeth Doyle, who specialise in estate and antique jewellery, will have that intimate, one-of-a-kind piece you're looking for, including engagement rings and eternity bands.

Edith & Daha

104 Rivington Street, between Essex & Ludlow Streets (1-212 979 9992). Subway: F to Delancey Street; J, M, Z to Delancey-Essex Streets. **Open** 1-8pm Mon-Fri; noon-8pm Sat, Sun. **Map** p59 E4 ⑦

Check out one of the city's best collections of (mostly) fine leather bags, not to mention an army of shoes, at this slightly below-street-level shop. There's no trash padding out the rails here – only the cream of the vintage crop. The front rack displays Edith & Daha's own line of clothing.

Foley & Corinna

114 Stanton Street, between Essex & Ludlow Streets (1-212 529 2338/www. foleyandcorinna.com). Subway: F to Delancey Street; J, M, Z to Delancey-Essex Streets. **Open** noon-8pm Mon-Sat; noon-7pm Sun. **Map** p59 E4 ⑦

Vintage-clothing fiends like Liv Tyler and Donna Karan know they can have it both ways: shoppers freely mix old (Anna Corinna's vintage finds) with new (Dana Foley's original creations, including lace tops, leather-belted pants and sheer wool knits) to compose a truly one-of-a-kind look. Encourage the boy in your life to spiff up at the men's store, just around the corner.

Guss' Pickles

85-87 Orchard Street, between Broome & Grand Streets. Subway: F to Delancey Street; J, M, Z to Delancey-Essex Streets. **Open** 9.30am-6.30pm Mon-Thur; 9.30am-4pm Fri; 10am-6pm Sun. **Map** p59 E4 ㉚

After moving twice in recent years, the Pickle King has settled down in this Lower East Side location, and the complete, delicious array of sours and half-sours, pickled peppers, watermelon rinds and sauerkraut is available to grateful New Yorkers once again.

Marmalade

172 Ludlow Street, between Houston & Stanton Streets (1-212 473 8070). Subway: F, V to Lower East Side-Second Avenue. **Open** noon-8.30pm Mon-Thur, Sun; noon-9.30pm Fri, Sat. **Map** p59 E4 ㉛

Marmalade, one of the cutest vintage-clothing stores on the Lower East Side, has some of the hottest 1970s and '80s threads to be found below Houston Street. That slinky cocktail dress or ruffled blouse is tucked away amid a selection of well-priced and well-cared-for items. Accessories, vintage shoes and a small selection of men's clothing are also available.

OdinTG-170

170 Ludlow Street, between Houston & Stanton Streets (1-212 995 8660/ www.tg170.com). Subway: F to Delancey Street; J, M, Z to Delancey-Essex Streets. **Open** noon-8pm daily. **Map** p59 E4 ㉜

Terri Gillis has an eye for emerging designers: she was the first to carry Built by Wendy and Pixie Yates. Nowadays you'll find Jared Gold and Liz Collins pieces in her newly expanded store.

Russ & Daughters

179 E Houston Street, between Allen & Orchard Streets (1-212 475 4880/ www.russanddaughters.com). Subway: F, V to Lower East Side-Second Avenue. **Open** 9am-7pm Mon-Sat; 8am-5.30pm Sun. **Map** p59 D4 ㉝

Russ & Daughters, open since 1914, sells eight kinds of smoked salmon and many Jewish-inflected Eastern European delectables, along with dried fruits, chocolates and caviar.

Nightlife

Arlene's Grocery

95 Stanton Street, between Ludlow & Orchard Streets (1-212 995 1652/ www.arlene-grocery.com). Subway: F to Delancey Street; J, M, Z to Delancey-Essex Streets. **Open** 6pm-4am daily. **Map** p59 E4 ㉞

A mid-level rung on the local-band ladder, Arlene's Grocery can pack in as many as six rock acts a night, often adding afternoon shows on Saturday. Monday night's live-band karaoke is an institution, even if the band that started it all has since moved on. A lively spot.

Bowery Ballroom

6 Delancey Street, between Bowery & Chrystie Street (1-212 533 2111/ www.boweryballroom.com). Subway: J, M, Z to Bowery; 6 to Spring Street. **Open** 8pm-late. **Map** p59 E4 ㉟

Probably the best venue in town for seeing indie bands either on the way up or holding their own, the Bowery nonetheless brings in a diverse range of artists from town and around the world, as well as offering a clear view and loud, bright sound from just about any spot. Not into an opening band? The spacious downstairs lounge is a great place to relax and socialise between (or during) sets.

Cake Shop

152 Ludlow Street, between Rivington & Stanton Streets (1-212 253 0036/ www.cake-shop.com). Subway: F, V to Lower East Side-Second Avenue. **Open** 8pm-late. No credit cards. **Map** p59 D4 ㊱

This narrow but clean-and-new basement space gets points for much more than its keen indie-rock bookings. For one thing, it's in the heart of the Lower East Side. What's more, it has pastries and coffee for sale upstairs. Better still (for late-night music junkies, at least) is the brightly lit back room on street level, which sells used vinyl and CDs, as well as a smattering of new releases, DVDs and other record-store ephemera.

Delancey

168 Delancey Street, at Clinton Street (1-212 254 9920/www.thedelancey. com). Subway: F to Delancey Street; J, M, Z to Delancey-Essex Streets. **Open** 8pm-late. **Cover** $6-$10. No credit cards. **Map** p59 E4 ㊲

Within spitting distance from the Williamsburg Bridge is the Delancey, which has quickly become one of Manhattan's hotter spots on account of its frequent bookings of hyped indie bands (Clap Your Hands Say Yeah, Youth Group) and DJs – and the lovely second-floor outdoor patio, which is always mobbed with beautiful young hipsters in the summer, doesn't hurt.

Element

225 E Houston Street, at Essex Street (1-212 254 2220). Subway: F, V to Lower East Side-Second Avenue. **Open** 10pm-4am daily. **Map** p59 E4 ㊳

See box p84.

Laugh Lounge nyc

151 Essex Street, between Rivington & Stanton Streets (1-212 614 2500/ www.laughloungenyc.com). Subway: F to Delancey Street; J, M, Z to Delancey-Essex Streets. **Shows** 8.30pm Tue-Thur; 8.30pm, 10.30pm Fri, Sat. **Map** p59 E4 ㊴

Although the off-peak nights occasionally offer line-ups as edgy as the Lower East Side location would imply, for the most part you can expect standard club-circuit fare from this relatively new venue.

Living Room

154 Ludlow Street, between Rivington & Stanton Streets (1-212 533 7235/ www.livingroomny.com). Subway: F to Lower East Side-Second Avenue; J, M, Z to Delancey-Essex Streets. **Open** 6pm-4am Mon, Tue; 2pm-4am Wed-Sat; 6pm-2am Sun. No credit cards. **Map** p59 E4 ㊵

Many local clubs try to lay claim to being the place where Norah Jones got her start, but Living Room really was. Still, that was in the venue's old (and drab) location; since moving to Lower East Side's version of Main Street, the stream of singer-songwriters that fill

Delancey

the schedule here has taken on a bit more gleam, and the warmly lit environs seem to be always bustling. Skilful guitarist Jim Campilongo appears regularly, as do local stalwarts such as Tony Scherr, Chris Lee and Matty Charles.

Mercury Lounge
217 E Houston Street, between Essex & Ludlow Streets (1-212 260 4700/ www.mercuryloungenyc.com). Subway: F, V to Lower East Side-Second Avenue. **Open** *Call for showtimes.* **Map** p59 E4 ③①
Mercury Lounge is both an old stand-by and pretty much the No.1 indie-rock club in town, with solid sound and sight lines (and a cramped bar in the front room). With four-band bills almost every night, you can catch plenty of locals and touring bands in the course of just one week.

Pianos
158 Ludlow Street, between Rivington & Stanton Streets (1-212 505 3733). Subway: F to Delancey Street; J, M, Z to Delancey-Essex Streets. **Shows** *start around 8pm.* **Map** p59 E4 ③②
On a Saturday night, Pianos can seem like either the centre of New York or the ninth circle of hell, depending on your tastes. But there's no denying that this style-conscious bar-cum-club brings in a weird, wild mix; one night you'll get trendy local bands (the Harlem Shakes, Unisex Salon) and the next you might get Prince Paul! Also a good bet is the emerging talent booked in the charming and free upstairs lounge.

Rothko
116 Suffolk Street, between Delancey & Rivington Streets (www.rothkonyc.com). Subway: F to Delancey Street; J, M, Z to Delancey-Essex Streets. **Shows** *start around 8pm.* **Cover** *free-$8. No credit cards.* **Map** p59 E4 ③③
The cloying vibe of trendiness that plagues a place like Pianos (above) is relatively absent at Rothko, just a few blocks away. This Lower East Side shoebox has a more refined definition

of hip, drawing DJing and electronic stars such as Diplo, Mu and Plaid in addition to rockers (Pilot to Gunner, Dance Disaster Movement, the Ponys). The monthly hip-hop karaoke is among the best of such events you'll find in town.

Sapphire

249 Eldridge Street, between Houston & Stanton Streets (1-212 777 5153/ www.sapphirenyc.com). Subway: F, V to Lower East Side-Second Avenue. **Open** 7pm-4am daily. **Map** p59 D4 **94**
Monday to Wednesday the music here falls somewhere along the techno-house-disco continuum, and local heroes E-man and Melvin Moore are joined by the occasional slumming-it big name. Hip hop and funk rule from Thursday to Saturday with beloved veteran DJ Jazzy Nice often running things. A word of warning, though: weekends can be brutally crowded, so dress to sweat.

Slipper Room

167 Orchard Street, at Stanton Street (1-212 253 7246/www.slipperroom. com). Subway: F, V to Lower East Side-Second Avenue. **Open** 8pm-4am Tue-Sat. **Map** p59 D4 **95**
New York has a healthy neo-burlesque scene, and the petite Slipper Room is, if not at that scene's nexus, then pretty darn near it. Many of the Victorian-looking venue's happenings, notably Friday's Hot Box hoedown, feature plenty of bump-and-grind action, with DJs spinning the appropriate beats; the occasional band completes the picture.

Subtonic Lounge at Tonic

107 Norfolk Street, between Delancey & Rivington Streets (1-212 358 7501/ www.tonicnyc.com). Subway: F to Delancey Street; J, M, Z to Delancey-Essex Streets. **Open** 7.30pm-2am Thur-Sat. **Map** p59 E4 **96**
Subtonic Lounge, the unadorned basement of the Lower East Side's avant-bohemian Tonic performance space, features the Friday night Bunker bash,

where DJs spin myriad underground beats ranging from challenging IDM to straight-up techno. The sound system might not be great, but the party throwers and the patrons (who rest on banquettes inside giant, ancient wine casks) make up for it with their sheer exuberance.

Arts & leisure

Landmark's Sunshine Cinema

143 E Houston Street, between First & Second Avenues (1-212 330 8182/ 1-212 777 3456). Subway: F, V to Lower East Side-Second Avenue. **Open** Call for showtimes. **Map** p59 E4 **97**
A beautifully restored 1898 Yiddish theatre has become one of New York's snazziest art house cinemas, presenting some of the finest new independent films in air-conditioned and stadium-seated luxury.

East Village

Scruffier than its genteel western counterpart, the East Village has a long history as a countercultural hotbed. The area east of Broadway between Houston and 14th Streets is less edgy today, but remnants of its spirited past endure. Check out the indie record shops, bargain restaurants, grungy bars, punky clubs and funky clothing stores.

Curry Row, on 6th Street, between First & Second Avenues, is one of several Little Indias in New York. Roughly two dozen Indian restaurants sit side by side and they remain popular with diners on an extremely tight budget. **Tompkins Square Park** is the community park of the East Village – and a place where Latino bongo beaters, longhairs playing acoustic guitars, punky squatters, mangy dogs, yuppie stroller-pushers and the homeless all mingle.

Aroma

Eating & drinking

Aroma

*36 E 4th Street, between Bowery &
Lafayette Street (1-212 375 0100).
Subway: 6 to Astor Place.* **Open** 6pm-
midnight Tue-Thur; 6pm-2am Fri;
12.30am-3.30pm, 6pm-2am Sat;
12.30am-3.30pm, 6pm-midnight Sun.
$$. Italian. Map p59 D3 🟢
This slender wine bar has been carved
out of a former streetwear boutique,
and the result is enchanting. Chef
Christopher Daly's dishes are carefully
conceived: a duck salad is loaded with
lardons, wild chicory and a soft-
poached egg. The excellent 'lamb three
ways' consists of a tower of braised
shoulder, a patty of neck meat, pine
nuts, raisins and capers, and a juicy,
rosemary-rubbed chop.

Buenos Aires

🆕 *513 E 6th Street, between Avenues
A & B (1-212 228 2775). Subway: F,
V to Lower East Side-Second Avenue;
6 to Astor Place.* **Open** noon-midnight
daily. **$. Argentinian. Map** p59 E3 🟢
Fat, succulent steaks; plump, snappy
sausages; juicy, lemony chicken —this
bustling, bright Argentine spot is a car-
nivore's playground, where even meat
may be served with a side of meat (a
jumbo slab of skirt steak comes with
blood sausage). Your breath will reek
for days, but that's a small price to pay
for a tasty meal, decent service and a
bill that won't break the bank.

Cafecito

*185 Avenue C, at 12th Street (1-212
253 9966). Subway: L to First Avenue.*
Open 6-10pm Tue, Thur, Sun; 6pm-
2am Fri, Sat. **$. Cuban.** No credit
cards. **Map** p59 E2 🔟
The relaxed outdoor bar is just one of
the authentic touches at Cafecito ('tiny
coffee'). You can sip a Mojito and nib-
ble green plantain chips as you con-
template the menu: the aborcito de
Cuba gives you a taste of each of the
small hot appetisers – the best of which

Savings and tones

An old bank gets a new club.

Clubbers of a certain age will remember the Bank, a downtown disco that was part of the East Village's once-thriving nightlife counterculture. Housed in a hulking former savings and loan building, the spot opened to much fanfare on New Year's Eve 1990, but the lustre faded over time. Now the venue has relaunched as the shiny new **Element**. One plus: the 600-person-capacity space, though totally redone, still has that soaring ceiling, the great mezzanine and the memorable downstairs vault. Another plus: the owners have hired a booking guy who really knows the city's underground dance-music scene – Stephen Schwartz, co-owner of the Halcyon vinyl emporium.

Element's recent grand opening featured electro-rock from Tommie Sunshine and technoid stylings by Adultnapper. And plenty more goods are on the way: the electro-techy Robots team plans to bring in the top German label Kompakt; deep-housers like Jeannie Hopper and Tedd Patterson are slated for a series of deck sessions; and distortion-disco king Larry Tee will be presiding over the action every Saturday.

In a nod to the building's past, Tee has dubbed his night Bank. With savvy like that, Element is sure to generate interest.

■ Element, 225 E Houston Street, at Essex Street (1-212 254 2200).

are bollos, corn and black-bean fritters. In addition to specials like char-grilled skirt steak with chimichurri sauce, the perfectly pressed Cuban sandwich is spot on.

Degustation

NEW *239 E 5th Street, between Second & Third Avenues (1-212 979 1012). Subway: 6 to Astor Place.* **Open** 6pm-11pm Mon-Sat. **$**. **Spanish**. Map p59 D3 **101**

This tiny 16-seat eatery is run by chef Wesley Genovart, a Spaniard who last worked at Jean-Georges Vongerichten's Perry Street. Genovart's small-plates menu blends French and Spanish cuisines in dishes such as slowly poached egg with *jamón serrano* and bread crumbs, foie gras with tarragon-caramel water and grapefruit, and cod in *salsa verde* with clams and cockles.

Jack's Luxury Oyster Bar

246 E 5th Street, between Second & Third Avenues (1-212 673 0338). Subway: F, V to Lower East Side-Second Avenue; 6 to Astor Place. **Open** 6-11pm Mon-Sat. **$$$$**. **Seafood**. Map p59 D3 **102**

Jack and Grace Lamb have transformed the first two floors of their romantic 5th Street townhouse into this doll's house of a restaurant. The real magic unfolds in the tiny upstairs dining room, where a mere dozen or so guests settle in near a fireplace for each night's dinner party – a phenomenal five-course feast conceived by chef Maxime Bilet.

Mermaid Inn

96 Second Avenue, between 5th & 6th Streets (1-212 674 5870). Subway: F, V to Lower East Side-Second Avenue. **Open** 5.30-11pm Mon-Thur; 11.30pm-midnight Fri, Sat; 5pm-10pm Sun. **$$**. **Seafood**. Map p59 D3 **103**

The chefs at the Mermaid dress seafood for New York palates. The menu changes seasonally, but they always have the overstuffed lobster roll and spaghetti with spicy shrimp, scallops and calamari, topped with arugula. Everything tastes even better in summer, when you can sit in the back garden.

One and One

76 E 1st Street, at First Avenue (1-212 598 9126). Subway: F, V to Lower East Side-Second Avenue. **Open** noon-2am Mon-Wed, Sun; noon-4am Thur-Sat. **Bar. Map** p59 D3 ❿

Not one, not two, but three paintings by Paul Joyce (great-nephew of James) adorn the back wall of this comfortable pub. That means we're in Irish territory. The name of this bar is, in fact, Emerald Isle slang for fish and chips, the house speciality. Order a basket and you'll get flaky beer-battered cod fillets with a pile of crisp fries, perfect for soaking up malt vinegar. The natural chaser: one of 12 beers on tap.

Poetessa

92 Second Avenue, between 5th & 6th Streets (1-212 387 0065). Subway: F, V to Lower East Side-Second Avenue; 6 to Astor Place. **Open** 5-11pm Mon-Thur; noon-4.30pm, 5pm-2am Fri, Sat; 5-10pm Sun. **$$. Italian. Map** p59 D3 ❺

The dining room is comfortably familiar – exposed brick walls, wood furniture and ceiling fans. Chef Pippa Calland follows through with a menu of flavourful Italian dishes: Parmesan-battered soft-shell crab with courgettes and fresh peas; sizzling home-made pork meatballs; and plenty of hearty pasta dishes.

Rififi

332 E 11th Street, between First & Second Avenues (212-677-1027). Subway: L to First Avenue, 6 to Astor Place. **Open** 6pm-2am Mon-Thur, Sun; 7pm-4am Fri, Sat. **Bar**. No credit cards. **Map** p59 D2 ❻

Hovering between unpretentious and run-down is Rififi, a dive bar with old-world charm. The popular back room screens movies several nights a week; there are also occasional bands and burlesque shows. Rififi (which takes its name from Jules Dassin's

heist-film masterpiece) has become a local hangout with clutches of hipsters engaged in serious conversation.

Spice Cove

326 E 6th Street, between First & Second Avenues (1-212 674 8884). Subway: F, V to Lower East Side-Second Avenue. **Open** 11.30am-midnight Mon-Fri; 11.30am-12.30am Sat, Sun. **$. Indian. Map** p59 D3 ❼

Bright orange walls, stone archways and candles provide a seductive setting; St Germain stands in for sitar music; and in place of an all-you-can-eat buffet are chef Muhammed Ahmed Ali's specialities. Expect properly spiced dishes such as chickpeas stir-fried with coriander, cumin and cinnamon, and fenugreek-scented Atlantic salmon crowned with tomato masala.

Starlight Bar & Lounge

167 Avenue A, between 10th & 11th Streets (1-212 475 2172/www. starlightbarlounge.com). Subway: L to First Avenue. **Open** 6pm-3am Mon-Thur, Sun; 6pm-4am Fri, Sat. **Bar. Map** p59 E2 ❽

This reliable gay lounge gets mobbed on weekends, but its calmer weeknight schedule brings a wonderful rotation of performances, including comedy on Wednesdays and readings and DJs at other times. On Sunday nights the popular lesbian party Starlette is still kicking, bringing in a mix of glamour gals, tomboys and college students.

Shopping

D/L Cerney

13 E 7th Street, between Second & Third Avenues (1-212 673 7033). Subway: N, R, W to 8th Street-NYU; 6 to Astor Place. **Open** noon-7.30pm daily. **Map** p59 D3 ❾

Specialising in timeless, original designs for stylish fellows, the store also carries menswear from the 1940s to the '60s. Mint-condition must-haves include hats (some pristine fedoras), ties and shoes. An adjacent shop carries D/L Cerney's new women's line.

Dave's Quality Meat

7 E 3rd Street, between Bowery & Second Avenue (1-212 505 7551/ www.davesqualitymeat.com). Subway: F, V to Lower East Side-Second Avenue. **Open** noon-7pm Mon-Sat; noon-6pm Sun. **Map** p59 D3 ⑩

Dave Ortiz – formerly of urban-threads label Zoo York – and professional skateboarder Chris Keefe stock top-shelf streetwear in their wittily designed shop, its decor complete with meat hooks and mannequins sporting butcher's aprons. Home-made graphic-print T-shirts are wrapped in plastic and displayed in a deli case.

Fabulous Fanny's

335 E 9th Street, between First & Second Avenues (1-212 533 0637/ www.fabulousfannys.com). Subway: L to First Avenue; 6 to Astor Place. **Open** noon-8pm daily. **Map** p59 D2 ⑪

The city's premier source of period eyeglasses for more than 17 years, this former booth at the 26th Street flea market now calls the East Village home. It has more than 10,000 pairs of spectacles, from World War II-era aviator goggles to 1970s rhinestone-encrusted Versace shades.

Kiehl's

109 Third Avenue, between 13th & 14th Streets (1-212 677 3171/ www.kiehls.com). Subway: L to Third Avenue; N, Q, R, W, 4, 5, 6 to 14th Street-Union Square. **Open** 10am-7pm Mon-Sat; noon-6pm Sun. **Map** p59 D2 ⑫

Although it is 154 years old and has recently expanded, this New York institution still gets mobbed. Check out the Motorcycle Room, full of vintage Harleys (the owner's obsession). Try one dab of Kiehl's moisturiser, lip balm or body lotion from the plentiful free samples, and you'll be hooked.

Local Clothing

NEW *328 E 9th Street, between First & Second Avenues (1-212 777 3850). Subway: L to Third Avenue.* **Open** noon-8pm Sun-Thur; noon-9pm Fri, Sat. **Map** p59 D3 ⑬

It's funny how vintage never gets old. NYC's latest instalment in aged threads is this women's vintage trove that focuses on garb from the Victorian era up to the first MTV generation.

Patricia Field

NEW *302 Bowery between Bleecker & Houston (1-212 966 4066/www. patriciafield.com). Subway: B, D, V, F to Broadway-Lafayette Street.* **Open** 11am-8pm Mon-Fri, Sun; 11am-9pm Sat. **Map** p59 D3 ⑭

Patricia Field is a virtuoso at blending eclectic club and street styles (she famously assembled the offbeat costumes for *Sex and the City*). Field recently relocated her idiosyncratic collection of jewellery, make-up and clothes to the East Village.

Nightlife

Ace of Clubs

9 Great Jones Street, at Lafayette Street (1-212 677 6924/www.aceof clubsnyc.com). Subway: B, D, F, V to Broadway-Lafayette Street; 6 to Bleecker Street. **Open** from 7pm. No credit cards. **Map** p58 C3 ⑮

All this cosy shoebox of a space had needed in the past was a booker with some taste. Ask and ye shall receive, as early in 2005 it morphed from the old Under Acme into Ace of Clubs and started bringing in a diverse mix of mostly local rock (the Giraffes), blues (Corey Harris) and progressive jazz (the Jazz Passengers' Bill Ware and his Urban Vibes project).

Continental

25 Third Avenue, at St Marks Place (1-212 529 6924/www.continentalnyc. com). Subway: N, R, W to 8th Street-NYU; 6 to Astor Place. **Open** from 4pm. No credit cards. **Map** p58 D3 ⑯

The Continental is surely the best rock club in the city for drinking: a titillating sign above the bar reads 'five shots of anything – $10'. But the real draw is Monday's Original Punk/Metal Karaoke Band. All-ages gigs on weekend afternoons are a long-standing tradition.

Joe's Pub

425 Lafayette Street, between Astor Place & E 4th Street (1-212 539 8770/ www.joespub.com) Subway: N, R, W to 8th Street-NYU; 6 to Astor Place. **Open** call for showtimes. **Map** p59 D3 **117**

This plush club and restaurant located within the Public Theater is both hip and elegant, and boasts an extraordinarily varied mix of performers (usually booked for just a single night). Among the rock, jazz and world-music acts, you will occasionally find a Broadway performer venturing into the world of cabaret.

Mo Pitkin's House of Satisfaction

NEW *34 Avenue A, between 2nd & 3rd Streets (1-212 777 5660/www. mopitkins.com). Subway: F, V to Lower East Side-Second Avenue.* **Open** 5pm, see website for prices and showtimes. **Map** p59 E3 **118**

The Brothers Phil and Jesse Hartman recently opened this irreverent Jewish-Latino restaurant on Avenue A, named after an eccentric uncle. Above the dining room lies a snug cabaret space that hosts a range of artists, from famous musicians to unknown stand-up comedians.

Nublu

62 Avenue C, between 4rth & 5th Streets (1-212 979 9925/www.nublu. net). Subway: F, V to Lower East Side-Second Avenue. **Open** 8pm-4am. No credit cards. **Map** p59 E3 **119**

Inversely proportional to its size has been Nublu's prominence on the local globalist club scene. A pressure cooker of creativity, the venue gave rise to the Brazilian Girls – who started jamming at one late-night session and haven't stopped yet – as well as starting New York City's romance with the Northern Brazilian style *forró*. Even on weeknights events usually start no earlier than 10pm – but if you show up early (once you've located the unmarked door), you'll find that the bar is well stocked and the staff is as warm as the music.

Pyramid

101 Avenue A, between 6th & 7th Streets (1-212 228 4888). Subway: F, V to Lower East Side-Second Avenue; L to First Avenue; 6 to Astor Place. **Open** 10pm-4am daily. **Map** p59 E3 **120**

In a clubbing era long gone, this was a cornerstone of forward-thinking queer club culture. In what could be considered a sign of the times, the venue's sole remaining gay soirée is Friday night's non-progressive '80s dance-fest, 1984. Otherwise, the charmingly decrepit space features the long-running drum 'n' bass bash Konkrete Jungle, as well as a rotating roster of goth and new wave.

Arts & leisure

Blue Man Group

Astor Place Theater, 434 Lafayette Street, between Astor Place & E 4th Street (1-212 254 4370/www.blue man.com). Subway: N, R, W to 8th Street-NYU; 6 to Astor Place. **Open** Call for showtimes. **Map** p59 D3 **121**

Three men endowed with extraterrestrial imaginations (and decorated with head-to-toe blue body paint) carry this long-time favourite – a show that is as smart as it is ridiculous.

Bowery Poetry Club

308 Bowery, at Bleecker Street (1-212 614 0505/www.bowerypoetry. com). Subway: B, D, F, V to Broadway-Lafayette Street; 6 to Bleecker Street. **Map** p59 D3 **122**

The name of this colourful joint on the Bowery reveals its roots in the poetry-slam scene, but it's also the truest current iteration of the East Village's legendary creative arts scene: all kinds of jazz, folk, hip hop and improv theatre can be found here routinely; if you have a taste for the bizarre and aren't easily offended, keep your eyes peeled for anything from the Jollyship to the Whiz-Bang musical-puppet crew. There is also a range of sandwiches and hot and cold drinks on offer.

NEW YORK BY AREA

Bowery Poetry Club p87

New York Theatre Workshop

79 E 4th Street, between Bowery & Second Avenue (1-212 460 5475/ www.nytw.org). Subway: F, V to Lower East Side-Second Avenue; 6 to Astor Place. **Map** p59 D3

Founded in 1979, NYTW works with emerging directors eager to take on challenging pieces. Besides plays by the likes of Caryl Churchill (*Far Away, A Number*) and Tony Kushner (*Homebody/Kabul*), this company also premièred *Rent*, Jonathan Larson's Pulitzer Prize-winning musical (still packing 'em in on Broadway).

Performance Space 122

150 First Avenue, at 9th Street (1-212 477 5288/www.ps122.org). Subway: L to First Avenue; 6 to Astor Place. **Map** p59 D2

This non-profit arts centre presents experimental dance, performance art, music, film and video. Eric Bogosian, Whoopi Goldberg, John Leguizamo and others have developed projects here; of more street-level interest is the monthly bloggers' night. Australian trend-setter Vallejo Gantner recently took over as artistic director, promising to make its programming more international in flavour.

Public Theater

425 Lafayette Street, between Astor Place & E 4th Street (1-212 539 8500/ Telecharge 1-212 239 6200/www. publictheater.org). Subway: N, R, W to 8th Street-NYU; 6 to Astor Place. **Map** p59 D3

Founded by the late Joseph Papp and dedicated to the work of new American playwrights and performers, this Astor Place landmark is also known for its Shakespeare productions. The venue houses five stages and Joe's Pub (p87).

Stomp

Orpheum Theater, 126 Second Avenue, between St Marks Place & E 7th Street (1-212 477 2477). Subway: N, R, W to 8th Street-NYU; 6 to Astor Place. **Map** p59 D3

This show is billed as a 'percussion sensation' because there's no other way to describe it. Using garbage-can lids, buckets, brooms, sticks and just about anything they can get their hands on, these aerobicised dancer-musicians make a lovely racket.

Greenwich Village

Stretching from Houston Street to 14th Street, between Broadway and Sixth Avenue, Greenwich Village's leafy streets have inspired bohemians for almost a century. Once the dingy but colourful stomping ground of Beat poets and folk and jazz musicians, the well-trafficked strip of **Bleecker Street** between La Guardia Place and Sixth Avenue is now simply an overcrowded stretch of poster shops, cheap restaurants and music venues for the college crowd.

Sights & museums

AIA Center for Architecture

536 La Guardia Place, between Bleecker & W 3rd Streets (1-212 683 0023/ www.aiany.org). Subway: A, B, C, D, E, F, V to W 4th Street. **Open** 9am-8pm Mon-Fri; 11am-5pm Sat. **Map** p59 C3 **127**

After five years of planning, the AIA Center for Architecture opened to acclaim in autumn 2003. The sweeping, light-filled design is a physical manifestation of AIA's goal of promoting transparency in its access and programming. Large slabs of flooring were cut away at the street and basement levels, converting underground spaces into suitably bright, museum-quality galleries.

Washington Square Park

Subway: A, B, C, D, E, F, V to W 4th Street-Washington Square. **Map** p59 C3 **128**

The hippies who turned up and tuned out in Washington Square Park, once a potter's field, are still there in spirit,

and often in person: the park hums with musicians and street artists. In warmer months this is one of the best people-watching spots in the city.

Eating & drinking

Blue Hill

75 Washington Place, between Washington Square West & Sixth Avenue (1-212 539 1776). Subway: A, B, C, D, E, F, V to W 4th Street. **Open** 5.30-11pm Mon-Sat; 5.30-10pm Sun. **$$$**. **French**. **Map** p58 C3 **129**

This beloved gourmand destination has a knack for scoring the best local produce all year round. Chefs Dan Barber and Michael Anthony succeed so consistently with their dishes because of their solid foundation in classical French cooking. When in season, Blue Hill's strawberries have more berry flavour, and its heirloom tomatoes are juicier, than anyone else's.

Jane

100 W Houston Street, between La Guardia Place & Thompson Street (1-212 254 7000). Subway: C, E to Spring Street; 1 to Houston Street. **Open** 11.30am-midnight Mon-Sat; 11am-11pm Sun. **$$**. **American**. **Map** p58 C3 **130**

This popular neighbourhood spot has warm lighting, plush banquette seating and sunny sidewalk tables; they all match well with the good vibe and pleasant menu. At brunch, hollandaise-glossed poached eggs top delicious crab and crawfish cakes.

La Lanterna di Vittorio

129 MacDougal Street, between 3rd & 4th Streets (1-212 529 5945). Subway: A, B, C, D, E, F, V to W 4th Street-Washington Square. **Open** 10am-3am Mon-Thur, Sun; 10am-4am Fri, Sat. **$**. **Italian**. **Map** p58 C3 **131**

Woo your darling by the fire or under the stars at a romantic Village spot that has been helping to smooth the course of true love for 28 years. The 200-year-old garden was once owned by Aaron Burr; in wintertime four fireplaces spark your courting. Choose a bottle from the extensive wine list to go with light café eats like panini, crostini, smoked duck breast with salad, or thin-crust pizza.

Las Ramblas

NEW *170 W 4th Street, between Cornelia & Jones Streets (646-415-7924). Subway: A, B, C, D, E, F, V to W 4th Street-Washington Square.* **Open** 4pm-2am daily. **$. Spanish. Map** p58 B3 **132**

Now that tapas has become the trendy misnomer for small-plate fare from any cuisine, it's no wonder you're grateful when you see the real Spanish deal. The authenticity of Las Ramblas is apparent in every *centímetro* of the place – the chef hails from Pamplona; three flavours of sangria are mixed to order; and the intimate space actually fosters interaction. Or maybe you just like the food: aged serrano ham, grilled chorizo, *patatas bravas*, *croquetas* and a selection of Spanish cheeses.

Lupa

170 Thompson Street, between Bleecker & Houston Streets (1-212 982 5089). Subway: A, B, C, D, E, F, V to W 4th Street. **Open** noon-3pm, 5-11.30pm Mon-Fri; 11.30am-2.30pm, 5-11.30pm Sat, Sun. **$$. Italian. Map** p58 C3 **133**

Fans of this 'poor man's Babbo' (celeb-chef Mario Batali's pricier restaurant around the corner) keep reclaiming their seats. Here's the ritual they recommend: first, a cutting board of fatty-delicious cured meats. Move on to sublime pasta. Then choose a meaty main, like oxtail *alla vaccinara* or a classic saltimbocca. By the time the panna cotta with apricot arrives, you'll be ready to become a regular too.

Peanut Butter & Co

240 Sullivan Street, between Bleecker & W 3rd Streets (1-212 677 3995). Subway: A, B, C, D, E, F, V to W 4th Street. **Open** 11am-9pm Sun-Thur; 11am-10pm Fri, Sat. **$. American. Map** p58 C3 **134**

Every day the staff at Peanut Butter & Co grinds out a fresh batch of peanut butter, which is used to create gooey mood-pacifiers like the popular Elvis – the King's infamous grilled favourite of peanut butter, banana and honey. Goober-free menu items, like tuna melts and bologna sandwiches, continue the brown-bag theme.

Prem-On Thai

138 W Houston Street, between Sullivan & MacDougal Streets (1-212 353 2338). Subway: C, E to Spring Street. **Open** noon-11.30pm Mon-Fri; noon-midnight Sat, Sun. **$$. Thai. Map** p58 C3 **135**

In one of several stylish rooms, you'll watch in awe as dramatically plated Thai dishes and cocktails are carried through the dining room. Prem-On doesn't hold back with the seasoning either: a whole fried sea bass fillet is served upright and loaded with basil and roasted-chilli-paste sauce.

Strip House

13 E 12th Street, between Fifth Avenue & University Place (1-212 328 0000). Subway: L, N, Q, R, W, 4, 5, 6 to 14th Street-Union Square. **Open** 5-11.30pm Mon-Thur; 5pm-midnight Fri, Sat; 5-11pm Sun. **$$$. Steakhouse. Map** p58 C2 **136**

Strip House cultivates a retro-sexy vibe with its suggestive name, red furnishings and vintage pin-ups. But it's still a modern meat shrine flaunting French influences. Executive chef David Walzog makes sure his New York strips arrive at your table still sizzling, seasoned with sea salt and peppercorns – they're a sublime combination of a perfectly charred outside with a luscious rare-red inside.

Nightlife

Blue Note

131 W 3rd Street, between MacDougal Street & Sixth Avenue (1-212 475 8592/www.bluenote.net). Subway: A, B, C, D, E, F, V to W 4th Street. **Open** 6pm-3am daily. **Map** p58 C3 **137**

Found on a bustling, slightly seedy block is the Blue Note, which prides itself on being 'the jazz capital of the world'. Bona fide musical titans (Cecil

Taylor, Abbey Lincoln) rub up against hot young talents (Matthew Shipp, Jason Lindner) on the calendar, while the tables in the club get patrons rubbing up against each other. The Late Night Groove series and the Sunday brunches are the best bargain bets.

Love

40 W 8th Street, at MacDougal Street (1-212 477 5683/www.musicislove.net). Subway: A, B, C, D, E, F, V to W 4th Street; R, W to 8th Street-NYU (W weekdays only). **Open** 10pm-4am Wed-Sat; 5pm-1am Sun. **Map** p58 C3 ⓳⓷⓼

Love, a recent addition to the city's clubbing landscape, is an anomaly; its focus is squarely on the music (mostly of the deep-house variety) and on building a scene. It's hardly a revolutionary concept, but in today's nightlife world of going for the quick buck, it helps Love to stand out. The main room is a sparsely furnished bare box, but the DJ line-up is impressive – names on the level of Kenny 'Dope' Gonzales, Body & Soul's Joe Claussell and Metro Area have all graced the decks here – and the sound system is one of New York's finest.

Sullivan Room

218 Sullivan Street, between Bleecker & W 3rd Streets (1-212 252 2151/www. sullivanroom.com). Subway: A, B, C, D, E, F, V to W 4th Street. **Open** 10pm-4am. **Map** p58 C3 ⓳⓷⓽

Where's the party? It's right here in this unmarked subterranean space, which hosts some of the best deep-house, tech-house and breaks bashes the city has to offer. It's an utterly unpretentious club, with little of the glitz that bigger clubs feature – but hell, all you really need are some thumpin' beats and a place to move your feet, right?

Village Vanguard

178 Seventh Avenue South, at Perry Street (1-212 255 4037/www.village vanguard.com). Subway: A, C, E, 1, 2, 3 to 14th Street; L to Eighth Avenue. **Open** Showtimes are 9pm and 11pm daily. **Map** p58 B2 ⓳⓸⓪

Seventy years old and still going strong, the Village Vanguard is one of New York's real jazz meccas. History surrounds you here: Coltrane, Miles Davis and Bill Evans have all grooved in this hallowed hall, and the walls are lined with photos and artefacts. The big names, old and new, continue to fill the Vanguard's line-up, and the 16-piece Vanguard Jazz Orchestra has been the Monday night regular for almost 40 years. Reservations are strongly recommended, and the Vanguard takes only cash or travellers' cheques at the door.

Zinc Bar

90 W Houston Street, between La Guardia Place & Thompson Street (1-212 477 8337/www.zincbar.com). Subway: A, B, C, D, E, F, V to W 4th Street. **Open** 6pm-3.30am daily. **Map** p58 C3 ⓳⓸⓵

Located where Greenwich Village meets Soho, Zinc Bar is the place to hoot and holler with die-hard night owls. The after-hours atmosphere is enhanced by the cool mix of African, flamenco, jazz and samba bands.

Arts & leisure

Angelika Film Center

18 W Houston Street, at Mercer Street (1-212 995 2000/www.angelika filmcenter.com). Subway: B, D, F, V to Broadway-Lafayette Street; N, R, W to Prince Street; 6 to Bleecker Street. Call for schedule. **Map** p58 C4 ⓳⓸⓶

The six-screen Angelika emphasises independent fare, both American and foreign. The complex is a zoo on weekends, so come extra early or visit the website to buy advance tickets.

West Village & Meatpacking District

The area west of Sixth Avenue to the Hudson River, from 14th Street to Houston Street, still possesses the features that moulded the Village's character. Only in this neighbourhood could West 10th

Street cross West 4th Street, and Waverly Place cross…Waverly Place. (The West Village's layout follows not the regular grid pattern but the original horse paths that settlers used to navigate it.) Locals and tourists fill the bistros along Seventh Avenue and Hudson Street (aka Eighth Avenue), the neighbourhood's main strips, and patronise the increasingly high-rent shops that line this newly hot end of Bleecker Street. The north-west corner of this area is known as the **Meatpacking District**; it was primarily a wholesale meat market until the 1990s, when it was also a choice haunt for prostitutes, many of them transsexual.

Eating & drinking

Arium

NEW *31 Little West 12th Street, between Greenwich & Washington Streets (1-212 463 8630). Subway: A, C, E to 14th Street.* **Open** 3-7pm Wed-Sat; 2-7pm. **$**. **Café**. **Map** p58 A2 ⓵⓸⓷
See box p93.

Brass Monkey

55 Little W 12th Street, between Washington Street & Tenth Avenue (1-212 675 6686). Subway: A, C, E to 14th Street; L to Eighth Avenue. **Open** noon-4am daily. **Bar**. **Map** p58 A2 ⓵⓸⓸
Most places in the Meatpacking District make a point of calling attention to their trendiness, but this pub plays it cool without feeling down-market. Like Pioneer, its sibling on the Bowery, the attitude here is relaxed and the decor is simple – just plain wooden chairs and tables. The crowd appreciates the rotating list of 20 beers on tap (including Hoegaarden, Chimay and Magic Hat), 45 bottled varieties, and tavern fare such as mussels, burgers, salads and shepherd's pie.

Buddha Bar

NEW *25 Little W 12th Street, between Ninth Avenue & Washington Street (1-212 647 7314). Subway: A, C, E,*

to 14th Street; L to Eighth Avenue. **Open** Call for details. **$$$**. **Asian**. **Map** p58 A2 ⓵⓸⓹
See box p93.

Chumley's

86 Bedford Street, between Barrow & Grove Streets (1-212 675 4449). Subway: 1 to Christopher Street-Sheridan Square. **Open** 4pm-midnight Mon-Thur; 4pm-2am Fri; 10am-4am Sat; 1pm-2am Sun. **Bar**. No credit cards. **Map** p58 B3 ⓵⓸⓺
The only thing wrong with Chumley's is that it's known the world over as a legendary New York watering hole, so out-of-towners and NYU students overcrowd the place at night and on weekends. The bar still offers an impressive selection of beers in bottles and on tap.

Corner Bistro

331 W 4th Street, at Jane Street (1-212 242 9502). Subway: A, C, E to 14th Street; L to Eighth Avenue. **Open** 11.30am-4am daily. No credit cards. **Bar**. **Map** p58 B3 ⓵⓸⓻
There's only one reason to come to this legendary pub: you'll find one of the city's best burgers ($5) – and beer is just $2 a mug (well, that makes two reasons.) The patties here are cheap, delish and no-frills, served on a flimsy paper plate. To get your hands on one, you may have to queue for a good hour or so, especially on weekend nights. Fortunately, the game is on the TV and a jukebox covers everything from Calexico to Coltrane.

Employees Only

510 Hudson Street, between Christopher & W 10th Streets (1-212 242 3021). Subway: 1 to Christopher Street-Sheridan Square. **Open** 6pm-4am daily. **Bar**. **Map** p58 B3 ⓵⓸⓼
Walk past the palm reader, sitting under a neon sign in the front window, and you'll find a bar with distinctive 1920s decor and a fashionably attired staff – waitresses in custom-designed deco-influenced dresses, bartenders in formal white chef coats. Speciality drinks like the Ginger Smash and the West Side are worth the wait.

Block party

Buddha Bar

The name of the street may be Little W 12th, but we assure you that this short stretch of road, in the trendy Meatpacking District, really packs a punch. First off, have a peek in at **Arium** (p92). Helmed by pastry chef Richard Guier and artist Jamie Titus, the new café/art studio/performance space/tea salon hosts visual art shows, recitals, readings and lectures throughout the year. Art lovers can quench their thirst with any of 86 exotic teas or a glass from the boutique wine list.

A few doors down, a New York offshoot of **Buddha Bar** (p92), the famous Parisian hotspot, has finally opened. Known less for its food than for its trendy patrons and seductive soundtracks (DJ Sam Popat has produced several CDs), the sure-to-be-swingin' venue is just the latest juggernaut to invade the area: the generous space features red Chinese chandeliers, tanks of live jellyfish and a 17-foot black lacquered Buddha. Chefs Keith Matsuoka and AJ Pike, both plucked from Paris, prepare an Asian menu accented with French touches. And wisely, the kitchen is open until 1am most nights.

Now that you're sated, and looking to burn off those extra calories, head over to **Cielo** (p99). Recently, at the fourth annual Club World Awards, Cielo came out on top in the polling for Best Club, which was yet another repeat victory. 'Actually, that's our third Club World Award in a row, if you count the Best Interior Design win from a couple of years ago,' says Cielo honcho Nicolas Matar. 'But winning doesn't mean we're going, "Oh, we've won. Now we can just sit around and not do anything." Really, the more awards we win, the harder we work – it just raises the bar higher.'

EN Japanese Brasserie

435 Hudson Street, at Leroy Street (1-212 647 9196). Subway: 1 to Houston Street. **Open** *5pm-2am Mon-Sat; 5pm-midnight Sun.* **$$.** **Japanese.** **Map** p58 B3 **149**

Bunkei and Reika Yo have created a strikingly diverse space within this multi-level restaurant. On the main floor, they built tatami-style rooms while, on the mezzanine level, they recreated the living room, dining room and library of a Japanese home from the Meiji era (1868-1912). Chef Koji Nakano runs with the homey theme by offering handmade miso paste, tofu and *yuba* (soy-milk skin) in dishes like Berkshire pork belly braised in sansho miso; foie gras and poached daikon steak with white miso vinegar.

Henrietta Hudson

438 Hudson Street, at Morton Street (1-212 924 3347/www.henrietta hudson.com). Subway: 1 to Christopher Street-Sheridan Square. **Open** *4pm-4am Mon-Fri; 1pm-4am Sat, Sun.* **Bar.** No credit cards. **Map** p58 B3 **150**

A long-time, well-loved lesbian bar, Henrietta Hudson used to be more of a grubby pub than glammy lounge. But following a glossy renovation, it's definitely more the latter now. It's still attracting young hottie girls from all over the New York area, especially the nearby burbs. Every night's a new DJ party, with Mamacita Sundays and Transcend Tuesdays among the diverse and well-attended line-up.

Pearl Oyster Bar

18 Cornelia Street, between Bleecker & W 4th Streets (1-212 691 8211). Subway: A, B, C, D, E, F, V to W 4th Street. **Open** *noon-2.30pm, 6-11pm Mon-Fri; 6-11pm Sat.* **$$.** **Seafood.** **Credit** MC, V. **Map** p58 B3 **151**

Thanks to a recently added dining room, Pearl is now twice its original size. But you'll still have to queue to enjoy chef Rebecca Charles's straightforward New England-style seafood. The gussied-up lobster roll – with chunky lobster salad spilling out of a toasted, butter-drenched hot dog

Employees Only p92

'sNice

NEW *45 Eighth Avenue, at 4th Street (1-212 645 0310). Subway: A, C, E to 14th Street; L to Eighth Avenue.* **Open** 7.30am-10pm Mon-Fri; 8am-10pm Sat, Sun. $. **Vegetarian café**. No credit cards. **Map** p58 B2 ⓓ

Someone who hasn't eaten meat for 20 years is bound to know a thing or two about what vegetarians like to eat. Mike Walter, now 33, opened this sandwich shop as a haven for the herbivore set – a simple, inviting place to spend a few hours reading, snacking or working on a laptop.

Shopping

Calypso Christiane Celle

654 Hudson Street, between Gansevoort & W 13th Streets (1-646 638 3000/www.calypso-celle.com). Subway: A, C, E to 14th Street; L to Eighth Avenue. **Open** 11am-7pm Mon-Sat; noon-7pm Sun. **Map** p58 A2 ⓓ

Christiane Celle has created a Calypso empire, of which this new outpost in the Meatpacking District is the jewel in the crown. Stop by any of the shops for gorgeous slip dresses, suits, sweaters and scarves, many from little-known French designers.

Chocolate Haven

NEW *350 Hudson Street, at King Street (1-212 414 2462). Subway: 1 to Houston Street.* **Open** 10.30am-7.30pm Mon-Sat; noon-5pm Sun. **Map** p58 B4 ⓓ

See box p98.

Diane von Furstenberg, the Shop

385 W 12th Street, between Washington Street & West Side Highway (1-646 486 4800/www.dvf.com). Subway: A, C, E to 14th Street; L to Eighth Avenue. **Open** 11am-6pm Mon-Wed, Fri; 11am-8pm Thur; 11am-5pm Sat; noon-5pm Sun. **Map** p58 A3 ⓓ

Although she's known for her classic wrap dress (she sold five million of them in the 1970s), indefatigable socialite Diane von Furstenberg has

bun – is her signature dish. Other fishy favourites include fresh steamers, clam chowder accented with smoky bacon, pan-roasted oysters and boiled or grilled whole lobster.

Plunge

Gansevoort Hotel, 18 Ninth Avenue, at 13th Street (212-206-6700). Subway: A, C, E to 14th Street; L to Eighth Avenue. **Open** noon-4am daily. **Bar**. **Map** p58 A2 ⓓ

The bar atop the Hotel Gansevoort offers a great aerial view of the Meatpacking District (it trumps Soho House by eight floors), but the experience comes at a premium: drinks are $14 apiece. The stylish executives and banker types who squeeze in here nightly can lounge at tables lining the stone terraces, or venture out to the crowded garden, where low sofas and wooden benches provide additional seating. What they can't do is take the plunge in the outdoor swimming pool on the hotel's rooftop. If you'd like to visit when it's calmer, come midweek.

Cielo p99

installed much more at this *soigné* space, which resembles the inside of a glittery jewel box. Whether you go for ultra-feminine dresses or sporty knits, you'll emerge from the changing room feeling just like a princess.

Girlshop

819 Washington Street, between Gansevoort & Little W 12th Streets (1-212 255 4985/www.girlshop.com). Subway: L to Eighth Avenue. **Open** 11am-7pm Mon-Wed; 11am-8pm Thur-Sat; noon-7pm Sun. **Map** p58 A2 ⑮⑦

Girlshop.com's bricks-and-mortar sibling offers instant gratification to shoppers who can now try on hot numbers available online by Keanan Dufty, Cigana, or any of the myriad labels – the perfect alternative for those who are short of patience, fall between two sizes or just have bad relationships with their FedEx men.

Jeffrey New York

449 W 14th Street, between Ninth & Tenth Avenues (1-212 206 1272). Subway: A, C, E to 14th Street; L to Eighth Avenue. **Open** 10am-8pm Mon-Wed, Fri; 10am-9pm Thur; 10am-7pm Sat; 12.30-6pm Sun. **Map** p58 A2 ⑮⑧

Jeffrey Kalinsky, a former Barneys shoe buyer, was a Meatpacking District pioneer with his namesake store, a branch of the Atlanta, Georgia, original. Designer clothing abounds here – Lang, Versace and YSL among other brands. But the centrepiece is the shoe salon, which features fabulous footwear by Manolo Blahnik, Prada and Robert Clergerie.

Magnolia Bakery

401 Bleecker Street, at 11th Street (1-212 462 2572). Subway: 1 to Christopher Street. **Open** noon-11.30pm Mon; 9am-11.30pm Tue-Thur; 9am-12.30am Fri; 10am-12.30am Sat; 10am-11.30pm Sun. **Map** p58 B3 ⑮⑨

Part sweet market, part meet market, Magnolia skyrocketed to fame thanks to *Sex and the City*. The pastel-iced cupcakes are much vaunted, but you can also pick up a cup of custardy,

Southern-style banana pudding (Brits: think trifle) or point yourself out a scoop from the summertime ice-cream cart. Then, sweetmeat in hand, join the other happy eaters clogging nearby apartment stoops.

Scoop

861 Washington Street, between 13th & 14th Streets (1-212 691 1905/ www.scoopnyc.com). Subway: A, C, E to 14th Street; L to Eighth Avenue. **Open** 11am-8pm Mon-Fri; 11am-7pm Sat; noon-6pm Sun. **Map** p58 A2 ⑯⓪

Scoop is the ultimate fashion editor's closet. Clothing from the likes of Juicy Couture, Diane von Furstenberg, Philosophy and others is arranged on the rails by hue, not label. The newest outposts, in the Meatpacking District, have fab finds for both genders at neighbouring stores.

Stella McCartney

429 W 14th Street, between Ninth & Tenth Avenues (1-212 255 1556/ www.stellamccartney.com). Subway: A, C, E to 14th Street; L to Eighth Avenue. **Open** noon-7pm Mon-Sat; 12.30-6pm Sun. **Map** p58 A2 ⑯①

Celeb designer McCartney, who won acclaim for her rock-star collections for Chloé, now showcases pricey lines of glam-sprite womenswear, shoes and accessories at her first-ever store.

Tracy Reese

NEW *641 Hudson Street, between Gansevoort & Horatio Streets (1-212 807 0505). Subway: A, C, E to 14th Street; L to Eighth Avenue.* **Open** 11am-7pm Mon-Wed; 11am-8pm Thur-Sat; noon-7pm Sun. **Map** p58 A2 ⑯②

With the opening of her eponymous Meatpacking District flagship, apostles of archfeminine designer Tracy Reese now have a house of worship. The 2,200 square feet of curvaceous walls, twinkly chandeliers and fuchsia cushioned settees pays tribute to all things femme – much like Reese's threads.

Yoya

636 Hudson Street, between Horatio & Jane Streets (1-646 336 6844/ www.yoyashop.com). Subway: A, C,

Haute chocolate

Chocolate Haven

CHAMPAGNE KISS
(Rosé Champagne)

Many of us obsess over chocolate. Some claim to be hopelessly addicted to it. Small children dress up in goofy costumes at Halloween to get their hands on some. The same can't be said of mayonnaise. No, chocolate is indeed on another level all together – and in recent years Manhattan has seen an explosion of new chocolate shops.

Legendary chocolatier Jacques Torres has unveiled his most irresistible creation yet: **Chocolate Haven**, an 8,000-square-foot factory that serves as the Manhattan hub for the pastry chef's growing chocolate empire. The space features a cocoa-pod shaped café overlooking the candy-making facilities, so visitors can indulge in chocolate treats and watch as cocoa beans are transformed into chocolate bars.

Another great boutique is the West Village's **Chocolate Bar**. The store stocks only candies, cookies and brownies from high-end local makers. This is also, as the name suggests, the place to score an updated version of the chocolate bar – worthwhile options include

the shop's hefty dark-chocolate bars flavoured liberally with mint or orange. For something more bite-size, check out the mojito truffle, flavoured with rum, lime and mint. Or a lemon-hazelnut one. Or peanut-butter caramel.

Boozehounds will fall head over heels for **Chocolat Michel Cluizel**. The French fine-chocolate producer opened his first stateside shop inside the Flatiron's ABC Carpet & Home, and even scored a liquor licence. His 'adult' bonbons are spiked with rum, vodka or whisky.

If you like candies on your chocolate, check out **Divalicious**. Here you'll find chocolate-covered everything – fortune cookies, graham crackers and pretzels – as well as chocolate lollipops and chocolate hearts.

■ Chocolate Bar, 48 Eighth Avenue, between Horatio & Jane Streets (1-212 366 1541).
■ Chocolate Haven p95.
■ Divalicious, 365 Broome Street, between Elizabeth & Mott Streets (1-212 343 1243).
■ Michel Cluizel, ABC Carpet & Home, 888 Broadway, at 19th Street (1-212 473 3000).

NEW YORK BY AREA

E to 14th Street; L to Eighth Avenue.
Open 11am-7pm Mon-Sat. **Map** p58
B2 **163**

A selection of Village sensibilities –
European, bohemian and hip – come
together in this store, which is aimed
at infants to six-year-olds. Labels such
as Erica Tanov, Temperley for Little
People, and Imps & Elves are available, as well as tiny-size (but not tiny-
priced) Diesel T-shirts.

Nightlife

APT

*419 W 13th Street, between Ninth
Avenue & Washington Street (1-212
414 4245/www.apt website.com).
Subway: A, C, E to 14th Street; L to
Eighth Avenue.* **Open** 7pm-4am daily.
Map p58 A2 **164**

This bi-level boîte is now the city's
prime place for hearing cool underground beats. Everyone from techno
deity Carl Craig to Zulu Nation founder
Afrika Bambaataa has played the plat-
ters here, in either the sleek basement
bar or the cosy, well-appointed street-
level room. The resident spinners
include lounge-kitsch Ursula 1000, the
electrofunky Negroclash crew, soulful-
house guru Neil Aline and deep-disco
master DJ Spun. APT becomes sar-
dine-packed at weekends and on head-
liner guest nights, but at least you're
squeezed in with one of the best-look-
ing crowds in town

Cielo

*18 Little W 12th Street, between Ninth
Avenue & Washington Street (1-212
645 5700/www.cieloclub.com). Subway:
A, C, E to 14th Street; L to Eighth
Avenue.* **Open** 10pm-4am daily.
Map p58 A2 **165**

It's a wonderful little joint – the urban-
ski-lodge decor looks terrific, and
the place boasts one of the city's clear-
est sound systems. (Weekends are a
slightly different matter, though, with
all of the tables reserved for those willing to drop a wad for a bottle of hooch.)
The club features top-shelf house from
world-class DJs, with everyone from

Masters at Work's Louie Vega to drum
'n' bass superstar Roni Size having
plied their trade here; every Monday
Cielo is treated to DJ deity François K's
dub-heavy Deep Space session. See
also box p93.

Lotus

*409 W 14th Street, between Ninth
Avenue & Washington Street (1-212
243 4420/www.lotusnewyork.com).
Subway: A, C, E to 14th Street; L to
Eighth Avenue.* **Open** 10pm-4am daily.
Map. p58 A2 **166**

Happily, this venue's trendy patina has
faded, and now Lotus can be fully
appreciated as a well-furnished restaurant, lounge and dance club where DJs
spin a mainstream mix of sounds to an
affluent bridge-and-tunnel crowd.
Friday nights are still the best but
getting past the doorman hasn't got
significantly easier, so make sure you
dress to impress.

Arts & leisure

Film Forum

*209 W Houston Street, between Sixth
Avenue & Varick Street (1-212 727
8110/www.filmforum.com). Subway:
1 to Houston Street.* **Map** p58 B4 **167**

Though the seats and sight lines
leave something to be desired, this
three-screen art theatre presents great
documentaries, new and repertory
films, and a cute crowd of budding
NYU auteurs and film geeks in horn-
rimmed glasses.

Merce Cunningham Studio

*11th Floor, 55 Bethune Street, between
Washington & West Streets (1-212 691
9751/www.merce.org). Subway: A, C, E
to 14th Street; L to Eighth Avenue.* No
credit cards. **Map** p58 A3 **168**

Located in the Westbeth complex on
the edge of the West Village, the venue
is rented to independent choreographers. As a result, performance quality varies, but some of the shows are
wonderful. The stage and seating area
are in a large dance studio; be prepared
to take off your shoes and arrive early,
or you may have to sit on the floor.

The Eagle

Midtown

Every day Midtown (occupying the slice of the island between 14th Street and 59th Street) earns its reputation as one of the most hectic, breathtaking urban landscapes on earth. The city's most famous landmarks – the **Empire State Building**, the **Chrysler Building**, **Rockefeller Center**, **Times Square** and **Grand Central Terminal** – are found here. High- and lowbrow fashion is conceived around Seventh Avenue, publicised on Madison and sold along Fifth. But there's more to Midtown than glistening towers and high-octane commerce. Cultural heavyweights such as the **Museum of Modern Art**, **Broadway** and the **Theater District**, **Carnegie Hall** and the **New York Public Library** draw their own crowds. Midtown is also where you'll find the folksy **Union Square Greenmarket** and the quaint tree-lined streets of **Chelsea**, **Tudor City** and **Gramercy Park**.

Chelsea

Chelsea is the epicentre of the city's gay life, but residents of all types inhabit the blocks between 14th and 29th Streets west of Fifth Avenue. There's a generous assortment of bars and restaurants, most of which are clustered along Eighth Avenue, the main hub of activity. The whole western edge of Chelsea is now the city's hottest art gallery zone.

Sights & museums
Museum of Sex
*233 Fifth Avenue, at 27th Street
(1-212 689 6337/www.museum
ofsex.org). Subway: N, R, W, 6 to 28th
Street.* **Open** 11am-6.30pm Mon-Fri,
Sun; 11am-8pm Sat. **Admission**
£14.50; £13.50 reductions. No under-
18s. **Map** p103 D3 ❶
Despite the subject matter, don't expect
too much titillation at this museum.
Instead, you'll find presentations of historical documents and items – many of
which were too risqué to be made public in their own time – that explore
prostitution, burlesque, birth control,
obscenity and fetishism. The museum
was lucky enough to acquire an extensive collection of pornography from a
retired Library of Congress curator
(apparently, he applied his professional skills to recreational pursuits as
well). Thus, the Ralph Whittington
Collection features thousands of items,
including 8mm films, videos, blow-up
dolls and other erotic paraphernalia.

Eating & drinking
Barracuda
*275 W 22nd Street, between Seventh
& Eighth Avenues (1-212 645 8613).
Subway: C, E, 1 to 23rd Street.* **Open**
4pm-4am daily. **Bar**. No credit cards.
Map p102 C4 ❷
While a recent makeover gets high
style points, this is still just a friendly
little neighbourhood place to have a
beer and watch drag shows. A pleasant mix of chilled-out locals converge
around the small stand-up tables up
front or in the back room, which is full
of inviting, get-comfy couches and a
pool table. Drinks are always stiff,
the crowd is good-looking, and DJs
keep the place pumping. The divine
drag shows take place from Sunday
to Thursday.

Bette
*461 W 23rd Street, at Tenth Avenue
(1-212 366 0404). Subway: C, E to
23rd Street.* **Open** 6-11.30pm Mon-Sat.
$$$. American. **Map** p102 B4 ❸

Amy Sacco, the beauty and brains
behind Bungalow 8 and Lot 61, has
opened a serious restaurant in Chelsea.
The space is relatively small, but
tastefully decorated with designer
touches: art by Richard Phillips and
stemware from Lalique. Executive
chef Tom Dimarzo – a Jean-Georges
protégé – serves lofty fare like lobster
gazpacho and seared tuna with basil,
capers and tapenade.

Cafeteria
*119 Seventh Avenue, at 17th Street
(1-212 414 1717). Subway: 1 to 18th
Street.* **Open** 24hrs. **$$. American.**
Map p102 C4 ❹
Cocktails and eye candy fuel a nonstop
cruising scene in the spare white
dining room. Cafeteria feeds the
fashionista hoards with down-home
favourites. Nostalgic pleasures include
a gravy-heavy meat loaf mac and
cheese, and a juicy charred burger with
blue cheese. On a liquid diet? Head
straight for the pint-size basement bar.

City Bakery
*3 W 18th Street, between Fifth & Sixth
Avenues (1-212 366 1414). Subway: L,
N, Q, R, W, 4, 5, 6 to 14th Street-
Union Square.* **Open** 7.30am-7pm Mon-
Fri; 7.30am-6.30pm Sat; 9am-6pm Sun.
$. American. **Map** p103 D4 ❺
Pastry whiz Maury Rubin has settled
nicely into this loft-size space jammed
with Chelsea shoppers loading up
on unusual salad-bar choices (grilled
pineapple with ancho chilli, bean
sprouts with smoked tofu). There's also
a small selection of soups, pizzas and
hot dishes. But to heck with all that: the
thick, rich hot chocolate with fat house-
made marshmallows is heaven in a
cup, and the moist 'melted' chocolate-
chip cookies are better than a marked-
down pair of Prada pumps.

The Eagle
*554 W 28th Street, between Tenth &
Eleventh Avenues (1-646 473 1866/
www.eaglenyc.com). Subway: C, E to
23rd Street.* **Open** 10pm-4am Mon-Sat;
5pm-4am Sun. **Bar**. No credit cards.
Map p102 A3 ❻

D

Helmsley Building

Grand Central
Terminal 107

Chrysler
Building

NY Public
Library

dinavia House:
Nordic Center
n America

Morgan
Library 27

Empire State
Building 6

um 1
ex

Madison
Square 31

R W

26
ron
ling

91

29

39

30 40

41
28

37

BROADWAY

FIFTH AVE

UNIVERSITY PL

FOURTH AVE

MADISON AVE

PARK AVE SOUTH

IRVING PL

LEXINGTON AVE

THIRD AVE

RUTHERFORD PL

SECOND AVE

NATHAN D
PERLMAN PL

MT CARMEL PL

FIRST AVE

ASSER LEVY PL

FRANKLIN D ROOSEVELT DR

AVENUE A

AVENUE B

E

109

E 48TH ST

E 46TH ST

E 44TH ST

E 42ND ST

E 40TH ST

E 38TH ST

E 36TH ST

E 34TH ST 38

E 32ND ST

E 30TH ST

E 28TH ST 42

26TH ST 43

E 26TH ST

E 24TH ST

E 23RD ST

E 22ND ST

E 18TH ST

E 16TH ST 35

114
Japan Society

108 United Nations
Headquarters

News
Building
117

TUDOR CITY PL

QUEENS-MIDTOWN TUNNEL

East River

300 m
300 yds

© Copyright Time Out Group 2006

Manhattan
Marina 70

Peter Cooper
Village

E 20TH ST

Stuyvesant
Town

E 14TH ST

E 13TH ST

E 12TH ST

E 11TH ST

E 10TH ST

E 9TH ST

Theodore
Roosevelt
Birthplace

Gramercy
Park

National
Arts Club 34

Stuyvesant
Square

Union
Square

GRAMERCY
PARK

St. Mark's Church
in-the-Bowery

Grace
Church

F

1

2

3

4

5

6

7 M 90

M S,4,5,6,7

M 6

M

6

6

M

M

M L

M L

L,M,N,Q,R,W,
4,5,6

A **B** **C**

W 72ND ST — 1,2,3 Ⓜ — B,C — Ⓜ Strawbe Fields

1

W 70TH ST

HENRY HUDSON PKWY
WEST END AVE
AMSTERDAM AVE
BROADWAY
COLUMBUS AVE
CENTRAL PARK WEST
WEST DR

W 68TH ST

FREEDOM PL

Sheep Meadov

W 66TH ST — Ⓜ — W 66TH ST

Tavern on the Green

RIVERSIDE BLVD

W 64TH ST

Lincoln Center   W 62ND ST

Heckscher Playground

2

W 60TH ST

A,B,C,D Ⓜ

Columbus Circle

99

98

97 — W 58TH ST

NY Visitors Bureau

96 — W 56TH ST

Ⓜ N,Q

W 57TH ST — 100

Carnegie Hall — 65

95

68

3 94 — W 54TH ST

CLINTON

96

92 — De Witt Clinton Park

W 52ND ST — 101

B,D,E

NYC Official Visitor Info Center

SEVENTH AVE

99 98

90 — W 50TH ST

72 — 83

TWELFTH AVE
ELEVENTH AVE
TENTH AVE
NINTH AVE

C,E Ⓜ

88 — W 48TH ST

1 Ⓜ Ⓜ N,F

Intrepid Sea-Air-Space Museum

86 95

THEATER DISTRICT

67

Times Sq Visitors' C

W 46TH ST — 106

102 63 61

52 51 50

84 — W 44TH ST

60 — TKTS

EIGHTH AVE

97 59

64 70 62 57

83 94

71 — Times Square

48

Port Authority Bus Terminal

A,C,E Ⓜ

58

54 49 69 — N,Q,E

Madame Tussaud's New York

1,2,3

NCOLN TUNNEL — W 42ND ST

81

5

W 40TH ST

78 — 104

W 38TH ST

GARMENT DISTRICT

SEVENTH AVE

76 — W 36TH ST

45

Javits Center

Macy's

W 34TH ST — A,C,E Ⓜ — 1,2,3 Ⓜ — 46

da Terrace
D
E 72ND ST
E
F

umburg
ndshell

**Asia Society
and Museum**

EAST DRIVE

**The Frick
Collection**

E 70TH ST

1 **Sights & museums**
1 **Eating & drinking**
1 **Shopping**
1 **Nightlife**
1 **Arts & leisure**

6
E 68TH ST

**China
Institute**
E 66TH ST

1

FIFTH AVE
PARK AVE
MADISON AVE
LEXINGTON AVE
THIRD AVE
SECOND AVE
FIRST AVE
FRANKLIN D ROOSEVELT DR

E 64TH ST

F

Zoo

**Rockefeller
University**

E 62ND ST

YORK AVE

2

ollman
emorial
Rink

TRAMWAY

N,R,W

**Grand Army
Plaza**

N,R,W
Bloomingdales
119

E 60TH ST

**QUEENSBORO
(59TH ST)BRIDGE**

4,5,6

E 58TH ST

113

SUTTON PL

86
89

E 57TH ST

SUTTON PL. SOUTH

93 **Trump Tower**
E 56TH ST

87

Art
eum
m
&

**Museum of
Modern Art**
111

E 54TH ST
110

73 76 84
75 85 77
E,V

E 52ND ST

MIDTOWN

**Radio City
Music Hall**
88

**Museum of TV
& Radio**

116

BEEKMAN PL

1 78
feller
er

80

St. Patrick's Cathedral
82

6
115
E 50TH ST
118
MITCHELL PL

NBC
92
**Saks
Fifth Ave**

109
112

Christie's
E 48TH ST

114
Japan Society

Helmsley Building
E 46TH ST

SECOND AVE

**Grand Central
Terminal**

E 44TH ST

108
**United Nations
Headquarters**

,D,F,V
90
107

**Chrysler
Building**

TUDOR CITY PL
FIRST AVE

7
S,4,5,6,7
E 42ND ST

**QUEENS-MIDTOWN
TUNNEL**

ryant
Park
79

**NY Public
Library**

**News
Building**
117

E 40TH ST

E 38TH ST

0

300 m

candinavia House:
he Nordic Center
in America

0
300 yds

27
**Morgan
Library**

LEXINGTON AVE
THIRD AVE

© Copyright Time Out Group 2006

5

E 36TH ST

V,N,Q,R,W **Empire State**

This classic Levi's-and-leather bar boasts a killer roof deck. Look out for beer blasts, leather soirées and simple nights of pool playing and cruising.

Naka Naka

NEW *458 W 17th Street, between Ninth & Tenth Avenues (1-212 929 8544). Subway: A, C, E to 14th Street; L to Eighth Avenue.* **Open** 6pm-midnight Tue-Sat. **$$. Japanese.** Map p102 B4 **7**

Tasty traditional dishes, starting with spicy lotus root, delicate mixed-vegetable tempura and deliciously dense shrimp dumplings. The sushi is neither phenomenal nor disappointing, but considering how difficult it is to find peace and quiet over dinner in this part of town, we can't complain.

Opus 22 Turntable Lounge

559 W 22nd Street, at Eleventh Avenue (1-212 929 7515). Subway: C, E to 23rd Street. **Open** Tue-Sat 11am-4am; Sun 10pm-4am. **Bar.** No credit cards. Map p102 A4 **8**

Sunsets over the Hudson remain the big draw at this revamped open-air room. The most significant improvements are the custom-designed sound system and DJ booth, where aspiring artists can show their stuff.

Pre:Post

NEW *547 W 27th Street, between Tenth & Eleventh Avenues (1-212 695 7270). Subway C, E to 23rd Street.* **Open** 5pm-midnight Tue, Wed; 5pm-2am Thur-Sun. **$$. American.** Map p102 A3 **9**

There's a seating option for every kind of clubby customer: cabanas for table-service types, regular tables for quiet wallflowers and private birch-wood log booths for couples. The menu wisely sticks to classic comfort food: burgers, sandwiches, meat loaf, chicken.

Red Cat

227 Tenth Avenue, between 23rd & 24th Streets (1-212 242 1122). Subway: C, E to 23rd Street. **Open** 5.30-11pm Mon-Thur; 5.30pm-midnight Fri, Sat; 5-10pm Sun. **$$. American.** Map p102 B4 **10**

Art-world luminaries and London Terrace residents descend on this comfortable, reliable, handsome eaterie, which is done out with red walls and crisp white tablecloths. Do not attempt to eat lightly here. The Red Cat specialises in all that's hearty: gargantuan pork chops, Parmesan-covered french fries, extra-juicy shell steak, and big-time sweets like banana splits.

Taj

48 W 21st Street, between Fifth & Sixth Avenues (1-212-620-3033). Subway: F, V, N, R, W to 23rd Street. **Open** 6pm-1am Tue; 5.30pm-4am Wed-Sat. **Bar.** Map p103 D4 **11**

Behind the sparkling crystal curtain is a vast, high-ceilinged room with dramatic South Asian decor. At night the restaurant morphs into a red-rope club with a no-sneakers dress code. Expect to share the dramatically lit dance floor with well-groomed chicks in trashy tops grooving to live drummers and Prince-ly Top 40 faves.

Tia Pol

205 Tenth Avenue, between 22nd & 23rd Streets (1-212 675 8805). Subway: C, E to 23rd Street. **Open** noon-3pm, 5pm-midnight Mon-Thur; noon-3pm, 5pm-1am Fri, Sat; 11am-3pm, 6pm-midnight Sun. **$. Spanish.** Map p102 B4 **12**

This tiny tapas restaurant keeps things simple with traditional tapas like sautéed cockles and razor clams. Other dishes showcase unlikely combinations: tomato-covered bread with lima-bean purée and chorizo and chocolate on bread rounds. The all-Spanish wine list is well priced, with selections that pair well with the spicy food.

Wild Lily Tea Room

511 W 22nd Street, between Tenth & Eleventh Avenues (1-212 691 2258). Subway: C, E to 23rd Street. **Open** noon-9pm Tue-Sun. **$. Pan Asian.** Map p102 B4 **13**

Goldfish swim among floating candles in a round pool at the front of this spare, peaceful space. The food is precious pan-Asian and often incorporates tea: black sticky-rice risotto with mascarpone shares space with steamed turbot and shiitake mushrooms in a slightly sweet jasmine-tea broth; a shrimp salad is delicately flavoured with a lavender-mint dressing.

xl

357 W 16th Street, between Eighth & Ninth Avenues (1-646 336 5574/ www.xlnewyork.com). Subway: A, C, E to 14th Street; L to Eighth Avenue. **Open** 4pm-4am daily. **Bar**. No credit cards. **Map** p102 B5 ⓮

This slick trilevel gay bar is a study in style: witness the giant aquarium in the unisex bathroom. Fashion divas, muscle men, fag hags and a few drag queens run amok under one roof.

Shopping

Billy's Bakery

184 Ninth Avenue, between 21st & 22nd Streets (1-212 647 9956/ www.billysbakerynyc.com). Subway: C, E to 23rd Street. **Open** 9am-11pm Mon-Thur, Sun; 9am-12.30am Fri, Sat. **Map** p102 B4 ⓯

Amid super-sweet retro delights such as coconut cream pie, Hello Dollies and Famous Refrigerator Cake, you'll find friendly service in a setting that will remind you of Grandma's kitchen.

The Garage

112 W 25th Street, between Sixth & Seventh Avenues (1-212 647 0707). Subway: F, V to 23rd Street. **Open** sunrise-sunset Sat, Sun. No credit cards. **Map** p102 C3 ⓰

Designers (and the occasional dolled-down celebrity) hunt regularly – and early – at this flea market inside an emptied parking garage. This spot specialises in old prints, vintage clothing, silver and linens; there's lots of household paraphernalia too.

Jazz Record Center

Room 804, 236 W 26th Street, between Seventh & Eighth Avenues (1-212 675 4480/www.jazzrecordcenter.com). Subway: C, E to 23rd Street; 1 to 28th Street. **Open** 10am-6pm Mon-Sat. **Map** p102 C3 ⓱

The city's best jazz store stocks current and out-of-print records, books, videos and other jazz-related merchandise. Worldwide shipping is available.

Kidding Around

60 W 15th Street, between Fifth & Sixth Avenues (1-212 645 6337). Subway: F, V to 14th Street; L to Sixth Avenue. **Open** 10am-7pm Mon-Sat; 11am-6pm Sun. **Map** p102 C5 ⓲

Loyal customers frequent this quaint shop for clothing and learning toys for the brainy baby. A play area will keep your little one occupied while you shop.

Nightlife

Avalon

660 Sixth Avenue, at 20th Street (1-212 807 7780). Subway F to 23rd Street; 1 to 23rd Street. **Open** 10pm-4am Fri, Sat. **Map** p102 C4 ⓳

Though many of the city's big clubs suffer from a conservative music policy, at least Avalon – the erstwhile Limelight – makes the effort occasionally to feature interesting beats, with the likes of techno wizard Robert Hood and Death in Vegas's Richard Fearless dropping by for a date on the decks.

Crobar

530 W 28th Street, between Tenth & Eleventh Avenues (1-212 629 9000/ www.crobar.com). Subway: C, E to 23rd Street. **Open** 5pm-4am Thur; 10pm-7am Fri, Sat. **Map** p102 A3 ⓴

The splendiferous Crobar is as close to a full-on superclub as NYC has to offer: it can squeeze 2,750 revellers into its main room and two smaller party dens, it has a great sound system and a dazzling repertoire of disco lights. Though the beats tend to lean towards the lowest-common-denominator end of the dance-music spectrum, this is a must-see on the city's after-dark circuit.

Spirit

530 W 27th Street, between Tenth & Eleventh Avenues (1-212 268 9477/ www.spiritnewyork.com). Subway: C, E to 23rd Street. **Open** 10pm-5am Fri, Sat. **Map** p102 A3 ㉑

NEW YORK BY AREA

Crobar p107

When Spirit first opened in 2004, it tried using forward-thinking house and techno; crowds were sparse. Next, the club tried an utterly mainstream approach, to much the same effect. Things have improved more recently with the Made Event crew occasionally taking over the space to feature DJs of the international calibre of prog-tech titan Danny Tenaglia from Tyrant, and Lee Burridge.

Arts & leisure

Chelsea Piers

Piers 59-62, W 17th through 23rd Streets, at Eleventh Avenue (1-212 336 6666/www.chelseapiers.com). Subway: C, E to 23rd Street. **Map** p102 A4 ㉒
This massive sports complex, which occupies a six-block stretch of riverfront real estate, offers just about every popular recreational activity in a bright, clean, well-maintained facility. Would-be Tigers can practise their swings at the Golf Club; bowlers can

set up their pins at the AMF Lanes. Or hit the Roller Rink and Skate Park. At the Sports Center gym, classes cover everything from triathlon training to hip-hop dance. Hours and fees vary; call or see the website for information.

Joyce Theater

175 Eighth Avenue, at 19th Street (1-212 242 0800/www.joyce.org). Subway: A, C, E to 14th Street; 1 to 18th Street; L to Eighth Avenue. **Map** p102 B4 ㉓
This intimate space, formerly a cinema, is one of the finest theatres in town. Of the 472 seats at the Joyce, there's not a single bad one. Companies and choreographers who present work here, including the Ballet Hispanico, David Parsons and Doug Varone, tend to be more traditional than experimental.

The Kitchen

512 W 19th Street, between Tenth & Eleventh Avenues (1-212 255 5793/ www.thekitchen.org). Subway: A, C, E to 14th Street; L to Eighth Avenue. **Map** p102 B4 ㉔

gives Downtown a run for its money in terms of cachet and cool. This chic enclave is full of shops as stylish as those below 14th Street, yet often less expensive.

You need a key to enter tranquil **Gramercy Park**, at the bottom of Lexington Avenue (between 20th and 21st Streets). The gated green square is the preserve of those lucky residents of the beautiful townhouses and apartments that ring the park. Anyone, however, can enjoy the charms of the surrounding district.

Murray Hill spans 30th to 40th Streets between Third and Fifth Avenues. Townhouses of the rich and powerful were once clustered around Madison and Park Avenues. Sniffen Court (150-158 E 36th Street, between Lexington & Third Avenues) is an unspoiled row of 1864 carriage houses.

Sights & museums

Flatiron Building

175 Fifth Avenue, between 22nd & 23rd Streets. Subway: N, R, W, 6 to 23rd Street. **Map** p103 D4 **26**
The 22-storey edifice is clad in white terracotta: its light colour was revealed again by cleaning and restoration in the early 1990s. The surrounding neighbourhood was christened in honour of the structure, which was the world's first steel-frame skyscraper.

Morgan Library

NEW *E 36th Street, between Madison & Park Avenues (1-212 685 0008/ www.morganlibrary.org). Subway: 6 to 34th Street.* **Open** 10.30am-5pm Tue-Thur; 10.30am-9pm Fri; 10am-6pm Sat; 11am-6pm Sun. **Admission** $12, $8 reductions. **Map** p103 D2/p105 E5 **27**
After undergoing a dramatic expansion, the library reopened its doors in spring 2006. Serving as both museum and research library, the impressive, light-filled space (glass walls in the main pavilion allow you to see more of the 1906 Charles McKim building and

Although the Kitchen is best known as an avant-garde theatre space, it also features experimental dance by inventive, often provocative artists. Choreographers Sarah Michelson and Dean Moss have worked here.

Laughing Lotus Yoga Center

3rd Floor, 59 W 19th Street, between Fifth & Sixth Avenues (1-212 414 2903/www.laughinglotus.com). Subway: F, V, N, R, W to 23rd Street. **Open** Call or see website for schedule. **Map** p102 C4 **25**
Roomy yogic community centre offering weekly workshops and classes. On the menu are midnight yoga, reflexology and absolute-beginner classes.

Flatiron District & Union Square

The Flatiron District, which extends from 14th to 29th Streets between Fifth and Park Avenues,

NEW YORK BY AREA

CityParks
Foundation
people + parks

the heart of the city

Central Park
SummerStage

free!

music

dance

film

word

in Central Park!

New Yorks's premiere **free** performing arts festi

www.SummerStage

Union Square

a naturally lit reading room tops the Madison Avenue structure) has an awe-inspiring collection of rare books, illuminated manuscripts, drawings and prints. Among the treats are etchings and drawings by Rembrandt and da Vinci, Mary Shelley's own copy of *Frankenstein* and one of the first copies of the Declaration of Independence.

Union Square

Subway L, N, Q, R, W, 4, 5, 6 to Union Square. **Map** p103 D5 ㉓
Union Square (from 14th to 17th Streets, between Union Square East & Union Square West) is the home of the Union Square Greenmarket (p113), which is fast becoming a New York institution.

Eating & drinking

Craftbar

900 Broadway, at 20th Street (1-212 461 4300). Subway: N, R, W, 6 to 23rd Street. **Open** noon-11pm Mon-Thur, Sun; noon-midnight Fri, Sat. **$$. American creative.**
Map p103 D4 ㉓

Tom Colicchio's flashy spin-off of his upscale restaurant Craft is in a bigger and brighter space around the corner from the original Craftbar. The dining room is still positively raucous, and the busy bar is jammed with chatty, wine-swigging groups. Appetisers rate highest. Desserts like chocolate pot de crème and steamed lemon pudding are sheer heaven.

Dévi

8 E 18th Street, at Fifth Avenue (1-212 691 1300). Subway: N, R, W, 6 to 23rd Street. **Open** noon-2.30pm, 5.30-10.30pm Mon-Thur; noon-2.30pm, 5.30-11pm Fri, Sat; 5.30-10.30pm Sun.
$$. Indian. Map p103 D4 ㉚
In this bi-level dining room decked out with multicoloured lanterns and gauzy saffron draperies, kick off your evening with a citrusy Dévi Fizz cocktail and some crisp samosas. Then pamper yourself with such inspired Indian dishes as velvety yam dumplings in a spiced tomato gravy; stuffed baby aubergine bathed

Country in the city

Geoffrey Zakarian gives another great reason to eat inside a hotel.

Many a restaurant's name has been used to sell a cookbook, but we'd never seen a magazine name inspire a restaurant name – which subsequently inspired a cookbook. Geoffrey Zakarian, who opened Town in the Chambers Hotel in 2001, recently unveiled **Country** in another boutique hotel, the Carlton, and published a cookbook, *Town/Country*, which plays off his two venues. Yet, aside from offering some typical rustic ingredients, Country is about as provincial as a ride on the subway. Hotshot designer David Rockwell has renovated the century-old space and restored the original beaux arts style, uncovering architectural gems such as a tiled floor and a Tiffany-style, green-and-white glass dome. The result is an elegant Parisian vibe.

Country actually comprises two eateries. A more informal, subterranean café and bar opened in late 2005. The serious cooking, however, takes place upstairs, where Zakarian has tapped Doug Psaltis as executive chef. His four-course, $85 prix fixe menu draws heavily on French influences, but adds American and Italian elements. Now city slickers can visit the country without leaving town.
■ Country, Carlton Hotel, 90 Madison Avenue at 29th Street (1-212 889 7100).

in spicy peanut sauce; or moist chunks of chicken with pistachios, cilantro (coriander) and green chillies.

Eleven Madison Park
11 Madison Avenue, at 24th Street (1-212 889 0905). Subway: R, W, 6 to 23rd Street. **Open** 11.30am-2pm, 5.30-11pm Mon-Thur; 11.30am-2pm, 5.30-11pm Fri, Sat; 5.30-10pm Sun.
$$$. American Creative.
Map p103 D4 ③
A five-course tasting menu here is a bragain at $65. The list might include melt-away sautéed sweetbreads, skate with a *grenobloise* twist, or flavour-packed *côte de boeuf* alongside fat, golden onion rings. The dining room, with its park views, soaring ceilings and attentive service, is sufficiently serious for business deals yet elegant enough for dates.

Encore
757 Sixth Avenue, between 25th & 26th Streets (1-212 414 4696). Subway: 1 to 28th Street. **Open** 9pm-4am Tue-Sat. **Bar. Map** p102 C3 ③
Karaoke junkies now have an upscale alternative to all those traditional seedy Japanese joints. This space boasts oversize portraits of Axl Rose and Jim Morrison, flat-screen TVs looping '80s videos and all kinds of speciality shots.

Flatiron Lounge
37 W 19th Street, between Fifth & Sixth Avenues (1-212 727 7741). Subway: F, V, R, W to 23rd Street. **Open** 5pm-2am Mon-Sun; 5pm-4am Thur-Sat. **Bar. Map** p103 D4 ③
To get to the 30ft mahogany bar, built in 1927, follow the arched hall-way, warmed by the soft glow of candles. Once inside, you'll find an art deco space with red leather booths, round wooden tables, flying-saucer-shaped lamps and an imaginative cocktail menu.

L'Express
249 Park Avenue South, at 20th Street (1-212 254 5858). Subway: 6 to 23rd Street. **Open** 24hrs daily. **$. French**. **Map** p103 D4 ③

It's 3am and, if you want to dodge that hangover, you'd better eat something. So why not consider this bustling bistro, which stays open 24 hours a day, seven days a week? The place is as lively in the wee hours as at 8pm and bistro standards like steak au poivre, seared tuna steak, along with monkfish and chorizo brochettes, are satisfying at any hour.

119

119 E 15th Street, between Union Square East & Irving Place (1-212 777 6158). Subway: L, N, Q, R, W, 4, 5, 6 to 14th Street-Union Square. **Open** 4pm-4am daily. **Bar**. No credit cards. **Map** p103 D5 ㉟

This rock 'n' roll bar, one of the few above 14th Street, has a lively after-show scene: bartenders have spotted Trent Reznor and some Strokes after their Irving Plaza performances. DJs, serious pool, and a juke that plays Jane's Addiction and early Nirvana – what else do you need?

Speak

28 E 23rd Street, between Madison Avenue & Park Avenue South (1-212 637 0100). Subway: 6 to 23rd Street. **Open** 4pm-4am Tue, Wed; 3pm-4am Thur, Fri; 6pm-2am Sat. **Bar**. **Map** p103 D4 ㊱

This lounge takes its cues from the heyday of Hollywood glamour: vintage wallpaper, oversized oval mirrors, French sconces, curved crimson banquettes and crystal chandeliers. Drink enough Blood Martinis (fresh-squeezed beet and orange juices) and Between the Sheets (passion fruit and lime mixed with rum and cognac), and you'll have a swingin' time indeed.

Tavalon Tea Bar

NEW *22 E 14th Street, between Fifth Avenue & University Place (1-212 807 7027). Subway: L, N, Q, R, W, 4, 5, 6 to 14th Street-Union Square.* **Open** 8am-10pm Mon-Fri; 8am-11pm Sat, Sun. **$**. **Café**. **Map** p103 D5 ㊲

With DJs and an Indian drummer, this Union Square tea salon aims to appeal to younger tea drinkers. You can sample house-blended loose leaf varieties or make it a meal by adding pastries, salads or sandwiches.

Underground

NEW *613 Second Avenue, between 33rd & 34th Streets (1-212 683 3000). Subway: 6 to 33rd Street.* **Open** 4pm-4am daily. **Bar**. **Map** p103 E2 ㊳

A third of the sprawling venue feels like a neighbourhood pub (lined with exposed brick), another section is a swanky, libraryesque lounge dotted with leather couches and low wooden tables, and the backyard functions as a sports bar.

Shopping

ABC Carpet & Home

888 Broadway, at 19th Street (1-212 473 3000/www.abchome.com). Subway: L, N, Q, R, W, 4, 5, 6 to 14th Street-Union Square. **Open** 10am-8pm Mon-Thur; 10am-7pm Fri, Sat; noon-6pm Sun. **Map** p103 D4 ㊴

At this shopping landmark, the selection of accessories, linens, rugs, and reproduction and antique furniture (Western and Asian) is unbelievable; so are the mostly steep prices. For bargains, head to ABC's warehouse outlet in the Bronx.

Barnes & Noble Union Square

33 E. 17th Street, between Park Avenue S and Broadway (1-212 253 0810/ www.barnesandnoble.com). Subway: L, N, Q, R, W, 4, 5, 6 to 14th Street-Union Square. **Open** 10am-10om daily. **Map** p103 D4 ㊵

Miles and miles of books await at this emporium of all things literary. Check out the awesome views of Union Square while you're browsing.

Union Square Greenmarket

From 16th to 17th Streets, between Union Square East & Union Square West (1-212 788 7476). Subway: L, N, Q, R, W, 4, 5, 6 to 14th Street-Union Square. **Open** 8am-6pm Mon, Wed, Fri, Sat. **Map** p103 D4 ㊶

TKTS p116

The unpretentious crowd and roadhouse atmosphere – not to mention the lack of a cover charge – make the Rodeo the city's best roots club, with a steady stream of rockabilly, country and related sounds. Rockabilly filly Rosie Flores is a regular, and bluegrass scion Chris Scruggs recently visited from Nashville.

Herald Square & Garment District

The beating heart of America's multibillion-dollar clothing industry is New York's **Garment District** (roughly from 34th to 40th Streets, between Broadway and Eighth Avenue), where platoons of designers – and thousands of workers – create the clothes we'll be wearing next season.

Beginning on 34th Street at Broadway and stretching all the way to Seventh Avenue, **Macy's** is still the biggest – and busiest – department store in the world. Across the street at the junction of Broadway and Sixth Avenue is **Herald Square**, named after a long-gone newspaper and surrounded by a retail wonderland. To the east, the many restaurants and shops of **Koreatown** line 32nd Street between Broadway and Madison Avenue.

Shop elbow-to-elbow with top chefs for all manner of regionally grown culinary pleasures at this farmer's market.

Nightlife

Paddy Reilly's Music Bar

519 Second Avenue, at 29th Street (1-212 686 1210). Subway: 6 to 28th Street. **Open** *11am-4am Mon-Sat; 11am-midnight Sun.* **Shows** *9.30pm Mon-Fri; 10pm, 11pm Fri, Sat; 4pm Sun.* **Map** *p103 E3* ㊷

Patrons flock to this Gramercy institution for the silky Guinness (the house's only draft) but they stay for the lively Irish folk and rock acts that bring the room to life. Popular pub-rockers the Prodigals are regulars on Fridays, while the rest of the weekend features Irish-rock and traditional jam sessions.

Rodeo Bar & Grill

375 Third Avenue, at 27th Street (1-212 683 6500). Subway: 6 to 28th Street. **Open** *4pm-4am daily.* **Map** *p103 E3* ㊸

Eating & drinking

Maru

11 W 32nd Street, between Broadway & Fifth Avenue (1-212 273 3413). Subway: A, C, E to 34th Street-Penn Station. **Open** *6pm-2am Mon-Wed, Sun; 6pm-3am Thur; 6pm-4am Fri, Sat.* **Bar.** **Map** *p103 D3* ㊹

This chic lounge in Koreatown is almost impossible to find. There's a discreet sign outside; you enter via a freight elevator that leads to the bar's third-floor location. When the doors swing open, you're greeted with a spectacular bi-level space, where white walls and soft lighting complement soaring ceilings and modern, wrap-around banquettes. Bartenders serve upscale drinks like lychee martinis and vodka mojitos.

Stitch

247 W 37th Street, between Seventh & Eighth Avenues (1-212 852 4826). Subway: A, C, E to 34th Street-Penn Station. **Open** 11am-1am Mon-Fri; 2pm-4am Sat. **Bar. Map** p102 C2/p104 C5 ⑮

The owner realised that the Garment District lacked a good postwork drink spot, so he converted a former apparel showroom into a spacious bar and lounge. The fashion theme is far from subliminal: antique sewing machines sit above the bar, and on the cocktail menu you'll find evocatively named drinks such as the Silk Scarf, Cashmere and, our favourite, the Stiletto.

Shopping

Macy's

151 W 34th Street, between Broadway & Seventh Avenue (1-212 695 4400/www.macys.com). Subway: B, D, F, N, Q, R, V, W to 34th Street-Herald Square; 1, 2, 3 to 34th Street-Penn Station. **Open** 10am-9pm Mon-Sat; 11am-8pm Sun. **Map** p102 C2/p104 C5 ⑯

Behold the real miracle on 34th Street. Macy's has everything: designer labels and lower-priced knockoffs, a pet-supply shop, a restaurant in the Cellar (the housewares section) and even a Metropolitan Museum of Art gift shop.

Arts & leisure

Madison Square Garden

Seventh Avenue, between 31st & 33rd Streets (1-212 465 6741/www.thegarden.com). Subway: A, C, E, 1, 2, 3 to 34th Street-Penn Station. **Map** p102 C3 ⑰

Madison Square Garden, the huge sports and concert complex, occupies the site of the old Pennsylvania Station, a McKim, Mead & White architectural masterpiece that was razed in the 1960s – an act so soulless, it spurred the creation of the Landmarks Preservation Commission. The railroad terminal, now known as Penn Station, lies beneath the Garden and serves approximately 600,000 people every day. Fortunately, the aesthetic tide has turned. The city has approved a $788 million restoration and development project to move Penn Station across the street, into the General Post Office.

Broadway & Times Square

Times Square is really just the elongated intersection of Broadway and Seventh Avenue, but it's also the heart of the **Theater District**. More than 40 stages showcasing extravagant dramatic productions are situated on the streets that cross Broadway. The streets west of Eighth Avenue are filled with eateries catering to theatregoers, especially along **Restaurant Row** (46th Street, between Eighth & Ninth Avenues). This stretch is also popular after the theatres let out, when the street's bars host stand-up comedy and campy drag cabaret.

Sights & museums

ABC Television Studios

7 Times Square (1500 Broadway), at 44th Street. Subway: A, C, E to 42nd Street-Port Authority; N, Q, R, W, 42nd Street S; 1, 2, 3, 7 to 42nd Street-Times Square. **Map** p102 C1/p104 C4 ⑱

The television network's studios draw dozens of early morning risers hoping to catch a glimpse of the *Good Morning America* crew.

Madame Tussaud's New York

234 W 42nd Street, between Seventh & Eighth Avenues (1-800 246 8872/www.nycwax.com). Subway: A, C, E to

42nd Street-Port Authority; N, Q, R, W, 42nd Street S, 1, 2, 3, 7 to 42nd Street-Times Square. **Open** 10am-8pm daily. **Map** p102 C1/p104 C4 ㊾

If you're a fan of frozen, life-sized celebs, every few months they roll out a new posse of waxed victims.

Times Square Visitors' Center

1560 Broadway, between 46th & 47th Streets, entrance on Seventh Avenue (1-212 869 1890/www.timessquarebid.org). Subway: N, R, W to 49th Street; 1 to 50th Street. **Open** 8am-8pm daily. **Map** p102 C1/p104 C4 ㊿

TKTS

Duffy Square, 47th Street, at Broadway (1-212 221 0013/www.tdf.org). Subway: N, Q, R, W, 42nd Street S, 1, 2, 3, 7 to 42nd Street-Times Square. **Open** 3-8pm Mon-Sat; 11am-7pm Sun. Matinée tickets 10am-2pm Wed, Sat; 11am-2pm Sun. No credit cards. **Map** p102 C1/p104 C4 (51)

TKTS has become a New York tradition. Broadway and Off Broadway tickets are sold at discounts of 25%, 35% and 50% for same-day performances; tickets to other highbrow events are also offered. The queue can be long, but tends to move quickly, and it's often worth the wait.

Eating & drinking

Blue Fin

W Times Square Hotel, 1567 Broadway, at 47th Street (1-212 918 1400). Subway: N, R, W to 49th Street. **Open** 7-11am, 11.30am-4pm, 5pm-midnight Sun, Mon; 7-11am, 11.30am-4pm, 5pm-12.30am Tue-Thur; 7-11am, 11.30am-4pm, 5pm-1am Fri, Sat. **$$$**. **Seafood**. **Map** p102 C1/p104 C4 (52)

This noisy, singles-friendly, packed-to-the-gills bar, just steps away from the TKTS booth (see above), has probably been the scene of more than a few hookups. Chef Paul Sale cranks out crowd-pleasers such as sesame-crusted bigeye tuna with ginger-soy vinaigrette and pan-seared halibut with green and white asparagus in a vanilla-flavoured brown butter.

The Carnegie Club

156 W 56th Street, between Sixth & Seventh Avenues (1-212 957 9676). Subway: F, N, Q, R, W to 57th Street. **Open** 4.30pm-2am Mon-Sat; 4.30pm-1am Sun. Fri two-drink minimum; Sat $30 plus two-drink minimum. **Bar**. **Map** p104 C3 (53)

The low-lit Carnegie Club is classy *and* quiet. A bartender in pinstripes expertly mixes classic cocktails, such as the Carnegie Cocktail (dark rum, Grand Marnier, passionfruit juice and champagne). On Saturdays, a singer plus 11-piece orchestra does Sinatra covers.

Dave & Busters

NEW *3rd Floor, 234 W 42nd Street, between Seventh & Eighth Avenues (1-646 495 2015). Subway N, Q, R, S, W, 1, 2, 3 to 42nd Street-Times Square.* **Open** 11am-12am Mon-Thur, Sun; 11am-2am Fri, Sat. **$**. **American**. **Map** p102 C1/p104 C4 (54)

The latest addition to Times Square's restaurant collection of giant theme-park eateries is this behemoth food-and-entertainment venue, which offers

NEW YORK BY AREA

virtual-reality simulators, video games galore and Skee-Ball – plus Philly cheese steaks, salads and burgers.

Heartland Brewery & Chop House

127 W 43rd Street, between Sixth Avenue & Broadway (1-646 366 0235). Subway: 42nd Street S, 1, 2, 3, 7 to 42nd Street-Times Square. **Open** 11.30am-midnight Mon-Sat; noon-9pm Sun. **Bar**. Map p102 C1/p104 C4 **55**
All of the microbrews served here come from a Fort Greene brewery, so there's a little touch of Brooklyn at the four Manhattan locations. Each franchise offers the Classic Voyage, a quintet of five-ounce brews including the award-winning Farmer Jon's Oatmeal Stout, a dark-roasted malt.

Rue 57

60 W 57th Street, at Sixth Avenue (1-212 307 5656). Subway: F to 57th Street. **Open** 7.30am-midnight Mon; 7.30pm-1am Tue-Fri; 9pm-1am Sat; 9pm-midnight Sun. **$$**. **French**. Map p105 D3 **56**

Serving steak tartare alongside tuna *tataki* sounds like the making of a culinary identity crisis. But Rue 57's spacious flower-decked dining room has a pleasing Parisian look, and the red leather banquettes are often full – for the most part with Midtown expensers and tourists.

Shopping

Toys 'R' Us Times Square

1514 Broadway, between 44th & 45th Streets (1-800 869 7787). Subway: N, Q, R, W, 42nd Street S, 1, 2, 3, 7 to 42nd Street-Times Square. **Open** 9am-10pm Mon-Sat; 11am-6pm Sun. **Map** p102 C1/p104 C4 **57**
The chain's flagship location is the world's largest toy store – big enough to accommodate a 60ft-high Ferris wheel inside and an animatronic tyrannosaur to greet you at the door. Brands rule here: a two-storey Barbie doll's house and a café with its very own sweetshop designed to look like the board game.

Dave & Busters

Nightlife

BB King Blues Club & Grill

237 W 42nd Street, between Seventh & Eighth Avenues (1-212 997 4144/ www.bbkingblues.com). Subway: A, C, E to 42nd Street-Port Authority; N, Q, R, W, 42nd Street S, 1, 2, 3, 7 to 42nd Street-Times Square. **Open** 11am-midnight daily. **Map** p102 C1/ p104 C4 ❸

Plays host to perhaps the widest variety of music in town: cover bands and soul tributes fill the gaps between big-names like Aretha Franklin, the Neville Brothers, Rodney Crowell and Judy Collins. Lately, the club has also proved a viable space for extreme metal bands (Napalm Death, Obituary, Hate Eternal) and neosoul and hip-hop acts (Angie Stone, Method Man, Ghostface, and assorted other Wu-Tangers). The best seats are at the dinner tables up front, but menu prices are steep. The Harlem Gospel Choir buffet brunch, on Sundays, raises the roof.

Birdland

315 W 44th Street, between Eighth & Ninth Avenues (1-212 581 3080/www. birdlandjazz.com). Subway: A, C, E to 42nd Street-Port Authority. **Open** 5pm-1am daily. **Map** p102 B1/p104 C4 ❹

The name means jazz but, perhaps in deference to its Theater District digs, Birdland is also a prime destination for cabaret. The jazz names are unimpeachable (Kurt Elling, Jim Hall, Paquito D'Rivera), the cabaret stars glowing (Christine Andreas, Christine Ebersole). Residencies are among the better ones in town: the Chico O'Farrill Afro-Cuban Jazz Orchestra on Sundays and David Ostwald's Louis Armstrong Centennial Band on Tuesdays; on Monday there's cabaret's waggish Jim Caruso and his Cast Party).

Danny's Skylight Room

Grand Sea Palace, 346 W 46th Street, between Eighth & Ninth Avenues (1-212 265 8130/1-212 265 8133/ www.dannysgsp.com). Subway: A, C, E to 42nd Street-Port Authority. **Open** 4pm-11pm Mon-Fri; 11.30am-midnight Sat, Sun; Piano bar 8-11pm daily. **Map** p102 B1/p104 C4 ❻

A pastel-hued nook in the Grand Sea Palace on Restaurant Row, Danny's features up-and-comers and more mature cabaret and jazz stand-bys such as the owlish John Wallowitch and the ageless Blossom Dearie.

Don't Tell Mama

343 W 46th Street, between Eighth & Ninth Avenues (1-212 757 0788/ www.donttellmama.com). Subway: A, C, E to 42nd Street-Port Authority. **Open** 9pm-4am daily. **Map** p102 B1/p104 C4 ❻

Showbiz pros and piano-bar buffs love this dank but homey Theater District stalwart, where acts range from the strictly amateur to potential stars of tomorrow. The nightly line-up may include pop, jazz or Broadway singers, as well as female impersonators, magicians, comedians or musical revues.

Nokia Theatre Times Square

NEW *1515 Broadway, at 44th Street (1-212 930 1950) Subway: N, Q, R, W to 42nd Street; S, 1, 2, 3, 7, to 42nd Street-Times Square.* **Open** call for show times. **Map** p102 C1/p104 C4 ❻

The new Nokia Theatre Times Square may well be the club-going experience NYC music fans have always deserved. And that assessment has relatively little to do with the crowd-pleasing bookings or extensive wiring job in the underground space. The 85ft marquee, plentiful plasma-TV screens, and phone-charging kiosks are all impressive features, for sure. But it's the music room itself that's most striking.

Swing 46

349 W 46th Street, between Eighth & Ninth Avenues (1-212 262 9554/ www.swing46.com). Subway: A, C, E to 42nd Street-Port Authority. **Open** 5pm-midnight Mon-Thur; 5pm-1am Fri, Sat; 5pm-11pm Sun. **Map** p102 B1/ p104 C4 ❻

Swing isn't just a trend at this supper club – whether peppy or sappy, these

$200 – for a T-shirt?

Vintage band tees are the latest must-have.

Cherry Vintage Rock Fashion

While you may be kicking yourself because your Def Leppard Hysteria tour T-shirt went the way of the Salvation Army years ago, who could have guessed it would become so valuable? You can still score retro concert tees, but be prepared to pay a lot more than you did at the merch table back in '87. In Midtown, look no further than **Cherry Vintage Rock Fashion** in the Virgin Megastore, which boasts a killer selection of rock garb ($45-$200). Because of its location, even around midnight the shop is often buzzing with people spilling in from Times Square. But are they really shelling out the big bucks for old T-shirts? 'You'd be surprised what people are willing to pay for a vintage T-shirt if they like it enough,' says shop clerk JD Stuntebeck. Many of the pricier shirts are pretty rare and in great condition. The must-have band? 'Right now it's definitely Stryper, but Pat Benatar is pretty popular too,' says Stuntebeck. And, it's not just people in their late 30s or

early 40s looking for a blast back to their freewheeling youth. 'We get a lot of twentysomethings in here who think these '80s shirts are just plain cool.'

If you can't find what you want here, check out downtown's **Screaming Mimi**'s; its hardy stash includes cheeseball favourites such as New Kids on the Block and Michael Jackson, ranging in price from around $45 to upwards of $100. At **What Comes Around Goes Around** you'll find the Holy Grails of concert tees, featuring Bruce Springsteen, Prince, Ted Nugent and the Police, but they'll cost you around $200 each.

■ **Cherry Vintage Rock Fashion** Virgin Megastore, 1540 Broadway, between 45th & 46th Streets, level B1 (1-646 624 5013).

■ **Screaming Mimi's** 382 Lafayette Street between Great Jones & E 4th Streets (1-212 677 6464).

■ **What Comes Around Goes Around** 351 West Broadway, between Broome & Grand Streets (1-212 343 9303).

NEW YORK BY AREA

American Folk Art Museum p122

cats mean it. Bands (with names like the Flying Neutrinos and the Flipped Fedoras) that jump, jive and wail await you, so be sure to wear your dancin' shoes. Dance lessons are available too.

Arts & leisure

Avenue Q

Golden Theater, 252 W 45th Street, between Broadway & Eighth Avenue (1-212 239 6200/www.avenueq.com). Subway: A, C, E to 42nd Street-Port Authority. **Shows** *8pm Tue-Fri; 2pm, 8pm Sat; 2pm, 7pm Sun. Length 2hrs 15 mins. One intermission.* **Map** *p102 C1/p104 C4* **64**

Mixing puppets and live actors with irreverent jokes and snappy songs, this clever, good-hearted musical comedy was a surprise hit. It garnered several 2004 Tonys, including Best Musical.

Carnegie Hall

154 W 57th Street, at Seventh Avenue (1-212 247 7800/www.carnegie hall.org). Subway: N, Q, R, W to 57th Street. **Map** *p104 C3* **65**

The stars – both soloists and orchestras – in the classical-music firmament continue to shine most brightly in the venerable Isaac Stern Auditorium, inside this renowned concert hall. Still, it's the spunky upstart Zankel Hall that has generated the most buzz; the below-street-level space offers an eclectic mix of classical, contemporary, jazz, pop and world music. Next door, Weill Recital Hall hosts intimate concerts and chamber-music programmes.

City Center

131 W 55th Street, between Sixth & Seventh Avenues (1-212 581 7907/www.nycitycenter.org). Subway: B, D, E to Seventh Avenue; F, N, Q, R, W to 57th Street. **Map** *p104 C3* **66**

Before the creation of Lincoln Center changed the city's cultural geography, this was the home of the American Ballet Theatre, the Joffrey Ballet and the New York City Ballet. The City Center's lavish decor is golden – as are the companies that pass through here.

Levitate Yoga

780 Eighth Avenue, between 47th & 48th Streets (1-212 974 2288/ www.levitateyoga.com). Subway: C, E to 50th Street. **Open** *Call or check website for schedule & prices.* **Map** *p102 C1/p104 C4* **67**

NEW YORK BY AREA

This modern-looking studio caters to beginners, tourists and casts and crews performing at nearby theatres. In the warm months, special classes are held on the 2,000sq ft rooftop terrace.

Manhattan Theatre Club

City Center, 131 W 55th Street, between Sixth & Seventh Avenues (1-212 581 1212/Telecharge 1-212 239 6200/www.mtc-nyc.org). Subway: B, D, E to Seventh Avenue. **Map** p104 C3 ⑱
Manhattan Theatre Club has a history of sending young playwrights to Broadway, as seen with such successes as David Auburn's *Proof* and John Patrick Shanley's *Doubt*. The club's two theatres are in the basement of City Center. The 275-seat Stage I Theater features four plays a year; the Stage II Theater offers works-in-progress, workshops and staged readings, as well as full-length productions.

Mary Poppins

NEW *New Amsterdam Theatre, 214 West 42nd Street, between Seventh & Eight Avenues (1-212 307 4747). Subway: A, C, E to 42nd Street-Port Authority; N, Q, R, W, 42nd Street S, 1, 2, 3, 7 to 42nd Street-Times Square.* **Map** p102 C1/p104 C4 ⑲
The world's most lovable nanny lands on Broadway in November 2006. Call theatre for details.

Monty Python's Spamalot

Shubert Theatre, 225 W 44th Street, between Broadway & Eighth Avenue (1-212 239 6200). Subway: A, C, E to 42nd Street-Port Authority; N, Q, R, W, 42nd Street S, 1, 2, 3, 7 to 42nd Street-Times Square. **Shows** 7pm Tue; 2pm, 8pm Wed, Sat; 8pm Thur, Fri; 3pm Sun. Length 2hrs 15mins. One intermission. **Map** p102 C1/p104 C4 ⑳
Monty Python founder Eric Idle is behind this 'lovingly ripped-off' musical adaptation of *Monty Python and the Holy Grail*. Veteran director Mike Nichols stages the mélange of greatest-hits laughs and Broadway-spoofing novelty. Winner of the 2005 Tony Award for Best Musical.

The Producers

St James Theatre, 246 W 44th Street, between Seventh & Eighth Avenues (1-212 239 6200/www.producerson broadway.com). Subway: N, Q, R, W, 42nd Street S, 1, 2, 3, 7 to 42nd Street-Times Square. **Shows** 7pm Tue; 2, 8pm Wed; 8pm Thur, Fri; 2, 8pm Sat; 3pm Sun. Length 2hrs 45 mins. One intermission. **Map** p102 C1/p104 C4 ㉑
Mel Brooks' ode to tastelessness mixes Broadway razzamatazz with Borscht Belt humour. Although the original stars – Nathan Lane and Matthew Broderick – have gone, the show still offers plenty of laughs.

Wicked

Gershwin Theatre, 222 W 51st Street, between Broadway & Eighth Avenue (1-212 307 4100). Subway: C, E, 1 to 50th Street. **Shows** 7pm Tue; 2, 8pm Wed; 8pm Thur, Fri; 2, 8pm Sat; 3pm Sun. Length 2hrs 45 mins. One intermission. **Map** p104 C3 ㉒
Based on novelist Gregory Maguire's 1995 riff on *The Wizard of Oz* mythology, *Wicked* provides a witty prequel to the classic children's book and movie. At press time, Joe Mantello's sumptuous production starred Megan

Chrysler Building p133

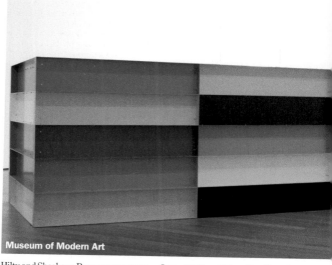

Museum of Modern Art

Hilty and Shoshana Bean as young versions of Glinda the Good Witch and the Wicked Witch of the West.

Fifth Avenue

Synonymous with the chic and moneyed, Fifth Avenue caters to the elite; it's also the main route for the city's many ethnic (and inclusive) parades: National Puerto Rican Day, St Patrick's Day, Gay and Lesbian Pride, and many more. The well heeled still shop here, but mall stores are nudging in. Whatever your pleasure, the gaggle of landmarks and first-rate museums never disappoint.

Sights & museums

American Folk Art Museum

45 W 53rd Street, between Fifth & Sixth Avenues (1-212 265 1040/ www.folkartmuseum.org). Subway: E, V to Fifth Avenue-53rd Street.
Open 10.30am-5.30pm Tue-Thur, Sat, Sun; 10.30am-7.30pm Fri. **Admission** $9; free-$7 reductions. Free to all 5.30-7.30pm Fri. **Map** p105 D3 ⑳
Celebrating traditional craft-based work is the American Folk Art Museum (formerly the Museum of American Folk Art). Designed by architects Billie Tsien and Tod Williams, the architecturally stunning eight-floor building is four times larger than the original Lincoln Center location (which is now a branch of the museum) and includes a café.

Empire State Building

350 Fifth Avenue, between 33rd & 34th Streets (1-212 736 3100/ www.esbnyc.com). Subway: B, D, F, N, Q, R, V, W to 34th Street-Herald Square. **Open** 9.30am-midnight daily (closed during extreme weather). Last elevator up 11.15pm. **Admission** $12; reductions free-$11. No credit cards. **Map** p103 D2 ⑳
Located smack-dab in the centre of Midtown, the magnificent building is visible from most parts of the city and

Previously known as the American Crafts Museum, this is the country's leading museum for contemporary crafts in clay, cloth, glass, metal and wood. It changed its name to emphasise the correspondences among art, design and craft. The museum plans to move to a new home in the former Huntington Hartford building at Columbus Circle in late 2007, but for now, visitors can come here to peruse the jewellery, ceramics and other objects displayed on four floors.

Museum of Modern Art (MoMA)

11 W 53rd Street, between Fifth & Sixth Avenues (1-212 708 9400/www. moma.org). Subway: E, V to Fifth Avenue-53rd Street. **Open** 10.30am-5.30pm Mon, Wed, Thur, Sat, Sun; 10.30am-8pm Fri. **Admission** (includes film programmes) $20; free-$16 reductions. Free to all 4-8pm Fri. **Map** p105 D3 ⑦₆

MoMA contains the world's finest and most comprehensive holdings of 20th-century art and, thanks to a sweeping redesign by architect Yoshio Taniguchi completed in 2004, it is now able to show off much more of its immense permanent collection in serene, high-ceilinged galleries that almost outshine the art on display. Inside, the soaring five-storey atrium is the central artery from which six curatorial departments – Architecture and Design, Drawings, Painting and Sculpture, Photography, Prints and Illustrated Books, and Film and Media – display works that include the best of Matisse, Picasso, van Gogh, Giacometti, Pollock, Rothko and Warhol, among many others. Outside, Philip Johnson's sculpture garden has been restored to its original, larger plan from 1953, and its powerful minimalist sculptures and sheer matt-black-granite-and-glass wall are overlooked by the sleek high-end restaurant and bar the Modern, run by Midas-touch restaurateur Danny Meyer. The museum's eclectic exhibition of design objects is a must-see, with examples of art nouveau, the

beyond. At night, it's illuminated in showy colours to celebrate a holiday or special event (the lights turn off at the stroke of midnight). To say they don't build 'em like they used to is an understatement. The Empire State Building was financed as a speculative venture by General Motors executive John J Raskob; builders broke the ground in 1930. It sprang up in 14 months with amazing speed, completed more than a month ahead of schedule and $5 million under budget. The 1,250ft tower snatched the title of world's tallest building from under the nose of the months-old, 1,046ft Chrysler Building, conveniently showing up Raskob's Detroit rival Walter P Chrysler.

Museum of Arts & Design

40 W 53rd Street, between Fifth & Sixth Avenues (1-212 956 3535/ www.americancraftmuseum.org). Subway: E, V to Fifth Avenue-53rd Street. **Open** 10am-6pm Mon-Wed, Fri-Sun; 10am-8pm Thur. **Admission** $9; free-$6 reductions; voluntary donation 6-8pm Thur. **Map** p105 D3 ⑦₅

NEW YORK BY AREA

Bauhaus and the Vienna Secession lining up alongside a vintage 1946 Ferrari and architectural drawings and models from the likes of Rem Koolhaas and Mies van der Rohe.

Event highlights 'Eye on Europe: Prints, Books, and Multiples, 1960 to Now' 15 Oct 2006-1 Jan 2007; 'Édouard Manet and *The Execution of Maximilian*' 5 Nov 2006-29 Jan 2007; 'Comic Abstraction: Image Breaking, Image Making' 4 March-11 June 2007; 'Richard Serra: 40 Years' summer 2007.

Museum of Television & Radio

25 W 52nd Street, between Fifth & Sixth Avenues (1-212 621 6800/ www.mtr.org). Subway: B, D, F, V to 47-50th Streets-Rockefeller Center; E, V to Fifth Avenue-53rd Street.
Open noon-6pm Tue-Sun; noon-8pm Thur. **Admission** $10; $5-$8 reductions. No credit cards.
Map p105 D3 ⑰

This nirvana for boob-tube addicts and pop-culture junkies contains an archive of more than 100,000 radio and TV programmes. Head to the fourth-floor library to search the computerised system for your favourite *Star Trek* or *I Love Lucy* episodes, then walk down one flight to take a seat at your assigned console. (The radio listening room operates the same way.) Screenings of modern cartoons, public seminars and special presentations are offered.

NBC

30 Rockefeller Plaza, 49th Street, between Fifth & Sixth Avenues (1-212 664 3700/www.nbc.com). Subway: B, D, F, V to 47-50th Streets-Rockefeller Center. **Admission** $17.95; $15.50 reductions; no under-6s.
Map p105 D4 ⑱
Peer through the *Today* show's studio window with a horde of fellow onlookers, or pay admission (at the NBC

Bryant Park

the Bill Blass Public Catalog Room, which offers free internet access. Lectures, author readings and special exhibitions are definitely worth checking out. Situated behind the library is Bryant Park, a well-cultivated green space that hosts a dizzying schedule of free entertainment during the summer, when it also attracts outdoor internet users with its free wireless service. In the winter it becomes an ice-skating rink; see box p131.

Radio City Music Hall

1260 Sixth Avenue, at 50th Street (1-212 247 4777/www.radiocity.com). Subway: B, D, F, V to 47-50th Streets-Rockefeller Center. **Map** p105 D3 ⑥⓪
Few rooms scream 'New York City!' more than this gilded hall, which has drawn Wilco, Alanis Morissette and Carole King as headliners. The greatest challenge for any performer is not to get upstaged by the awe-inspiring art deco surroundings. Radio City was the world's largest cinema when it was built in 1932 (the backstage tour is one of the best in town).

Rockefeller Center

From 48th to 51st Streets, between Fifth & Sixth Avenues (1-212 632 3975/tickets 1-212 664 7174/www. rockefellercenter.com). Subway: B, D, F, V to 47-50th Streets-Rockefeller Center. **Admission** $18; $16 seniors and 6-16s; no under-6s. **Map** p105 D4 ③①
Veer off Fifth Avenue into the 19 buildings of Rockefeller Center and you'll see why this interlacing of public and private space is so lavishly praised. The centre is filled with murals, sculptures, mosaics and other artwork. On weekday mornings, a crowd of (mainly) tourists gathers at NBC television network's glass-walled, ground-level studio (where the *Today* show is shot), at the south-west corner of Rockefeller Plaza and 49th Street. Exploring the centre is free. For guided tours in and around the historic buildings, however, advance tickets are necessary and available by phone, online or at the NBC Experience Store. The recently opened Top of

Experience Store, www.shopnbc.com) for a guided tour of the studios. The tours are led by pages, many of whom – Ted Koppel, Kate Jackson, Michael Eisner, Marcy Carsey, and others – have gone on to bigger and better things in showbiz.

New York Public Library

455 Fifth Avenue, at 42nd Street (1-212 930 0830/www.nypl.org). Subway: B, D, F, V to 42nd Street-Bryant Park; 7 to Fifth Avenue. **Open** 11am-7.30pm Tue, Wed; 10am-6pm Thur-Sat. **Admission** free. **Map** p103 D1/p105 D5 ⑦⑨
When people mention 'the New York Public Library,' most are referring to this imposing beaux arts building. Two massive stone lions, dubbed Patience and Fortitude by former mayor Fiorello La Guardia, flank the main portal. Free guided tours (at 11am and 2pm) stop at the beautifully renovated Rose Main Reading Room and

the Rock (1-212 698 2000/www.topof therocknyc.com), an observation deck at 30 Rockefeller Center, offers jaw-dropping views.

St Patrick's Cathedral

Fifth Avenue, between 50th & 51st Streets (1-212 753 2261). Subway: B, D, F to 47-50th Streets-Rockefeller Center; E, V to Fifth Avenue-53rd Street. **Open** 6.30am-8.45pm daily. **Admission** free. **Map** p105 D3 ❷
St Patrick's adds gothic grace to Fifth Avenue. The diocese of New York bought the land for an orphanage in 1810, but then in 1858 it switched gears and began construction on what would become the country's largest Catholic church. Today, the white marble spires are dwarfed by Rockefeller Center, but inside the vaulted ceilings, stained-glass windows from Charres and altars by Tiffany & Co are still stunning.

Eating & drinking

Le Bernardin

155 W 51st Street, between Sixth and Seventh Avenues (1-212 489 1515). Subway: B, D, F, V to 47-50th Streets-Rockefeller Center; N, R, W to 49th Street. **Open** noon-2.30pm, 5.30-10.30pm Mon-Thur; noon-2.30pm, 5.30-11pm Fri; 5.30-11pm Sat. **$$$$**. **Seafood**. **Map** p104 C3 ❸
Eric Ripert's seafood shrine is, by nearly all measures, the most consistently acclaimed restaurant in New York. A true Frenchman, Ripert rarely lets a bite go sauceless, drizzling plates with rich truffle-butter vinaigrette, black-pepper-and-brandy-butter sauce or pungent sweet-garlic sauce with chorizo essence.

The Modern

NEW *9 W 53rd Street between Fifth and Sixth Avenues (1-212 333 1220) Subway: E, V to Fifth Avenue-53rd Street.* **Open** noon-2.15pm, 6-9.30pm Mon-Thur; noon-2.15pm, 5.30-10.30pm Fri; 5.30-10.30pm Sat. **$$$**. **American creative**. **Map** p105 D3 ❹
From the moment he was tapped to run the renovated MoMA's flagship

restaurant, chef Gabriel Kreuther set about creating modern art of his own – inspired dishes that would do justice to any setting, even a dining room over-looking the museum's famed sculpture garden filled with priceless works. Every element – slickly dressed servers, Christofle silverware, flower displays – shows attention to detail.

'21' Club

21 W 52nd Street, between Fifth and Sixth Avenues (1-212 582 7200). Subway: B, D, F, V to 47-50th Streets-Rockefeller Ctr; E, V to Fifth Avenue-53rd Street. **Open** noon-10pm Mon-Thur; noon-11pm Fri; 5.30-11pm Sat. **$$$$**. **American**. **Map** p105 D3 ❺
After 75 years this clubby sanctum for the rich and powerful remains true to its past while thriving in the present. In addition to ever-changing seasonal fare, the menu lists '21 Classics', such as steak Diane, flambéed tableside, which was on the restaurant's first menu. The famous burger mixes lean ground meats with duck fat – for $29.

Shopping

Bergdorf Goodman

754 Fifth Avenue, at 57th Street (1-212 753 7300/www.bergdorf goodman.com). Subway: E, V to Fifth Avenue-53rd Street; N, R, W to Fifth Avenue-59th Street. **Open** 10am-7pm Mon-Wed, Fri, Sat; 10am-8pm Thur; noon-6pm Sun. **Map** p105 D3 ❻
Barneys aims for a young, trendy crowd; Bergdorf's is dedicated to an elegant, understated clientele that has plenty of disposable income. Luxury clothes, accessories and even stationery are found here, along with an over-the-top Beauty Level. The famed men's store is across the street (745 Fifth Avenue).

Henri Bendel

712 Fifth Avenue, at 56th Street (1-212 247 1100/www.henribendel. com). Subway: E, V to Fifth Avenue-53rd Street; N, R, W to Fifth Avenue-59th Street. **Open** 10am-8pm Mon-Sat; noon-7pm Sun. **Map** p105 D3 ❼

St Patrick's Cathedral

Intrepid Sea-Air-Space Museum

Bendel's lavish quarters resemble an opulently appointed townhouse. Naturally there are elevators – no one expects you to walk; this is Fifth Avenue – but it's nicer to saunter up the elegant, winding staircase. Prices are comparable with those of other upscale stores, but the merchandise somehow seems more desirable here – we guess it must be those darling brown-striped shopping bags.

Jimmy Choo

645 Fifth Avenue, at 51st Street (1-212 593 0800/www.jimmychoo. com). Subway: E, V to Fifth Avenue-53rd Street. **Open** 10am-6pm Mon-Wed, Fri, Sat; 10am-7pm Thur; noon-5pm Sun. **Map** p105 D3 ⓰

The British luxury footwear label has conquered America with this six-year-old emporium, showcasing chic boots, sexy stilettos, curvaceous pumps and kittenish flats. Prices start at $450.

Louis Vuitton

1 E 57th Street, at Fifth Avenue (1-212 758 8877/www.vuitton.com). Subway: F to 57th Street; N, R, W to Fifth Avenue-59th Street. **Open** 10am-7pm Mon-Wed, Fri, Sat; 10am-8pm Thur; noon-6pm Sun. **Map** p105 D3 ⓰

The four-storey, glass-encased retail cathedral certainly gives cause for jubilation: crane your neck to view the three-floor-high LED wall screen and antique Vuitton trunks suspended from the ceiling. The much coveted bags and ready-to-wear collection are here as well.

Nat Sherman

500 Fifth Avenue, at 42nd Street (1-212 764 5000/www.natsherman. com). Subway: B, D, F, V to 42nd Street-Bryant Park; 7 to Fifth Avenue. **Open** 10am-8pm Mon-Fri; 10am-7pm Sat; 11am-5pm Sun. **Map** p103 D1/ p105 D4 ⓰

Just across the street from the New York Public Library, Nat Sherman offers its own brand of slow-burning cigarettes, as well as cigars and related accoutrements. Flick your Bic in the upstairs smoking room.

Otto Tootsi Plohound

137 Fifth Avenue, between 20th & 21st Streets (1-212 460 8650). Subway: N, R, W to 23rd Street. **Open** 11.30am-8pm Mon-Fri; 11am-8pm Sat; noon-7pm Sun. **Map** p103 D4 ⓰

One of the best places to head if you're looking for the latest shoe styles, Otto Tootsi Plohound has a wide selection

and began to create sensational art nouveau jewellery. Today the design stars are the no-less august Paloma Picasso and Elsa Peretti. Three floors are stacked with precious jewels, silver, watches, porcelain and the classic Tiffany engagement rings. FYI: breakfast is not served.

Midtown West

West of Times Square, in the vicinity of the Port Authority Bus Terminal (on Eighth Avenue) and the Lincoln Tunnel's traffic-knotted entrance, is an area historically known as **Hell's Kitchen**, where a gang- and crime-ridden Irish community scraped by during the 19th century. Italians, Greeks, Puerto Ricans, Dominicans and other ethnic groups followed. The neighbourhood maintained its tough reputation into the 1970s, when, in an effort to invite gentrification, local activists renamed it **Clinton**, after the one-time mayor (and governor) DeWitt Clinton.

Sights & museums

Circle Line Cruises
Pier 83, 42nd Street, at the Hudson River (1-212 563 3200/www.circle line.com). Subway: A, C, E to 42nd Street-Port Authority. **Tours** Call or visit website for schedule. **Tickets** $28; $15-£23 reductions. **Map** p102 A1/p104 A4 ❾❹
Circle Line's famous three-hour, guided circumnavigation of Manhattan is one of the best ways to take in the city's sights. Themed tours, such as a New Year's Eve cruise or fall foliage trip to the Hudson Valley, are also offered.

Intrepid Sea-Air-Space Museum
USS Intrepid, Pier 86, 46th Street, at the Hudson River (1-212 245 0072/ www.intrepidmuseum.org). Subway: A, C, E to 42nd Street-Port Authority, then M42 bus to Twelfth Avenue.

of trendy – and slightly overpriced – imports for both women and men.

Saks Fifth Avenue
611 Fifth Avenue, at 50th Street (1-212 753 4000). Subway: E, V to Fifth Avenue-53rd Street. **Open** 10am-7pm Mon-Wed, Fri, Sat; 10am-8pm Thur; noon-6pm Sun. **Map** p105 D3 ❸❷
The store features all the big names in women's fashion, from Armani to Yves St Laurent, plus an excellent menswear department and a children's section. There are also fine household linens, La Prairie skincare and attentive customer service. New management is exploring the possibility of a major overhaul this year; at press time, Frank Gehry's name had made the rumour mill as the architect.

Tiffany & Co
727 Fifth Avenue, at 57th Street (1-212 755 8000/www.tiffany.com). Subway: E, V to Fifth Avenue-53rd Street; F to 57th Street; N, R, W to Fifth Avenue-59th Street. **Open** 10am-7pm Mon-Fri; 10am-6pm Sat; noon-5pm Sun. **Map** p105 D3 ❸❸
The heyday of Tiffany's was at the turn of the 20th century, when Louis Comfort Tiffany, the son of founder Charles Lewis Tiffany, took the reins

NEW YORK BY AREA

Open *Apr-Sept* 10am-5pm Mon-Fri;
10am-6pm Sat, Sun. *Oct-Mar* 10am-5pm
Tue-Sun. Last admission 1hr before
closing. **Admission** $16.50; free-$12.50
reductions. **Map** p102 A1/p104 A4 **95**

Climb inside a model of a wooden
Revolutionary-era submarine, try out
a supersonic-flight simulator, and
explore dozens of military helicopters,
fighter planes and more aboard this
retired aircraft carrier – but only until
the end of October 2006, because after
that the august *Intrepid* is scheduled
for repairs and renovations, due to
reopen some time in 2008. It will be
towed to New Jersey amid much fanfare, hopefully on 11 November,
Veterans Day, tides allowing; keep an
eye on the website for confirmation.

Eating & drinking

El Centro

NEW *824 Ninth Avenue, at 54th Street*
(1-646 763 6585). Subway C, E to 50th
Street. **Open** 5-11pm Mon, Tue, Sun;
5pm-midnight Wed-Sat. **$. Mexican.**
Map p104 B3 **96**

To start the party right, indulge in
one of the fine frozen Margaritas,
available with guava and raspberry.
The menu's tried-and-true offerings –
tacos, burritos, enchiladas, fajitas and
so on – are all solid. We especially
liked a quesadilla made with fat
chunks of shrimp and melted Monterey
Jack cheese, and a tostada appetiser
with black beans, lettuce, tomato, sour
cream and thick, juicy slices of grilled
skirt steak.

Kemia Bar

630 Ninth Avenue, at 44th Street
(1-212 582-3200). Subway: A, C, E
to 42nd Street-Port Authority. **Open**
6pm-2am Tue-Sat. **Bar. Map** p102
B1/p104 B4 **97**

Descending into this lush Middle
Eastern oasis is like penetrating the
fourth wall of a brilliant stage set.
Gossamer fabric billows from the
ceiling, ottomans are clustered around
low tables, and dark-wood floors are
strewn with rose petals. The libations
are equally luscious.

Sortie

NEW *329 W 51st Street, between*
Eighth & Ninth Avenues (1-212 265
0650). Subway: C, E to 50th Street.
Open 5pm-4am Tue-Sat. **Bar. Map**
p104 C3 **98**

The owners of this sultry bordello-like
bar made sure their subterranean
space would never be boring. They
painted the walls a deep red and added
velvet banquettes and studded black-
leather café tables. They also hired
flamenco dancers and serious guest
DJs, and came up with a menu that
specialises in tapas, cocktails and 30
artisanal beers.

Vlada Lounge

NEW *331 W 51st Street, between Fifth*
& Sixth Avenues (1-212 974 8030/
www.vladabar.com). Subway C, E to
50th Street. **Open** 4pm-4am daily.
Bar. Map p104 C3 **99**

This super chic and sleek bar attracts
a mostly gay crowd looking to chill out
and indulge in one of the 15 special
infused vodkas.

Whym

889 Ninth Avenue, between 57th
& 58th Streets (1-212 315 0088).
Subway: A, B, C, D, 1 to 59th Street-
Columbus Circle. **Open** 11.30am-3pm,
5-11pm Mon-Thur, Sun; 11.30am-3pm,
5pm-midnight Fri, Sat. **$$. American.**
Map p104 B3 **100**

Crowds come to this sleek 80-seat
eaterie for its menu of traditional
American dishes punched up with
exotic spices and sauces. Among the
appetisers, a shrimp tamale balances
fat grilled shrimp dressed with roast-
ed-chilli pesto on top of soft, couscous-
like quinoa.

Xing

785 Ninth Avenue, between 52nd &
53rd Streets (1-646 289 3010).
Subway: C, E to 50th Street. **Open**
5-11pm Mon, Tue, Sun; 5pm-midnight
Wed, Thur; 5pm-1am Fri, Sat. **$$.**
Chinese. Map p104 B3 **101**

Of all the reinterpreted ethnic cuisines
in New York, highfalutin Chinese has
proved to be one of the most difficult

Ice, ice baby!

Pond at Bryant Park

With the opening of a new skating rink in Midtown, getting time on the ice is as easy as falling down. Try your double axel at one of these picturesque outdoor spots.

The new **Pond at Bryant Park**, on the lawn behind the New York Public Library, is a boon for winter sports. From mid-November to mid-January, the 17,000-square-foot rink will offer free ice-skating sessions. Expect the same long queues you'd find at Rockefeller Center and Wollman Rink, but admission is free and skate rental reasonable. Hot chocolate and snacks await at the Ice Café.

The queues are simply hellish at the **Rink at Rockefeller Center** and prices are sky-high, but few things say 'winter in New York' better than the Rock's art deco pit. Twirling around under the giant Prometheus and sipping hot cocoa afterwards can't be topped.

In 1986 Donald Trump helped put up the money needed to keep the **Wollman Rink**, an insanely romantic rink hosting skaters young and old under the bare branches of Central Park. Expect to queue for up to an hour at the height of the holiday season and on weekends. Your best bet is to go weeknights when it's open until 10pm. If you don't want to battle the crowds, head north to Central Park's lower-profile **Lasker Rink**.

■ Lasker Rink, Central Park, between 106th & 108th Streets (1-917 492 3856/www.wollman skatingrink.com). Mid Oct-March.
■ Pond at Bryant Park, Bryant Park, Sixth Avenue, between 41st & 42nd Streets (1-212 768 4242/www.bryantpark.org). Nov-mid Jan.
■ Rink at Rockefeller Center, 50th Street, between Fifth & Sixth Avenues (1-212 332 7654). Nov-March.
■ Wollman Rink, Central Park, at 62nd Street (1-212 439 6900, www.wollmanskatingrink.com). Mid Oct-March.

Copacabana

to master. The better dishes are the ones that don't try so hard to be different, like fiery-hot Szechuan-peppered scallops, or a pile of succulent pork ribs bathed in finger-lickin' sauce.

Shopping

Amy's Bread
672 Ninth Avenue, between 46th & 47th Streets (1-212 977 2670/ www.amysbread.com). Subway: C, E to 50th Street; N, R, W to 49th Street. **Open** *7.30am-11pm Mon-Fri; 8am-11pm Sat; 9am-6pm Sun. No credit cards.* **Map** p102 B1/p104 B4 102
Whether you want sweet (chocolate-chubbie cookies) or savoury (semolina-fennel bread, hefty French sourdough boules), this wonderful bakery-kitchen never disappoints. Coffee and sandwiches are served on the premises.

B&H Photo
420 Ninth Avenue, at 34th Street (1-212 444 5040/www.bhphotovideo. com). Subway: A, C, E to 34th Street-Penn Station. **Open** *9am-7pm Mon-Thur; 9am-2pm Fri; 10am-5pm Sun.* **Map** p102 B2 103
B&H is the ultimate one-stop shop for all your photographic, video and audio needs – stock includes professional audio equipment and discounted Bang & Olufsen products. Note that the store is closed Friday after 2pm, all day Saturday and on Jewish holidays.

Hell's Kitchen Flea Market
39th Street, between Ninth & Tenth Avenues (1-212 243 5343). Subway: A, C, E to 34th Street-Penn Station. **Open** *sunrise-sunset Sat, Sun. No credit cards.* **Map** p102 B2/p104 B5 104
The once-expansive Annex Antiques Fair & Flea Market on 26th Street lost its lease to a property developer, so many of the vendors packed up and moved to this stretch of road in Hell's Kitchen. Anyone familiar with the mind-boggling array of goods on offer at the former site is likely to feel a bit cheated in the new space, but there are treasures to be found and momentum is still growing.

Nightlife

Copacabana
560 W 34th Street between Tenth & Eleventh Avenues (1-212 239 2672/ www.copacabanany.com). Subway: A, C, E to 34th Street-Penn Station. **Cover** *$10-$40, $30 at tables.* **Map** p102 A2 105
The city's most iconic destination for Latin music has now become a fully fledged party palace. It's still a prime

stop for salsa, cumbia and merengue, but in addition to booking world-renowned stars (Ruben Blades, El Gran Combo, and Tito Nieves with Conjunto Clasico), the Copa now has an alternative nook called the House Room, where dancers can spin to disco, house and Latin freestyle.

Pacha

NEW *618 W 46th Street, between Eleventh & Twelfth Avenues (1-212 209 7500). Subway C, E to 50th Street.* **Open** 10pm-4am daily. **Map** p102 A1/p104 A4

The worldwide glam-clubbing chain Pacha, with outposts in nightlife hotspots such as Ibiza, London and Buenos Aires, has finally hit the US market with a swanky outpost helmed by superstar spinner Erick Morillo.

Midtown East

The area east of Fifth Avenue may seem less appealing to visitors than Times Square or Rockefeller Center. Although the neighbourhood is home to some of the city's most recognisable landmarks – the **United Nations, Grand Central Terminal** and the distinctive art deco **Chrysler Building** – the grid of busy streets is lined with large, imposing buildings, and the bustling sidewalks are all business. The area is a little thin on plazas and street-level attractions, but it compensates with a dizzying array of world-class architecture including the **MetLife Building, Waldorf-Astoria, Lever House** and the **Seagram Building**.

Sights & museums

Grand Central Terminal

From 42nd to 44th Streets, between Vanderbilt & Lexington Avenues. Subway: 42nd Street S, 4, 5, 6, 7 to 42nd Street-Grand Central. **Tours** Call 1-212 697 1245 for information. **Map** p103 D1/p105 E4

The 1913 beaux arts train station is the city's most spectacular point of arrival. Grand Central played an important role in the nation's historic preservation movement, after a series of legal battles that culminated in the 1978 Supreme Court decision affirmed NYC's landmark laws. Since its 1998 renovation, the terminal itself has become a destination, with classy restaurants and bars, such as the Campbell Apartment cocktail lounge (off the West Balcony, 1-212 953 0409), the expert Grand Central Oyster Bar & Restaurant (Lower Concourse, 1-212 490 6650) and star chef Charlie Palmer's Métrazur (East Balcony, 1-212 687 4600). The Lower Concourse food court spans the globe with its fairly priced lunch options. One notable oddity: the constellations on the Main Concourse ceiling are drawn in reverse, as if seen from outer space.

United Nations Headquarters

UN Plaza, First Avenue, between 42nd & 48th Streets (1-212 963 7710/tours 1-212 963 8687/ www.un.org). Subway: 42nd Street S, 4, 5, 6, 7 to 42nd Street-Grand Central. **Admission** $10.50; $8 seniors; $7 students; $6 5-14s; under-5s not admitted. **Map** p103 F1/p105 F4

The grounds and the Peace Garden along the East River are off-limits for security reasons. Unless you pay for a guided tour, the only accessible attractions are the exhibitions in the lobby and the bookstore and gift shop on the lower level.

Eating & drinking

Avra

141 E 48th Street, between Lexington & Third Avenues (1-212 759 8550). Subway: E, V to Lexington Avenue-53rd Street; 6 to 51st Street. **Open** noon-4pm, 5pm-midnight Mon-Fri; 11am-4pm, 5pm-midnight Sat; 11am-4pm, 5-11pm Sun. **$$$**. **Seafood**. **Map** p103 E1/p105 E4 (109)

Arched doorways and a limestone floor evoke an Ionian seaside village; fabric draped like sails over wooden ceiling beams adds to the breezy feel. Starters such as grilled whole sardines and feta-and-tomato-stuffed squid whet the appetite for the main attraction: impeccably fresh fish, priced by the pound and laid out on a bed of ice. Whole fish – a flaky royal dorado, for example – is charcoal grilled and dressed with lemon juice, olive oil and oregano.

Branch

226 E 54th Street, between Second & Third Avenues (1-212 688 5577). Subway: E, V to Lexington Avenue-53rd Street; 6 to 51st Street. **Open** 6pm-4am Thur; 10:30pm-4am Fri, Sat. **Admission** $10. **Bar**. **Map** p105 E3 (110)

This elegant lounge-club caters to local lawyer and banker types and out-of-towners in for a little weekend fun.

Caviar Russe

538 Madison Avenue between 54th and 55th Streets (1-212-980-5908). Subway: E, V to Fifth Avenue-53rd Street. **Open** noon-10pm Mon-Sat. **Caviar bar**. **Map** p105 D3 (111)

Fish eggs are serious business at this small bar. At the seven-seat caviar bar facing the open kitchen, every detail has been designed for an experience that's refined but not fussy.

Manchester Pub

920 Second Avenue, at 49th Street (1-212 935 8901). Subway: E, V to Lexington Avenue-53rd Street; 6 to 51st Street. **Open** 11am-4pm daily. **Bar**. Map p105 E4 (112)

A little bit of Northern English grit near the United Nations, this proto-typical pub offers all the amenities (Boddingtons and Guinness on tap, greasy pub food and grungy bathrooms) to make a Mancunian homesick. Soccer fans pack the place for Manchester United games; live broadcasts are shown at peculiar hours.

March Restaurant

405 E 58th Street, between First Avenue & Sutton Place (1-212 754 6272). Subway: N, R, W to Lexington Avenue-59th Street; 4, 5, 6 to 59th Street. **Open** 5.30-10.30pm daily. **$$$$**. **American creative**. **Map** p105 F2 (113)

Housed in an elegantly appointed turn-of-the-century townhouse, March is a rare breed: an expensive, top-notch restaurant that's neither stuffy nor pretentious. Unusual combinations add up to more than the sum of their parts; we liked the spring pea tortelloni with pecorino, lemon and toasted almond froth.

Megu Midtown

NEW *845 UN Plaza, Trump World Tower, First Avenue, at 47th Street (1-212 964 7777). Subway: E, V to Lexington Street; 6 to 51st Street.* **Open** 5.30-10.30pm Mon-Wed; 5.30-11.30pm Thur-Sat **$$$$**. **Japanese**. **Map** p103 E1/p105 F4 (114)

The 115-seat dining room has 24ft ceilings, 16ft-long lampshades, black wood panelling, a monumental mural of white tigers poised to pounce and, like the original, a Buddha ice sculpture. Inside the open kitchen, an army of chefs produce pristine sushi and meat dishes (kobe beef, lamb, foie gras) the likes of which you won't find elsewhere. If the $70 four-course prix fixe menu isn't enough to impress, ask about the 'wagon service', featuring rare ingredients – jetted in daily.

Mint

NEW *150 E 50th Street, between Lexington & Third Avenues (1-212 644 8888). Subway E, V to Lexington Avenue-53rd Street; 6 to 51st Street.* **Open** 11.30am-3pm, 5-11pm daily. **$$.** **Indian**. **Map** p105 E3 ⑮

At this Indian eatery, chefs pull all sorts of traditional baked goods out of the fiery clay oven – fluffy nan, roti and *kulcha* – but the best is the *aloo paratha*: warm, chewy and slightly charred rounds with a layer of soft, spicy potato in the middle. The secret is in the seasoning and the precisely heated oven.

Montparnasse

230 E 51st Street, between Second & Third Avenues (1-212 758 6633). Subway: E, V to Lexington Avenue-53rd Street; 6 to 51st Street. **Open** noon-3pm, 5-11pm Mon, Sun; noon-3pm, 5pm-midnight Tue-Fri; 5pm-midnight Sat. **$$.** **French.** **Map** p105 E3 ⑯

Both decor and menu are bistro standard, but the food is fresher, prettier and tastier than what's on offer at many cookie-cutter French joints. Top dishes here include seared hanger steak in red-wine sauce and bouillabaisse – the saffron-accented broth has an abundant tumble of seafood.

Phoenix Garden

242 E 40th Street, between Second & Third Avenues (1-212 983 6666). Subway: 42nd Street S, 4, 5, 6, 7 to 42nd Street-Grand Central. **Open** 11.30am-9.45pm Mon-Fri; noon-9.45pm Sat, Sun. **$.** **Chinese.** No credit cards. **Map** p103 E2/p105 E5 ⑰

Here's proof that you don't have to go to Chinatown to get the good stuff. Everything here tastes incredible, especially dumplings stuffed with chives and crisp sea bass with shredded pork and black mushrooms. Don't overlook casseroles, like the robust eggplant with minced pork and ham.

Top of the Tower

Beekman Tower, 3 Mitchell Place, at First Avenue (1-212 980 4796). Subway: E, V to Lexington Avenue-

Grand Central Terminal p133

53rd Street; 6 to 51st Street. **Open** 5pm-1am Mon-Thur, Sun; 5pm-2am Fri, Sat. **Bar.** **Map** p105 F3 ⑱

Sweeping views of Midtown and the East River are not the only draws at this swanky lounge with two small outdoor terraces, perched on the 26th floor of the art deco landmark Beekman Tower Hotel. There's also live jazz piano (Thursday to Saturday) and sippable signature cocktails such as the chocolatey Gotham Martini.

Shopping

Bloomingdale's

1000 Third Avenue, at 59th Street (1-212 705 2000/www.bloomingdales. com). Subway: N, R, W to Lexington Avenue-59th Street; 4, 5, 6 to 59th Street. **Open** 10am-8.30pm Mon-Fri; 10am-7pm Sat; 11am-7pm Sun. **Map** p105 E2 ⑲

Bloomies is a gigantic, glitzy department store offering everything from handbags and cosmetics to furniture and designer duds. Brace yourself for the crowds – this store ranks among the city's most popular tourist attractions, right up there with the Empire State Building. Check out the cool new little-sister branch in Soho.

Central Park

Uptown

As you get above 57th Street in Manhattan, you'll notice that the crowds thin out and the frenetic pace slows down considerably: welcome to Uptown. While it's definitely calmer up here, there are still plenty of attractions to get your heart racing. For starters, there's **Central Park**, the city's gigantic outdoor playground. The cultural offerings found uptown are stellar: **Lincoln Center, the Metropolitan Museum of Art, the Guggenheim** and the **Studio Museum in Harlem**, to name just a few. The city's wealthiest residents are huddled together in spectacular mansions on the Upper East Side – we guarantee a walk up Fifth Avenue will leave you breathless. The very northern tip of Manhattan not only provides glorious views of the Hudson River,

but take a look back: the medieval castle of the **Cloisters** sits majestically in Fort Tryon Park.

Central Park

Two and a half miles long and half a mile wide, this patch of the great outdoors was the first man-made public park in the US. In 1853, the newly formed Central Park Commission chose landscape designer Frederick Law Olmsted and architect Calvert Vaux to turn this vast tract of rocky swampland into a rambling oasis of greenery. In 2003, the park celebrated its 150th anniversary, and it has never looked better, thanks to the Central Park Conservancy, a private non-profit civic group formed in 1980 that has been instrumental in restoration and maintenance.

The park is dotted with landmarks. **Strawberry Fields**, near the West 72nd Street entrance, commemorates John Lennon, who lived in the nearby Dakota Building. The statue of Balto, a heroic Siberian husky (East Drive, at 67th Street), is a favourite sight for tots. Slightly older children appreciate the statue of Alice in Wonderland, just north of the **Conservatory Water** at the East 74th Street park entrance.

In winter, ice-skaters lace up at **Wollman Rink**, where the skating comes with a picture-postcard view of the fancy hotels surrounding the park. A short stroll to about 64th Street brings you to the **Friedsam Memorial Carousel**, still a bargain at a $1.50 per ride.

Come summer, kites, frisbees and soccer balls fly every which way across **Sheep Meadow**, the designated quiet zone that begins at 66th Street. East of Sheep Meadow, between 66th and 72nd Streets, is the **Mall**, where you'll find volleyball courts and plenty of in-line skaters. East of the Mall's **Naumburg Bandshell** is **Rumsey Playfield** – site of the annual Central Park SummerStage series, an eclectic roster of free and benefit concerts held from Memorial Day weekend to Labor Day weekend. One of the most popular meeting places in the park is the grand **Bethesda Fountain and Terrace**, near the midpoint of the 72nd Street Transverse Road. North of it is the **Loeb Boathouse** (midpark, at 75th Street), where you can rent a rowing boat or gondola to take out on the lake, which is crossed by the elegant Bow Bridge. The bucolic park views enjoyed by diners at the nearby **Central Park Boathouse Restaurant** (midpark, at 75th Street, 1-212 517 2233) make it a lovely place for brunch or drinks, with an outdoor terrace and bar that are idyllic in summer. The **Great Lawn** (midpark, between 79th and 85th Streets) is a sprawling stretch of grass that doubles as a rally point for political protests and a concert spot for just about any act that can rally a six-figure audience, as well as free shows courtesy of the Metropolitan Opera and the New York Philharmonic in summer.

Upper East Side

Along the expanse of Fifth, Madison and Park Avenues from 61st to 81st Streets – you'll see the great old mansions, many of which are now foreign consulates. The structure at 820 Fifth Avenue (at 64th Street) was one of the earliest luxury-apartment buildings on the avenue. Philanthropic gestures made by the moneyed class over the past 130 years have helped to create a cluster of art collections, museums and cultural institutions. In fact, Fifth Avenue from 82nd to 104th Streets is known as Museum Mile.

Sights & museums

Asia Society & Museum

725 Park Avenue, at 70th Street (1-212 288 6400/www.asiasociety.org). Subway: 6 to 68th Street-Hunter College. **Open** 11am-6pm Tue-Thur, Sat, Sun; 11am-9pm Fri. **Admission** $10; free-$7 reductions; free 6-9pm Fri. No credit cards. **Map** p139 D4 ❶

The Asia Society sponsors study missions and conferences while promoting public programmes in the US and abroad. The headquarters' striking galleries host major exhibitions of art from dozens of countries and time periods – from ancient India and medieval Persia to contemporary Japan – and assembled from public and private collections, including the permanent Mr and Mrs John D Rockefeller III collection of Asian art. There are

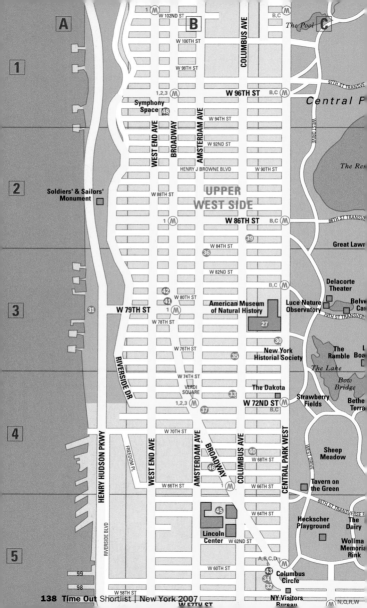

A
B
C

1
W 102ND ST
W 100TH ST
W 98TH ST
COLUMBUS AVE
B,C M
The Pool

W 96TH ST
1,2,3 M
B,C M
Central P

Symphony Space 48
W 94TH ST
W 92ND ST
WEST END AVE
BROADWAY
AMSTERDAM AVE
HENRY J BROWNE BLVD
W 90TH ST

2
Soldiers' & Sailors' Monument
W 88TH ST
UPPER WEST SIDE
The Res

1 M
W 86TH ST
B,C M
Great Lawn

39
W 84TH ST
36
W 82ND ST

3
31
42
41
W 80TH ST
W 79TH ST
1 M
W 78TH ST
American Museum of Natural History
27
B,C M
Luce Nature Observatory
Delacorte Theater
Belve Cas

30
New York Historial Society
35
W 76TH ST
The Ramble
L Boa

RIVERSIDE DR
W 74TH ST
VERDI SQUARE
33
The Dakota
The Lake
Bow Bridge

1,2,3 M
37
W 72ND ST
B,C M
Strawberry Fields
Bethe Terra

4
W 70TH ST
W 68TH ST
40
AMSTERDAM AVE
BROADWAY
46
COLUMBUS AVE
CENTRAL PARK WEST
WEST DRIVE
Sheep Meadow

HENRY HUDSON PKWY
FREEDOM PL
WEST END AVE
W 66TH ST
1 M
Tavern on the Green

65TH ST TRANSVERSE
45
W 64TH ST
Heckscher Playground
The Dairy

RIVERSIDE BLVD
Lincoln Center
W 62ND ST
Wollma Memoria Rink

5
99
98
W 60TH ST
W 58TH ST
A,B,C,D M
43
34
32
Columbus Circle
NY Visitors Bureau
N,Q,R,W M

138 Time Out Shortlist | New York 2007

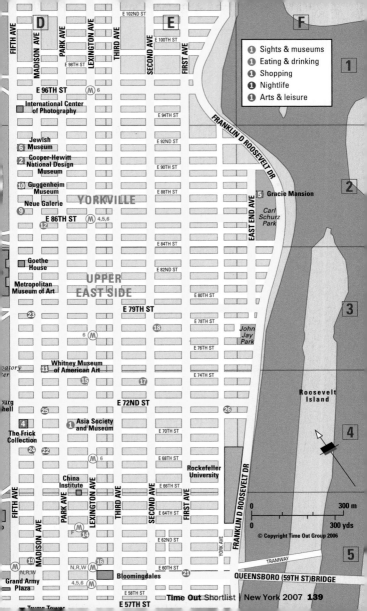

D | PARK AVE | LEXINGTON AVE | THIRD AVE | E | F

FIFTH AVE · MADISON AVE · PARK AVE · LEXINGTON AVE · THIRD AVE · SECOND AVE · FIRST AVE

E 102ND ST
E 100TH ST
E 98TH ST
1
1 Sights & museums
1 Eating & drinking
1 Shopping
1 Nightlife
1 Arts & leisure

E 96TH ST
Ⓜ 6
International Center
of Photography

E 94TH ST

FRANKLIN D ROOSEVELT DR

6 Jewish
Museum
E 92ND ST

2 Cooper-Hewitt
National Design
Museum
E 90TH ST

10 Guggenheim
Museum
E 88TH ST

Neue Galerie
9
YORKVILLE

5 Gracie Mansion

EAST END AVE

Carl
Schutz
Park

2

12
E 86TH ST Ⓜ 4,5,6

E 84TH ST

UPPER
EAST SIDE
Goethe
House
E 82ND ST

Metropolitan
Museum of Art
E 80TH ST

3
23
E 79TH ST
E 78TH ST

6 Ⓜ
18
E 76TH ST
John
Jay
Park

Whitney Museum
11 of American Art
15
17
E 74TH ST

Roosevelt
Island

E 72ND ST
urg
hell
25
26
4

1 Asia Society
and Museum
E 70TH ST

The Frick
Collection
24 **22**
Ⓜ 6
E 68TH ST
Rockefeller
University
servatory
ter

FRANKLIN D ROOSEVELT DR

China
Institute
E 66TH ST

FIFTH AVE · MADISON AVE · PARK AVE · LEXINGTON AVE · THIRD AVE · SECOND AVE · FIRST AVE

E 64TH ST
Ⓜ F
14
E 62ND ST

YORK AVE

0 ——— 300 m
0 ——— 300 yds
© Copyright Time Out Group 2006

19
N,R,W
Grand Army
Plaza
N,R,W Ⓜ
16
E 60TH ST
21
TRAMWAY

4,5,6 Ⓜ
Bloomingdales
QUEENSBORO (59TH ST)BRIDGE

E 58TH ST
Time Out Shortlist | New York 2007 **139**

Trump Tower
E 57TH ST

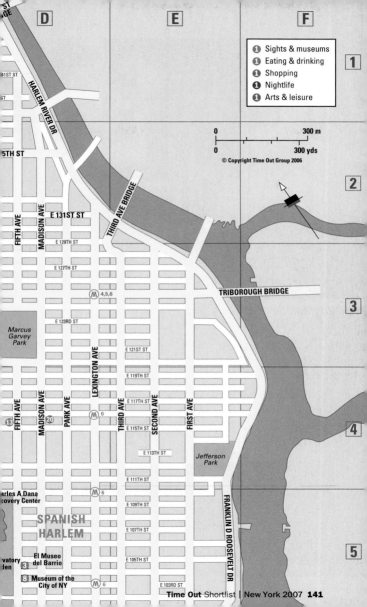

D **E** **F**

1

Sights & museums
Eating & drinking
Shopping
Nightlife
Arts & leisure

HARLEM RIVER DR

31ST ST

5TH ST

0   300 m
0   300 yds
© Copyright Time Out Group 2006

2

FIFTH AVE
MADISON AVE

E 131ST ST

THIRD AVE BRIDGE

E 129TH ST

E 127TH ST

TRIBOROUGH BRIDGE

3

M 4,5,6

E 123RD ST

Marcus
Garvey
Park

LEXINGTON AVE

E 121ST ST

E 119TH ST

FIFTH AVE
MADISON AVE
PARK AVE
THIRD AVE
SECOND AVE
FIRST AVE

E 117TH ST

13

20

M 6

E 115TH ST

4

E 113TH ST

Jefferson
Park

E 111TH ST

arles A Dana
covery Center

M 6

E 109TH ST

FRANKLIN D ROOSEVELT DR

SPANISH
HARLEM

E 107TH ST

E 105TH ST

vatory
Jen

3

El Museo
del Barrio

5

8

Museum of the
City of NY

E 103RD ST

M 6

Central Park p136

a spacious, atrium-like café with a pan-Asian menu and a beautifully stocked gift shop.

Cooper-Hewitt, National Design Museum

2 E 91st Street, at Fifth Avenue (1-212 849 8400/www.cooper hewitt.org). Subway: 4, 5, 6 to 86th Street. **Open** 10am-5pm Tue-Thur; 10am-9pm Fri; 10am-6pm Sat; noon-6pm Sun. **Admission** $10; free-$7 reductions. **Map** p139 D2 ❷

The Smithsonian's National Design Museum was once the home of industrialist Andrew Carnegie (there is still a lovely lawn behind the building). Now it's the only museum in the US dedicated to domestic and industrial design, and it boasts a fascinating roster of temporary exhibitions.

Event highlights Until July 2007, the museum stages the 'National Design Triennial: Design Life Now', which examines experimental projects and innovations in architecture, fashion, graphics and product design.

El Museo del Barrio

1230 Fifth Avenue, between 104th & 105th Streets (1-212 831 7272/ www.elmuseo.org). Subway: 6 to 103rd Street. **Open** 11am-5pm Wed-Sun. **Admission** $6; free-$4 reductions. Seniors free Thursday. **Map** p141 D5 ❸

Located in Spanish Harlem (aka El Barrio), El Museo del Barrio is dedicated to the work of Latino artists who reside in the US as well as Latin-American masters. The 8,000-piece collection ranges from pre-Columbian artefacts to contemporary installations.

Frick Collection

1 E 70th Street, between Fifth & Madison Avenues (1-212 288 0700/ www.frick.org). Subway: 6 to 68th Street-Hunter College. **Open** 10am-6pm Tue-Sat; 1-6pm Sun. **Admission** $12; $5-$8 reductions (under-10s not admitted). **Map** p139 D4 ❹

The opulent 1914 residence that houses this private collection of great masters (from the 14th to the 19th centuries) was originally built for industrialist Henry Clay Frick, with a beautiful interior court and reflecting pool. The permanent collection boasts world-class paintings, sculpture and furniture by the likes of Rembrandt, Vermeer and Renoir.

Gracie Mansion Conservancy

Carl Schurz Park, 88th Street, at East End Avenue (1-212 570 4751). Subway: 4, 5, 6 to 86th Street. **Tours** Mar-mid Nov 10am, 11am, 1pm, 2pm Wed; tours last 45 minutes. **Admission** $7; free-$4 reductions; reservations required, same-day reservations not permitted. No credit cards. **Map** p139 F2 ❺

At the eastern end of 88th Street is the only Federal-style mansion in Manhattan, and it's been New York's official mayoral residence since 1942 – the current mayor, billionaire Michael Bloomberg, famously eschewed this traditional address in favour of his own beaux arts mansion at 17 East 79th Street (between Fifth and Madison Avenues). The green-shuttered yellow edifice, built in 1799 by Scottish merchant Archibald Gracie was originally constructed as a country house for the wealthy businessman.

Jewish Museum

1109 Fifth Avenue, at 92nd Street (1-212 423 3200/www.thejewish museum.org). Subway: 4, 5 to 86th Street; 6 to 96th Street. **Open** 11am-5.45pm Mon-Wed, Sun; 11am-9pm Thur; 11am-3pm Fri. Closed Jewish holidays. **Admission** $10; free-$7.50 reductions; donation 5-8pm Thur. **Map** p139 D2 ❻

The Jewish Museum, in the 1908 Warburg Mansion, contains a fascinating collection of more than 28,000 works of art, artefacts and media installations. A two-floor permanent exhibition, 'Culture and Continuity: The Jewish Journey', examines the survival of Judaism and the essence of Jewish identity. The Museum's Café Weissman features a menu of contemporary kosher fare.

Dakota Building p137

medieval armour – a huge favourite with adults and children alike – was recently enriched by gifts of European, North American, Japanese and Islamic armaments.

The museum has also made significant additions to its modern-art galleries, including major works by American artist Eric Fischl and Chilean surrealist Roberto Matta. Contemporary sculptures are displayed each year in the Iris and B Gerald Cantor Roof Garden (May to late autmn, weather permitting).

Event highlights 'Cézanne to Picasso: Ambroise Vollard, Patron of the Avant-Garde' mid Sept 2006-7 Jan 2007; 'Witness to History: The Face in Medieval Sculpture' 26 Sept 2006-18 Feb 2007; 'Glitter and Doom: German Portraits from the 1920s' 14 Nov 2006-18 Feb 2007; 'Barcelona and Modernity: Gaudi to Dali' 7 Mar-3 June 2007; 'Venice and the Islamic World, 828-1797' 27 March-8 July 2007.

NEW YORK BY AREA

Metropolitan Museum of Art

1000 Fifth Avenue, at 82nd Street (1-212 535 7710/www.metmuseum. org). Subway: 4, 5, 6 to 86th Street. **Open** 9.30am-5.30pm Tue-Thur, Sun; 9.30am-9pm Fri, Sat. No strollers Sun. **Admission** suggested donation (incl same-day admission to the Cloisters) $12; free-$7 reductions. **Map** p139 D3 ❼

It could take weeks to cover the Met's two million square feet of gallery space, so it's best to be selective. Besides the enthralling temporary exhibitions, there are excellent collections of African, Oceanic and Islamic art, along with more than 3,000 European paintings from the Middle Ages up through the fin de siècle period, including major works by Titian, Brueghel, Rembrandt, Vermeer, Goya and Degas. Egyptology fans should head straight for the glass-walled atrium housing the Temple of Dendur. The Greek and Roman halls have received a graceful makeover, and the incomparable collection of

Museum of the City of New York

1220 Fifth Avenue, between 103rd & 104th Streets (1-212 534 1672/www. mcny.org). Subway: 6 to 103rd Street. **Open** 10am-5pm Tue-Sun. **Admission** suggested donation $7; $5 seniors, students, children; $15 families. **Map** p139 D5 ❽

This institution contains a wealth of city history and includes paintings, sculptures, photographs, military and naval uniforms, theatre memorabilia, manuscripts, ship models and rare books. The toy collection, full of New Yorkers' playthings dating from the colonial era to the present, is especially well loved.

Neue Galerie

1048 Fifth Avenue, at 86th Street (1-212 628 6200/www.neuegalerie. org). Subway: 4, 5, 6 to 86th Street. **Open** 11am-6pm Mon, Sat, Sun; 11am-9pm Fri. **Admission** $10; $7 reductions; under-12s not admitted. **Map** p139 D2 ❾

This elegant museum is devoted entirely to late 19th- and early 20th-century

German and Austrian fine and decorative arts. The creation of the late art dealer Serge Sabarsky and cosmetics mogul Ronald S Lauder, the Neue Gallerie has the largest concentration of works by Gustav Klimt and Egon Schiele outside Vienna.

Solomon R Guggenheim Museum

1071 Fifth Avenue, at 89th Street (1-212 423 3500/www.guggenheim. org). Subway: 4, 5, 6 to 86th Street. **Open** 10am-5.45pm Mon-Wed, Sat, Sun; 10am-8pm Fri. **Admission** $15; free-$10 reductions; half-price 5-8pm Fri. **Map** p139 D2 ❿

Even if your schedule doesn't allow time to view the collections, you must get a glimpse (if only from the outside) of this dramatic spiral building, designed by Frank Lloyd Wright. In addition to works by Manet, Kandinsky, Picasso, Chagall and Louise Bourgeois, the museum owns Peggy Guggenheim's haul of cubist, surrealist and abstract expressionist works, along with the Panza di Biumo Collection of American minimalist and conceptual art from the 1960s and '70s. A ten-storey tower provides space for a sculpture gallery (with views of Central Park), an auditorium and a café.

Whitney Museum of American Art

945 Madison Avenue, at 75th Street (1-212 570 3676/1-800 944 8639/ www.whitney.org). Subway: 6 to 77th Street. **Open** 11am-6pm Wed, Thur, Sat, Sun; 1-9pm Fri. **Admission** $12; free-$9.50 reductions; donation 6-9pm Fri. **Map** p139 D3 ⓫

Like the Guggenheim, the Whitney is set apart by its architecture: it's a Marcel Breuer-designed gray granite cube with an all-seeing upper-storey 'eye' window. When Gertrude Vanderbilt Whitney, a sculptor and art patron, opened the museum in 1931, she dedicated it to living American artists. Today, the Whitney holds about 15,000 pieces by nearly 2,000 artists, including Alexander Calder, Willem de Kooning, Edward Hopper (the museum

Metropolitan Museum of Art

holds his entire estate), Jasper Johns, Louise Nevelson, Georgia O'Keeffe and Claes Oldenburg. Still, the museum's reputation rests mainly on its temporary shows, particularly the exhibition everyone loves to hate, the Whitney Biennial. Held in even-numbered years, the Biennial remains the most prestigious (and controversial) assessment of contemporary art in America.

Event highlights 'Picasso and American Art' 28 Sept 2006-28 Jan 2007; 'Albers and Moholy-Nagy: From the Bauhaus to the New World' 2 Nov 2006-21 Jan 2007; Lorna Simpson Feb 7-6 May 2007.

Eating & drinking

Centolire

1167 Madison Avenue, between 85th & 86th Streets (212-734 7711). Subway: 4, 5, 6 to 86th Street. **Open** noon-3.30pm, 5.30-11pm Mon-Fri; 6-11pm Sat; noon-3.30pm, 6-10pm Sun. **$$$. Italian. Map** p139 D2 ⓬

'Up or down?' the host will probably ask when you arrive. Head upstairs, where potted sunflowers light up a room overlooking Madison Avenue. The service is delightful; waiters offer advice and don't hesitate to mention prices for specials. The menu includes a variety of inventive pastas as well as traditional dishes such as veal *milanese*.

Ginger

NEW *1400 Fifth Avenue, at 116th Street (212-423 1111). Subway 2, 3, to 116th Street-Lenox Avenue; 6 to 116th Street-Lexington Avenue.* **Open** 5.30-10.30pm Mon-Thur; 5.30-11.30pm Fri; 11.30am-4.30pm, 5.30-11.30pm Sat; 5.30-10.00pm Sun. **$$. Chinese. Map** p141 D4 ⑬
What's novel about this recently opened organic Chinese restaurant is what executive chef James Marshall won't do to the food: there will be no deep-frying and no excessive usage of oil or salt. Instead, fresh vegetables and lean meats are doused in citrusy sauces; the menu lists pineapple-and-mango-glazed pork chop as well as apricot-glazed chicken.

Jovia

NEW *135 E 62nd Street, between Park & Lexington Avenues (212-752 6000). Subway: F to Lexington Avenue-63rd Street.* **Open** 5.30-10.30pm Sun-Thur; 5.30-11.30pm Fri, Sat. **$$$. American Creative. Map** p139 D5 ⑭
Jovia's chef Josh DeChellis focuses on American cuisine with Italian influences – curing his own salumi, melding warm scallops with saffron-pickled melon and prosciutto, and cooking venison and chestnuts over a bed of pine and juniper branches. Fireplaces in the upstairs dinning rooms, downstairs offers sleek plasma TVs and a mahogany bar.

Payard Pâtisserie & Bistro

1032 Lexington Avenue, between 73rd & 74th Streets (212-717 5252). Subway: 6 to 77th Street. **Open** noon-3pm, 5.45-10.30pm Mon-Thur; noon-3pm, 5.45-11pm Fri, Sat. Tea: 3.30-5pm Mon-Sat. **$-$$$. French. Map** p139 D4 ⑮

Glance past the espresso machines at this Parisian-style bakery and restaurant, and you'll spy an elegant panelled dining room with glittering belle epoque mirrors. Contemporary dishes such as seared scallops in vanilla *nage,* and classics like rack of lamb and a steak in four-peppercorn sauce are winners.

Subway Inn

143 E 60th Street, between Lexington & Third Avenues (212-223 8929). Subway: N, R, W to Lexington Avenue-59th Street; 4, 5, 6 to 59th Street. **Open** 8am-4am. **Bar. Map** p139 D5 ⑯
The bar near the Lexington Avenue and 60th Street subway exit is a 73-year-old watering hole that really is a hole. And we like that way. The clientele varies based on the time of day, but you're likely to see a mix of what appears to be Bowery-bum-like boozers, regular guys, and confused tourists seated in decrepit booths or at the bar. Drinks are lost in a time warp – beer starts at $3.50.

Üsküdar

1405 Second Avenue, between 73rd & 74th Streets (212-988 2641). Subway: 6 to 77th Street. **Open** noon-11pm daily. **$$. Turkish. Map** p139 E4 ⑰

Barneys New York

Named after an ancient, famously beautiful neighbourhood in Istanbul, this narrow, no-frills restaurant may not live up to its namesake in the looks department, but you won't be disappointed by the food. The service is a bit slow, but in a friendly mom-and-pop kind of way.

Uva

NEW *1486 Second Avenue, at 77th Street (1-212 472 4552). Subway: 6 to 77th Street.* **Open** noon-1am Sun-Thur; noon-2am Fri, Sat. Wine Bar. **Map** p139 E3 ⑱

A great wine bar requires more than a well-stocked cellar: the smartly selected, not-too-pricey wines (35 of them available by the glass) come in just the right package – a rustic brick-walled room dimly lit with chandeliers and flickering ruby-red tea lights. Along with the extensive leather-bound wine list comes an equally comprehensive dinner menu.

Shopping

Barneys New York

660 Madison Avenue, at 61st Street (1-212 826 8900/www.barneys.com). Subway: N, R, W to Fifth Avenue-59th Street; 4, 5, 6 to 59th Street. **Open** 10am-8pm Mon-Fri; 10am-7pm Sat; 11am-6pm Sun. Map p139 D5 ⑲

The top designers are represented at this bastion of New York style. At Christmas time, Barneys has the most provocative windows in town. Its Co-op boutique branches carry young designers as well as secondary lines from heavyweights like Marc Jacobs and Theory. Every February and August the Chelsea Co-op (236 West 18th Street, 1-212 593 7800) hosts the Barneys Warehouse Sale, when prices are reduced up to 80%.

Casa de las Velas

60 E 116th Street, between Madison & Park Avenues (1-212 289 0378). Subway: 6 to 116th Street. **Open** 10am-6pm Mon-Sat; noon-6pm Sun. **Map** p139 D4 ⑳

Whatever your problem, the Santeria superstore (New York's oldest existing botanica, established in 1921) has got a candle to cure it. And if a wick won't do the trick, the emporium's shelves are also packed with a profusion of helpful herbs, charms, incense, icons and bath preparations. This is one of the last remaining botanicas on fast-gentrifying 116th Street.

Myla

Conran Shop

*407 E 59th Street, between First &
York Avenues (1-212 755 9079).
Subway: N, R, W to Lexington Avenue-
59th Street; 4, 5, 6 to 59th Street.*
Open 11am-8pm Mon-Fri; 10am-7pm
Sat; noon-6pm Sun. **Map** p139 E5 **㉑**
Nestled under the Queensboro Bridge,
Terence Conran's shop stocks a vast
selection of trendy products for every
room of the house. The range includes
cabinets, dishes, lighting, rugs, sofas,
draperies, beds, linens, kitchen gadgets
and much more.

Donna Karan New York

*819 Madison Avenue, between 68th &
69th Streets (1-212 861 1001/www.
donnakaran.com). Subway: 6 to 68th
Street-Hunter College.* **Open** 10am-6pm
Mon-Wed, Fri, Sat; 10am-7pm Thur;
noon-6pm Sun. **Map** p139 D4 **㉒**
Created around a central garden with
a bamboo forest, Donna Karan's
upscale flagship caters to men, women
and the home. Check out the organic
café at the nearby DKNY store, as well
as Donna-approved reads, clothing,
shoes and vintage furniture.

La Maison du Chocolat

*1018 Madison Avenue, between 78th
& 79th Streets (1-212 744 7117/
www.lamaisonduchocolat.com). Subway:*
6 to 77th Street. **Open** 10am-7pm Mon-
Sat; noon-6pm Sun. **Map** p139 D3 **㉓**
This suave cocoa-brown boutique, the
creation of Robert Linxe, packages
refined (and pricey) examples of edible
Parisian perfection like fine jewellery.
A small café serves hot and cold chocolate drinks and a selection of sweets.

Myla

*20 E 69th Street, between Fifth &
Madison Avenues (1-212 570 1590)
Subway: 6 to 68th Street-Hunter
College.* **Open** 10am-6pm Mon-Sat.
Map p139 D4 **㉔**
London-based naughty-nineties empo-
rium Myla sells elegant lingerie
and boudoir accessories, including
tasteful (yet nipple-exposing) 'peep-
hole' bras, silk wrist-ties and blind-
folds, plus a handful of sculptural,
Brancusi-esque vibrators.

Ralph Lauren

*867 Madison Avenue, at 72nd Street
(1-212 606 2100/www.polo.com).
Subway: 6 to 68th Street-Hunter
College.* **Open** 10am-7pm Mon-Wed,
Fri, Sat; 10am-8pm Thur; noon-5pm
Sun. **Map** p139 D4 **㉕**
Ralph Lauren spent $14 million turn-
ing the old Rhinelander mansion into
an Ivy League dream of a superstore:
it's filled with oriental rugs, English

paintings, leather club chairs, old mahogany and fresh flowers. The young homeboys, skaters and bladers who've adopted Ralphie's togs head to Polo Sport across the street.

Sotheby's

1334 York Avenue, at 72nd Street (1-212 606 7000/www.sothebys.com). Subway: 6 to 68th Street-Hunter College. **Open** 10am-5pm Mon-Sat (weekend hours change seasonally). **Admission** free. **Map** p139 E4 ㉖

With offices in cities from London to Singapore, Sotheby's is the world's most famous auction house. The New York branch regularly holds public sales of antique furniture and jewellery in one lot, and pop-culture memorabilia in another. Spring and autumn see the big sales of modern and contemporary art. Public viewings are held prior to each auction; call or visit Sotheby's website for details of dates and times.

Upper West Side

This four-mile-long stretch west of Central Park is culturally rich and cosmopolitan. As on the Upper East Side, New Yorkers were drawn here in the late 19th century, after the completion of Central Park, the opening of local subway lines and Columbia University's relocation to Morningside Heights. The gateway to the Upper West Side is **Columbus Circle**, where Broadway meets 59th Street, Eighth Avenue, Central Park South and Central Park West – a rare rotary in a city of right angles.

The Upper West Side's seat of highbrow culture is **Lincoln Center**, a complex of concert halls and auditoriums built in the 1960s. It is home to the New York Philharmonic, the New York City Ballet and the Metropolitan Opera, along with a host of other arts organisations. The big circular fountain in the central plaza is a popular gathering spot, especially

in summer, when amateur dancers converge on it to dance alfresco at Midsummer Night Swing.

Sights & museums

American Museum of Natural History/Rose Center for Earth & Space

Central Park West, at 79th Street (1-212 769 5100/www.amnh.org). Subway: B, C to 81st Street-Museum of Natural History. **Open** 10am-5.45pm daily. **Admission** $13 suggested donation; free-$10 reductions. **Map** p138 C3 ㉗

The thrills begin when you cross the threshold of the Theodore Roosevelt Rotunda, where you're confronted with a towering barosaurus rearing up to protect its young from an attacking allosaurus. This impressive welcome to the world's largest museum of its kind acts as a reminder to visit the dinosaur halls, on the fourth floor.

The rest of the museum is equally dramatic. The Hall of Biodiversity examines the world's ecosystems and environmental preservation, and a life-size model of a blue whale hangs from the cavernous ceiling of the Hall of Ocean Life. The impressive Hall of Meteorites was brushed up and reorganised in 2003. From October to May, the museum installs a tropical butterfly conservatory in the Hall of Oceanic Birds, where visitors can mingle with 500 live specimens.

The spectacular $210 million Rose Center for Earth and Space – dazzling at night – is a giant silvery globe where you can discover the universe via 3-D shows in the Hayden Planetarium and light shows in the Big Bang Theater. An IMAX screens larger-than-life nature programmes, and you can always learn something new from the innovative temporary exhibitions, an easily accessible research library (with vast photo and print archives) and several cool gift shops.

Event highlights 'Gold' Nov 2006-19 Aug 2007; 'Mythic Beasts' May 2007-Jan 2008.

Cathedral Church of St John the Divine

1047 Amsterdam Avenue, at 112th Street (1-212 316 7540/www.stjohn divine.org). Subway: B, C, 1 to 110th Street-Cathedral Parkway. **Open** 8am-6pm daily. **Admission** $5; $4 reductions. **Map** p138 B4 ㉓

Construction on 'St John the Unfinished' began in 1892 in Romanesque style, was put on hold for a Gothic Revival redesign in 1911, then ground to a halt in 1941, when the US entered World War II. It resumed in earnest in 1979, but a fire in 2001 destroyed the church's gift shop, further delaying completion. In addition to Sunday services, the cathedral hosts concerts and tours. It bills itself as a place for all people – and it means it. Annual events include both winter and summer solstice celebrations; the Blessing of the Animals during the Feast of St Francis, which draws pets and their people from all over the city; and, would you believe it, the Blessing of the Bikes, which kicks off the bicycle season each spring.

General Grant National Memorial

Riverside Drive, at 122nd Street (1-212 666 1640). Subway: 1 to 125th Street. **Open** 9am-5pm daily. **Admission** free. **Map** p138 A3 ㉙

Who's buried in Grant's Tomb? Technically, no one – the crypts of Civil War hero and 18th president Ulysses S Grant and his wife Julia are in full above-ground view. Note: the memorial is closed on Thanksgiving, Christmas and New Year's Day.

New-York Historical Society

170 Central Park West, between 76th & 77th Streets (1-212 873 3400/www. nyhistory.org). Subway: B, C to 81st Street-Museum of Natural History. **Open** 10am-6pm Tue-Sun. **Admission** $10; free-$5 reductions. No credit cards. **Map** p138 C3 ㉚

New York's oldest museum, founded in 1804, was one of America's first cultural and educational institutions. Highlights in the vast Henry Luce III Center for the Study of American Culture include George Washington's

American Museum of Natural History p149

Valley Forge camp cot, a complete series of watercolours from Audubon's *The Birds of America* and the world's largest collection of Tiffany lamps.

Riverside Park

Map p138 A1-4/p140 A1-5 ③①
A sinuous stretch of riverbank that starts at 72nd Street and ends at 158th Street, between Riverside Drive and the Hudson River. The stretch of park below 72nd Street, called Riverside Park South, includes a pier and beautiful patches of grass with park benches. You'll see yachts, along with several houseboats, berthed at the 79th Street Boat Basin; in the summertime, there's an open-air café in the adjacent park where New Yorkers unwind with a beer and watch the sun set over the Hudson River.

Time Warner Center

10 Columbus Circle, at Broadway. Subway: A, B, C, D, 1 to 59th Street-Columbus Circle. **Open** 8am-10pm daily. **Map** p138 C5 ③②
The Shops at Columbus Circle takes up the first seven levels of the enormous glass complex and includes dozens of retail shops, J Crew, Borders Books, Whole Foods and numerous bars and gourmet restaurants.

Eating & drinking

Alice's Teacup

102 W 73rd Street, between Columbus & Amsterdam Avenues (1-212 799 3006). Subway B, C, 1, 2, 3 to 72nd Street. **Open** 8am-8pm Mon-Thur; 8am-10pm Fri; 10am-10pm Sat; 10am-8pm Sun. **$. Café. Map** p138 B4 ③③
A quaint, homey space with mismatched furniture and scribbles from Lewis Carroll's classic text on the walls. Tea snobs will appreciate the impressive menu of 140 black, green and white blends from all over the globe, and cakes on proper stands.

Bouchon Bakery

NEW *Third Floor, Time Warner Center, 10 Columbus Circle, at Broadway (1-212 823 9366). Subway: A, C, B, D, 1 to 59th Street-Columbus Circle.* **Open** 7am-7.30pm daily; closed Sun. **$. French. Map** p138 C5 ③④

Ring it on

Lincoln Center

In the world of opera, one central pillar of repertoire looms taller than all others: Richard Wagner's *Der Ring des Niebelungen*, a massive, four-performance cycle in which mythological gods, fearsome giants and star-crossed warriors alike fall prey to all-too-human passions and weaknesses. In New York, a stately, traditional production at the Metropolitan Opera has held the stage since its debut in 1987. But, in July 2007, the Lincoln Center Festival presents a new vision of the classic saga, created in 2003 for Russia's most revered troupe, the Kirov Opera of the Mariinsky Theatre in St Petersburg.

Two complete Ring Cycles – one of them on four consecutive evenings, as the composer intended – will be conducted by the Mariinsky Theatre's artistic and general director, Valery Gergiev. One of the world's foremost conductors, Gergiev has long maintained close ties with both the Lincoln Center Festival and the Metropolitan Opera, whose imposing house will host the visiting Kirov company. 'We have had a close relationship with Valery Gergiev since the beginning of the festival in 1996, and he was eager that this production be seen in New York City,' says Lincoln Center Festival director Nigel Redden. 'We worked closely with the Metropolitan Opera to make it happen.'

According to Redden, the designers of the Kirov *Ring* conceived their colourful, fantastically lit vision of Wagner's epic by drawing upon a wealth of ancient sources. 'It is a very contemporary *Ring*, which draws from many different aspects of world culture,' he explains. 'Gergiev and designer George Tsypin have drawn on ideas from Russian, Caucasian and especially Scythian folk mythology, but there are traces of voodoo and African elements, and a monumental pre-Christian European element. It is a radically different *Ring* from the Met's production, the only one seen in New York in recent years.'

The radical production has drawn mixed reviews from critics worldwide, but potential audiences have been less ambivalent: tickets for a Kirov Ring Cycle presented at the Wales Millennium Centre last winter sold out in four hours. Granted, the Metropolitan Opera House holds considerably more visitors; even so, planning ahead is mandatory.

■ www.lincolncenter.org

It has taken chef Thomas Keller, of Per Se, three years to open the New York outpost of his famous French bistro and boulangerie. The sleek 60-seat café on the third floor of the mall also has a chic take-away shop around the corner. The menu – served throughout the space whether you sit at the espresso/wine bar, the communal table or a marble four-top – includes savoury tartines, hearty soups, rustic pâtés, chocolate tarts and other affordable treats.

Dive 75
101 W 75th Street, at Columbus Avenue (1-212 362 7518). Subway: B, C, 1, 2, 3 to 72nd Street. **Open** 5pm-4am Mon-Fri; noon-4am Sat, Sun. **Bar.** **Map** p138 B3 35
This 'dive' attracts spruced-up West Siders with its living-room vibe and dedication to play. You'll find games on DirecTV-equipped sets and on your table: settle in for a round of Connect Four, Battleship or Yahtzee. Free chicken wings are served during Monday Night Football; on other nights, you can flip through the stack of order-in menus.

Good Enough to Eat
483 Amsterdam Avenue, between 83rd & 84th Streets (1-212 496-0163). Subway: 1 to 86th Street. **Open** 8am-10.30pm Mon-Thur; 8am-11pm Fri; 9am-11pm Sat; 9am-10.30pm Sun. **$.** **American.** **Map** p138 B3 36
Brunchers crowd Good Enough to Eat's farmhouse-style space for the fluffy eggs, fruit-packed apple pancakes and plump buttermilk biscuits with strawberry butter. Everything – even the chopped salad tossed with bacon and a pinch of sugar – is aimed at hearty appetites and served in grizzly-bear portions. If home cooking were really this good, we'd still be living there.

Gray's Papaya
2090 Broadway, at 71st Street (1-212 799 0243) Subway: 1, 2, 3 to 72nd Street. **Open** 24 hours. **$.** **American.** **Map** p138 B4 37

Many New Yorkers think that Gray's Papaya serves up the classic New York hot dog. The meat itself (all beef) boasts the ever-alluring combination of salty and sweet. Toppings are another matter – and debates rage on about how you should garnish your wiener – but you'll find mustard, sauerkraut, sautéed onions and ketchup on the counter.

La Rosita
2809 Broadway, between 108th & 109th Streets (1-212 663 7804). Subway: 1 to 110th Street-Cathedral Parkway. **Open** 7am-midnight daily. **$.** **Mexican.** **Map** p138 B5 38
Your voyage of discovery at this divey, bustling cuisine catch-all might include tasty *tostones rellenos* (fried green plantains stuffed with tomato-laced chicken stew) or fiery Mexican-style shrimp in tomato-chilli sauce.

Loft
NEW *505 Columbus Avenue, between 84th & 85th Streets (1-212 362 6440). Subway: B, C to 86th Street.* **Open** 6pm-midnight Sun-Thur; 6pm-4am Fri, Sat. **Bar.** **Map** p138 B2 39
At the sexy Moroccan-accented lounge and restaurant Loft, the addition of pungent spices makes for some profoundly unusual drinking. The Sirocco, a blast of bourbon and lime juice, gets its sweet and vicious snap from lavender-flower honey. And for its basil mojito, Loft boils down sugarcane.

Telepan
NEW *72 W 69th Street, at Columbus Avenue (1-212 580 4300). Subway: B, C to 72nd Street; 1 to 66th Street-Lincoln Center.* **Open** 5-11pm Mon, Tue; 11.30am-2.30pm, 5-11pm Wed, Thur; 11.30am-2.30pm, 5pm-midnight Fri; 11am-2.30pm, 5pm-midnight Sat; 11am-2.30pm, 5-10.30pm Sun. **$$$.** **American.** **Map** p138 B4 40
The place isn't fancy, but it does get things right. Diners can customise their $55 prix-fixe dinners by selecting three dishes from any three columns on the menu; they can ask for assistance and get smart feedback; and they can

count on fresh, Greenmarket-inspired fare featuring ingredients such as hen-of-the-woods mushrooms, brook trout and organic lamb.

Shopping

H&H Bagels

2239 Broadway, at 80th Street (1-212 595 8003). Subway: 1 to 79th Street. **Open** 24 hours daily. **Map** p138 B3 ④

For a taste of the real, old-fashioned (boiled and baked) thing, head straight to H&H, which lays claim to being the city's largest bagel purveyor.

Zabar's

2245 Broadway, at 80th Street (1-212 787 2000/www.zabars.com). Subway: 1 to 79th Street. **Open** 8am-7.30pm Mon-Fri; 8am-8pm Sat; 9am-6pm Sun. **Map** p138 B3 ④

Zabar's is more than just a food store – it's a New York landmark. You might leave the place feeling a little light in the wallet, but you can't beat the top-flight foods. Besides the famous smoked fish and rafts of Jewish delicacies, Zabar's has fabulous selections of bread, cheese and coffee – and an entire floor of well-priced gadgets and housewares.

Nightlife

Dizzy's Club Coca-Cola – Jazz at Lincoln Center

Broadway, at 60th Street (1-212 258 9595/www.jazzatlincolncenter.org). Subway: A, B, C, D, 1 to 59th Street-Columbus Circle. **Shows** at 7.30pm, 9.30pm. **Map** p138 C5 ④

Seductively lit, decorated with elegant photography and blessed with clear sight lines and a gorgeous view of 59th Street and Central Park South, Dizzy's Club Coca-Cola might be a Hollywood cinematographer's ideal vision of what a Manhattan jazz club ought to be. The swanky, intimate club – a regular hangout for some of the most outstanding players in the business – is a class act in all but its clunky, commercialised name.

Smoke

2751 Broadway, between 105th & 106th Streets (1-212 864 6662/ www.smokejazz.com). Subway: 1 to 103rd Street. **Shows** 9pm, 11pm, 12.30am Mon-Sat; 6pm Sun. **Map** p138 B5 ④

Not unlike a swanky living room, Smoke is a classy little joint that acts as a haven for local jazz legends and any touring artists looking to play in an intimate space. Early in the week, evenings are themed: on Sunday, it's Latin jazz; Tuesday, organ jazz. On weekends, internationally renowned jazzers (Hilton Ruiz, Tom Harrell, Eddie Henderson) hit the stage, relishing the opportunity to play informal gigs uptown.

Arts & leisure

Lincoln Center

Columbus Avenue, at 65th Street (1-212 546 2656/www.lincolncenter. org). Subway: 1 to 66th Street-Lincoln Center. **Map** p138 B5 ④

The listing above is the main entry point for Lincoln Center, although the venues that follow are spread out across the square of blocks from 62nd to 66th Streets, between Amsterdam and Columbus Avenues.

Built in the 1960s, this massive complex is the nexus of Manhattan's performing arts scene. Lincoln Center hosts lectures and symposia in the Rose Building, in addition to events in the main halls: Alice Tully Hall, Avery Fisher Hall, Metropolitan Opera House, New York State Theater, the Vivian Beaumont and Mitzi E Newhouse Theaters and the Walter Reade Theater.

Alice Tully Hall *1-212 875 5050.*
Home to the Chamber Music Society of Lincoln Center (1-212 875 5788, www. chambermusicsociety.org), Alice Tully Hall somehow manages to make its 1,096 seats feel cosy. It has no centre aisle, and the seating offers decent legroom. The venue's Art of the Song series ranks among Lincoln Center's most inviting offerings.

Avery Fisher Hall *1-212 875 5030.*
This handsome, comfortable 2,700-seat hall is the headquarters of the New York Philharmonic (1-212 875 5656, www.nyphilharmonic.org), the country's oldest symphony orchestra (founded in 1842) and one of its finest. The acoustics, which range from good to atrocious depending on who you ask, stand to be improved. Inexpensive, early evening 'rush hour' concerts and open rehearsals are presented on a regular basis.

Metropolitan Opera House *1-212 362 6000/www.metopera.org.*
The Met is the grandest of the Lincoln Center buildings, so it's a spectacular place to see and hear opera. It hosts the Metropolitan Opera from September to May, and major visiting companies during the summer. Opera's biggest stars (think Domingo, Fleming and Voigt) appear here regularly, and artistic director James Levine has turned the orchestra into a true symphonic force. Audiences are knowledgeable and fiercely partisan, with subscriptions remaining in families for generations. Still, the Met has become more inclusive; digital English-language subtitles, which appear on screens affixed to railings in front of each seat, are convenient for the novice and unobtrusive to their more seasoned neighbour. Tickets are expensive, and unless you can afford good seats, the view won't be great; standing-room-only tickets start at $15, and you'll have to queue on Saturday morning to buy them. At least you'll be able to see the eye-popping, gasp-inducing sets that remain the gold standard.

New York State Theater *1-212 870 5570.*
NYST houses the New York City Ballet (www.nycballet.com) as well as the New York City Opera (www.nycopera.com). The opera company has tried to overcome its second-best reputation by being both ambitious and defiantly populist. Rising young American singers often take their first bows at City Opera (many of them

eventually make the trek across the plaza to the Met), where casts and productions tend to be younger and sexier than those of its more patrician counterpart. Known for its fierce commitment to the unconventional – from modern American works and musical-theatre productions to intriguing Handel stagings and forgotten *bel canto* gems – City Opera is considerably cooler than its neighbour and about half the price. But truly splashy grand spectacle remains the province of the Met.

Walter Reade Theater
1-212 875 5600/www.filmlinc.com. No credit cards.
The Walter Reade Theater's acoustics are less than fabulous; still, the Chamber Music Society uses the space regularly, and the Great Performers series offers Sunday morning events fuelled by pastries and hot beverages sold in the lobby.

Merkin Concert Hall

Kaufman Center, 129 W 67th Street, between Broadway & Amsterdam Avenue (1-212 501 3330/www. kaufman-center.org). Subway: 1 to 66th Street-Lincoln Center. **Map** p138 B4 ⑯
Tucked away on a side street in the shadow of Lincoln Center, this unimposing gem of a concert hall offers a robust mix of early music and avant-garde programming, as well as an increasing amount of jazz, folk and some more eclectic fare. Here the New York Festival of Song has finally found a comfortable home, while regular performances sponsored by WNYC-FM afford opportunities for casual interaction with composers and performers.

Miller Theatre at Columbia University

Broadway, at 116th Street (1-212 854 7799/www.millertheatre.com). Subway: 1 to 116th Street-Columbia University. **Map** p138 B4 ⑰
Columbia's Miller Theatre has single-handedly made contemporary classical music sexy in New York. The credit belongs to executive director George

Steel, who proved that presenting challenging fare by composers such as Babbitt, Ferneyhough and Scelsi in a casual, unaffected setting could attract a young audience – and hang on to it. Miller's early-music offerings, many conducted by Steel, are also exemplary.

Symphony Space

2537 Broadway, at 95th Street (1-212 864 5400/www.symphonyspace.org). Subway: 1, 2, 3 to 96th Street. **Map** p138 B1 ㊽

Despite its name, Symphony Space provides programming that is anything but symphony-centric: recent seasons have featured saxophone quartets, Indian classical music and politically astute performances of Purcell's *Dido and Aeneas*. The annual Wall to Wall marathons serve up a full day of free music focusing on a particular composer, from Bach to Sondheim.

Harlem & beyond

Harlem is not just a destination on Manhattan island – it's the cultural capital of black America. West Harlem, between Fifth and St Nicholas Avenues, is the Harlem of popular imagination, and 125th Street is its lifeline. Harlem's historic districts continue to gentrify. The **Mount Morris Historic District** (from 119th to 124th Streets, between Malcolm X Boulevard (Lenox Avenue) & Mount Morris Park West) contains charming brownstones and a collection of religious buildings in a variety of architectural styles.

These days, new boutiques, restaurants and pavement cafés dot the walk down the double-wide **Malcolm X Boulevard** (Lenox Avenue). Another area with a historic past is **Strivers' Row**, also known as the St Nicholas Historic District. Running from 138th to 139th Streets, between Adam Clayton Powell Jr Boulevard (Seventh Avenue) and Frederick Douglass Boulevard (Eighth Avenue), these blocks of majestic houses were developed in 1891. East of Fifth Avenue is East

Harlem, sometimes called Spanish Harlem but better known to its primarily Puerto Rican residents as El Barrio.

At the northern tip of Manhattan in pretty Fort Tryon Park, you'll find the **Cloisters**, a museum built in 1938 incorporating segments of medieval cloisters shipped from Europe by the Rockefeller clan. It currently houses the Metropolitan Museum of Art's permanent medieval art collection, including the exquisite *Unicorn Tapestries*, woven around AD 1500.

Sights & museums

Abyssinian Baptist Church

132 W 138th Street, between Malcolm X Boulevard (Lenox Avenue) & Adam Clayton Powell Jr Boulevard (Seventh Avenue) (1-212 862 7474/www. abyssinian.org). Subway: 2, 3 to 135th Street. **Open** 9am-5pm Mon-Fri. **Admission** free. **Map** p138 C1 ㊾

The place where Harlem's controversial 1960s congressman Adam Clayton Powell Jr once preached is celebrated for its history, political activism and rousing gospel choir. A small museum is dedicated to Powell, the first black member of New York's City Council.

Cloisters

Fort Tryon Park, Fort Washington Avenue, at Margaret Corbin Plaza (1-212 923 3700/www.metmuseum. org). Subway: A to 190th Street, then M4 bus. **Open** *Mar-Oct* 9.30am-5.15pm Tue-Sun. *Nov-Feb* 9.30am-4.45pm Tue-Sun. **Admission** suggested donation (includes admission to the Metropolitan Museum of Art on the same day) $15; free-$10 reductions.

Set in a lovely park overlooking the Hudson River, the Cloisters houses the Met's medieval art and architecture collections. A path winds through the peaceful grounds to a castle that seems to have survived from the Middle Ages. (It was built a mere 70 years ago, using pieces from five medieval French cloisters.) Be sure to see the famous

Unicorn Tapestries, the 12th-century Fuentidueña Chapel and Robert Campin's *Annunciation Triptych*.

Hispanic Society of America

Audubon Terrace, Broadway, between 155th & 156th Streets (1-212 926 2234/www.hispanicsociety. org). Subway: 1 to 157th Street. **Open** 10am-4.30pm Tue-Sat; 1-4pm Sun. **Admission** free.

The Hispanic Society has the largest assemblage of Spanish art and manuscripts outside Spain. Look for two portraits by Goya and the lobby's bas-relief of Don Quixote. The collection is dominated by religious artefacts, but there are also decorative art objects and thousands of black-and-white photographs documenting Spanish and Latin-American life from the 19th century to the present.

Morris-Jumel Mansion

65 Jumel Terrace, between 160th & 162nd Streets (1-212 923 8008/www. morrisjumel.org). Subway: C to 163rd Street-Amsterdam Avenue. **Open** 10am-4pm Wed-Sun. **Admission** $4; free-$3 reductions. No credit cards.

Built in 1765, Manhattan's only surviving pre-Revolutionary manse was originally the heart of a 130-acre estate that stretched from river to river (on the grounds, a stone marker points south with the legend 'new york, 11 miles'). George Washington planned the battle of Harlem Heights here in 1776, after the British colonel Roger Morris moved out. The handsome 18th-century Palladian-style villa offers fantastic views.

Studio Museum in Harlem

144 W 125th Street, between Malcolm X Boulevard (Lenox Avenue) & Adam Clayton Powell Jr Boulevard (Seventh Avenue) (1-212 864 4500/www. studiomuseum.org). Subway: 2, 3 to 125th Street. **Open** noon-6pm Wed-Fri, Sun; 10am-6pm Sat. Guided tours by appointment. **Admission** suggested donation $7; free-$3 reductions. No credit cards. **Map** p138 C3 ㊿

Life in the fast lanes

'Four years ago my Aunt Gail and I were walking down the street and she asked me what I thought Harlem needed,' recalls Sharon Joseph. 'I remember saying, "We need a bowling alley" because my sister loves to bowl,' she adds with a laugh. Today, Joseph, a longtime Harlem resident, along with her aunt, Gail Richards, are the proud owners of Harlem Lanes – the neighbourhood's first bowling alley since the last one closed in the 1980s.

Located on the third and fourth floor of the historic Alhambra Ballroom, it houses 24 lanes, a sports bar, arcade games and a lounge. On a recent Saturday night the place was hopping.

'We want Harlem Lanes to be an epicentre for the community, a place where people can come together and enjoy themselves,' says Joseph. 'We're overwhelmed by the response of the community.

An 86-year-old woman came the other day and wanted to know why we didn't open it ten years ago.'

Owning a business in Harlem is not new territory for Richards, who opened one of the first $10 shops here, and the two women have watched the area's popularity grow: former president Bill Clinton keeps an office on 125th Street. But has Harlem's gentrification been a positive thing?

'Yes, it's great to see the ethnic and economic diversity,' says Joseph. 'There's concern about Harlem becoming pricey, but it's no different than the rest of the city in needing more affordable housing. People use the word 'gentrification', but I really think we're seeing another renaissance – for Harlem and for bowling too.' ■ Harlem Lanes, 2110-2118 Adam Clayton Powell Jr Boulevard, at 126th Street (1-212 678 2695/ www.harlemlanes.com).

When the Studio Museum opened in 1968, it was the first black fine arts museum in the country, and it remains the place to go for historical insight into African-American art and that of the African diaspora. Under the leadership of director Lowery Stokes Sims (formerly of the Met) and chief curator Thelma Golden (formerly of the Whitney), it has evolved into the city's most exciting showcase for contemporary African-American artists.

Eating & drinking

Amy Ruth's

113 W 116th Street, between Malcolm X Boulevard (Lenox Avenue) & Adam Clayton Powell Jr. Boulevard (Seventh Avenue) (1-212 280 8779). Subway: 2, 3 to 116th Street. **Open** 7.30am-11pm Sun-Thur; 24hrs Fri, Sat. **$**. **American Regional**. Map p138 C4 🟡

Some of the city's better Southern cooking. Fried chicken is nearly perfect: its crunchy, peppery coating holds up even when dipped in fresh honey (harvested from the restaurant's rooftop apiary) or paired with waffles and drenched in maple syrup.

Coogan's

4015 Broadway, at 169th Street (1-212 928 1234). Subway: A, C, 1 to 168th Street-Washington Heights. **Open** 11am-4am daily. **Bar**.

All types pop up at this uptown Irish bar. Tuesdays and Saturdays are dedicated to belting out bilingual karaoke (in Spanish and English).

Kitchenette Uptown

1272 Amsterdam Avenue, between 122nd & 123rd Streets (1-212 531 7600). Subway: 1 to 125th Street. **Open** 8am-11pm Mon-Fri; 9am-11pm Sat, Sun. **$**. **American**. Map p138 B3 🟡

Uptown emphasises the rich side of country fare, which is fine with local families and Columbia brainiacs. Fried chicken soaked in buttermilk and honey is plump and moist. Each main dish scores two sides, such as wilted greens and four-cheese macaroni.

New Leaf Café

Fort Tryon Park, 1 Margaret Corbin Drive (1-212 568 5323). Subway A to 190th Street; take elevator to Ft. Washington Avenue, then walk into Fort Tryon Park. **Open** 6-10pm Tue; noon-3pm, 6-10pm Wed-Sat; 11am-4pm, 5.30-9.30pm Sun. **$$**. **American**.

Whether you enjoy smoked trout and pear salad on the garden patio, or a Bloody Mary with brunch in the dining room of the 1930s stone building, you'll be surrounded by the park's natural beauty, and you'll be helping to conserve it. The views are more dazzling than the mildly adventurous food, but this is one case where everybody wins.

Soundz Lounge

3155 Broadway, between 123rd & 124th Streets (1-212 537 7660). Subway: 1 to 125th Street. **Open** 4pm-4am daily. **Bar**. Map p138 B3 🟡

During happy hour, this comfortable, cavelike hangout, just south of the elevated subway station at 125th Street, serves fresh watermelon martinis, sugary 'shotz' like the Bomb Diggity Bomb (blue curaçao, Myers's rum and pineapple juice) and 24 varieties of $3 pints. And, when it comes to those 'soundz', you'll hear 1980s, retro, neo-soul and reggae, depending on the night.

Shopping

Harlemade

174 Lenox Avenue, between 118th & 119th Streets (1-212 987 2500/www.harlemade.com). Subway 2, 3 to 116th Street. **Open** 11.30am-7.30pm Tue-Sat; noon-5pm Sun. Map p138 C4 🟡

Sells T-shirts with Afro- and Harlem-centric messages and images, along with postcards, books and other neighbourhood memorabilia.

Hue-Man Bookstore & Café

2319 Frederick Douglass Boulevard (Eighth Avenue), between 124th & 125th Streets (1-212 665 7400/www.huemanbookstore.com). Subway:

Apollo Theater

Nightlife

Apollo Theater

253 W 125th Street, between Adam Clayton Powell Jr Boulevard (Seventh Avenue) & Frederick Douglass Boulevard (Eighth Avenue) (1-212 531 5305/www.apollotheater.com). Subway: A, B, C, D, 1 to 125th Street. **Map** p138 C3 ⑰

Visitors might think they know Harlem's venerable Apollo from TV's *Showtime at the Apollo*, but as the saying goes, the small screen adds about ten pounds. Inside, the elegant yet lived-in theatre – still the city's home of R&B and soul music – is actually quite cosy. Known for launching the careers of Ella Fitzgerald, Michael Jackson and D'Angelo, to name just a few, the Apollo continues to bring in veteran talent while offering wannabe stars a legendary stage.

Lenox Lounge

288 Malcolm X Boulevard (Lenox Avenue), between 124th & 125th Streets (1-212 427 0253/www.lenox lounge.com). Subway: 2, 3 to 125th Street. **Open** noon-4am daily. **Map** p138 C3 ⑯

This classy art deco lounge in Harlem once hosted Billie Holiday and has been drawing stars since the late '30s. Saxist Patience Higgins's Sugar Hill Jazz Quartet jams on Monday nights.

Arts & leisure

Schomburg Center for Research in Black Culture

515 Malcolm X Boulevard (Lenox Avenue), at 135th Street (1-212 491 2200). Subway: 2, 3 to 135th Street. **Open** noon-8pm Tue, Wed; noon-6pm Thur, Fri; 10am-6pm Sat. **Admission** free. **Map** p138 C3 ⑲

An extraordinary trove of vintage literature and historical memorabilia relating to black culture and the African diaspora is housed in an institution founded in 1926 by its first curator, bibliophile Arturo Alfonso Schomburg. The centre also hosts jazz concerts, films, lectures and tours.

A, B, C, D to 125th Street. **Open** 10am-8pm Mon-Sat; 11am-7pm Sun. **Map** p138 C3 ⑮

The emphasis is on African-American work at this spacious Harlem bookstore and café. Hue-Man features frequent readings as well as in-store appearances by authors (Bill Clinton, whose office is nearby, held a signing of his memoir here) and other events.

N

NEW *114 W 116th Street, between Malcolm X Boulevard (Lenox Avenue) & Adam Clayton Powell Jr Boulevard (Seventh Avenue) (1-212 961 1036/ www.nharlemnewyork.com). Subway: 2, 3 to 116th Street; A, C, E to 116th Street.* **Open** 11.30am-8pm Tue-Thur; 11.30am-9pm Fri, Sat; noon-5pm Sun. **Map** p138 C4 ⑯

N aspires to pioneer upscale retail in Harlem just as the downtown fashion megastore did in the Meatpacking District. Owners Larry Ortiz, Nikoa Evans and Lenn Shebar provide their fellow neighbourhood locals with 4,000sq ft of elegant urban garb.

Brooklyn p163

The Outer Boroughs

Bronx

Bronx Zoo/Wildlife Conservation Society

Bronx River Parkway, at Fordham Road (1-718 367 1010/www.bronx zoo.org). Subway: 2, 5 to West Farms Sq-East Tremont Avenue. **Open** *Apr-Oct* 10am-5pm Mon-Fri; 10am-5.30pm Sat, Sun, holidays. *Nov-Mar* 10am-4.30pm daily. **Admission** Apr-Oct $12; $9 reductions. Nov-Mar $8; $6 reductions. Voluntary donation Wednesday. (Some rides and exhibitions extra.)

The elusive snow leopard wanders across the peaks of the Himalayan Highlands, and more than 30 species of Rodentia coexist in the Mouse House. Birds, giraffes, lions and reptiles abound in a zoo that is home to more than 4,500 creatures. For visitors who want a bird's-eye view, the 'Skyfari', an aerial tram ride over the zoo, is wonderful. Groundcrawlers can jump on the Zoo Shuttle, which provides rides (for a few dollars) through the zoo. Tiger Mountain is a three-acre permanent display devoted to Siberian tigers, the largest of the big cats. Highlights include an underwater viewing area, kiosks to educate visitors about tigers and conservation, as well as talks and demonstrations. The Butterfly Garden is a big hit with children, featuring more than 1,000 colourful butterflies fluttering about in an enclosed habitat.

New York Botanical Garden

Bronx River Parkway, at Fordham Road (1-718 817 8700/www.nybg. org). Travel: D, 4 to Bedford Park Boulevard, then Bx26 bus to Garden gate; or Metro-North (Harlem Line local) from Grand Central Terminal to Botanical Garden. **Open** *Apr-Oct*

Bronx Zoo p161

10am-6pm Tue-Sun, holidays. Nov-Mar 10am-5pm Tue-Sun. **Admission** $6; $1-$3 reductions; free Wednesday.
The basic $6 fee is for the grounds only; a $13 Garden Passport ($11 seniors and students, $5 children 2-12) includes admission to the Adventure Garden, the Haupt Conservatory and tram tours. If you're traveling from Manhattan, a Getaway ticket (available at Grand Central Terminal) buys you round-trip travel on Metro-North's Harlem train line and a Garden Passport. The winter holiday model train is super festive.

New York Yankees

Yankee Stadium, River Avenue, at 161st St, Bronx (1-718 293 6000/www.yankees.com). Subway: B, D, 4 to 161st St-Yankee Stadium. **Open** Box office 9am-5pm Mon-Sat; 10am-4pm Sun; and during games. **Tickets** $8-$95.
It's not, to the few impartial observers, America's most lovely stadium – huge, concrete and without fancy concessions – but, hell, it's home to the New York Yankees, baseball's most glamorous team.

Brooklyn

Brooklyn Botanic Garden

900 Washington Avenue, at Eastern Parkway, Prospect Heights (1-718 623 7200/www.bbg.org). Subway: B, Q, Franklin Avenue S to Prospect Park; 2, 3 to Eastern Parkway-Brooklyn Museum. **Open** *Apr-Sept* 8am-6pm Tue-Fri; 10am-6pm Sat, Sun. *Oct-Mar* 8am-4.30pm Tue-Fri; 10am-4.30pm Sat, Sun. **Admission** $5; $3 reductions; free Tue; free late Nov-Feb Tue-Fri.
Fifty-two acres of luscious greenery awaits you. During spring hightail it out here for the blooming of more than 220 cherry blossoms. The newly renovated Eastern Parkway entrance and the Osborne Garden – a three-acre Italian-style formal garden – are also worth a peek.

Brooklyn Museum

200 Eastern Parkway, at Washington Avenue, Prospect Heights, Brooklyn
(1-718 638 5000/www.brooklynmuseum.org). Subway: 2, 3 to Eastern Parkway-Brooklyn Museum. **Open** 10am-5pm Wed-Fri; 11am-6pm Sat, Sun. First Sat of the month (except Sept) 11am-11pm. **Admission** $8; free-$4 reductions; free 5-11pm 1st Sat of mth (except September).
Brooklyn's premier institution is a tranquil alternative to Manhattan's big-name exhibition spaces; it's rarely crowded. Among the museum's many assets is a rich, 4,000-piece Egyptian collection, which includes a gilded-ebony statue of Amenhotep III and, on a ceiling, a large-scale rendering of an ancient map of the cosmos. You can even view a mummy preserved in its original coffin.
Masterworks by Cézanne, Monet and Degas, part of an impressive European painting and sculpture collection, are displayed in the museum's skylighted beaux arts Court. On the fifth floor, American paintings and sculptures include native son Thomas Cole's *The Pic-Nic* and Louis Rémy Mignot's *Niagara*, a stunning vista of the falls. Don't miss the renowned Pacific Island and African galleries (this was the first American museum to display African objects as art).

Coney Island

1208 Surf Avenue, at W 12th Street, Coney Island (1-718 372 5159/www.coneyislandusa.com). Subway: D, F, N, Q to Coney Island-Stillwell Avenue. **Open** Call or visit website for schedule. **Admission** $5; $3 under-12s.
Coney Island is a summertime destination. After decades of decay, the weirdly wonderful community – known for its amusement park, beach and boardwalk – has made a comeback. If you're a thrill-seeker, take a spin on the Cyclone at Astroland Amusement Park; although a ride on the 80-year-old wooden roller coaster lasts less than two minutes, the first drop is nearly vertical and the cars clatter along the 2,640 feet of track at speeds of up to 60 miles per hour. A stroll along the boardwalk will take you to the New York Aquarium

Coney Island p163

(1-718 265 3474, www.nyaquarium.com) where a family of beluga whales is in residence. The oddball Sideshows by the Seashore are put on by Coney Island USA an organisation that keeps the torch burning for early 20th-century Coney life – you won't want to miss a minute of the show which includes legendary locals like contortionist Ravi, Bendable Boy, snake charmer Princess Ananka and the heavily tattooed Tyler Fyre, whose talents include sword swallowing.

Queens

Aqueduct Racetrack

110-00 Rockaway Boulevard, at 110th Street, Jamaica, Queens (1-718 641 4700/www.nyra.com/aqueduct). Subway: A to Aqueduct Racetrack. **Races** Thoroughbred Oct-May Wed-Sun. **Admission** Clubhouse $2; grandstand $1. Free early Jan-early March. **No credit cards.**
The Wood Memorial – a test run for promising three-year-old horses – is held here each spring. Betting is, of course, legal at all New York tracks.

New York Mets

Shea Stadium, 123-01 Roosevelt Avenue, at 126th Street, Flushing, Queens (1-718 507 8499/www. mets.com). Subway: 7 to Willets Point-Shea Stadium. **Open** Box office 9am-5.30pm Mon-Fri; 9am-2pm Sat, Sun. **Tickets** $5-$53.
The Mets are New York's 'other' baseball team, although in terms of on-field success they have been closing the gap slightly.

New York Hall of Science

47-01 111th Street, at 47th Avenue, Flushing Meadows-Corona Park, Queens (1-718 699 0005/www. nyscience.org). Subway: 7 to 111th Street. **Open** *July, Aug* 9.30am-5pm Mon-Fri; 10am-6pm Sat, Sun. *Sept-June* 9.30am-2pm Mon-Thur; 9.30am-5pm Fri; 10-6pm Sat, Sun. **Admission** $11; $8 reductions; free 2-5pm Fri, Sept-June. Science playground (Mar-Dec, weather permitting) $3 plus general admission).

The fun-for-all-ages New York Hall of Science, built for the 1964 World's Fair and recently expanded, demystifies its subject through colourful hands-on exhibits about biology, chemistry and physics, with topics such as 'The Realm of the Atom' and 'Marvelous Molecules.' Kids can burn off surplus energy – and perhaps learn a thing or two – in the 30,000sq ft outdoor science playground.

Noguchi Museum

9-01 33rd Road, between Vernon Boulevard & 10th Street, Long Island City, Queens (1-718 204 7088/ www.noguchi.org). Travel: N, W to Broadway, then take the Q104 bus to 11th St; or 7 to Vernon Boulevard-Jackson Avenue, then take the Q103 bus to 10th Street. **Open** 10am-5pm Wed-Fri; 11am-6pm Sat, Sun. **Admission** $5; $2.50 reductions. No credit cards.

In addition to his famous lamps, artist Isamu Noguchi (1904-88) designed stage sets for Martha Graham and George Balanchine, as well as large-scale sculptures of supreme simplicity and beauty. The museum is located in a 1920s-era factory in Queens; galleries surround a serene sculpture garden that was designed by Noguchi himself. The building, which was recently renovated to the tune of $13.5 million, now stays open year-round. Look for the second-floor galleries devoted to Noguchi's interior design, a new café and a shop. A shuttle service from Manhattan is available at weekends (call the museum or visit the website for more information).

US Open

USTA National Tennis Center, Flushing Meadows-Corona Park, Queens (1-866 673 6849/www. usopen.org). Subway: 7 to Willets Point-Shea Stadium. **Tickets** $22-$120. Tickets go on sale late in the spring for this grand-slam thriller, which the United States Tennis Association (USTA) says is the highest-attended annual sporting event in the world. Check the website for match schedules.

Coney Island's Astroland p163

PS 1 Contemporary Art Center

22-25 Jackson Avenue, at 46th Avenue, Long Island City, Queens (1-718 784 2084/www.ps1.org). Subway: E, V to 23rd St-Ely Avenue; G to 21st Street-Jackson Avenue; 7 to 45th Road-Court House Square. **Open** noon-6pm Mon, Thur-Sun. **Admission** suggested donation $5; $2 reductions.

Cutting-edge shows and an international studio programme make each visit to this freewheeling contemporary-art space a treasure hunt, with artwork turning up in every corner, from the stairwells to the basement. In a distinctive Romanesque-revival building that still bears some resemblance to the public school it once was, PS 1 mounts shows that appeal to adults and children. PS 1 became an affiliate of the Museum of Modern Art in 1999, but it has a wholly independent schedule of temporary exhibitions, along with a decidedly global outlook. Be sure to check out the summer Warm Up dance party series (see website for schedule).

NEW YORK BY AREA

Essentials

Hotels

First, the good news: tourism has surged since the post-9/11 slump. Now, here's the bad: city hotels have responded by hiking rates. As this guide went to press, the average nightly rate for a place to rest one's head in Manhattan was hovering around $225 – with no sign of relenting.

'Hotel room rates are expected to increase by ten per cent this year over last year,' says John Fox of PKF Consulting, a New York City-based hotel industry advisory firm. What's more, Manhattan's skyrocketing real estate market is making matters worse. Many hotel owners are simply opting to cash in on their valuable property by converting it into luxury condos (see box p180). Still, there is a lot of chatter of late about the 5,000 new hotel rooms that are expected to up

the overall inventory by 2007's end. But with so many conversions afoot, even this four-figure increase isn't expected to make much of an overall gain, notes Fox. 'However, we are anticipating an increase in mid-priced hotel rooms,' he says.

So, what's a budget-minded traveller to do? We hate to say it, but we're not entirely sure. Even the recently opened Hotel QT (p178), which has been offering rooms at the low price of $125 a night, told us that those days are over – its lowest rate is now $175 – and you may need to book five months in advance even for that.

Money matters

The best way to begin your hotel search is to choose the price range and neighbourhood that interest you. Make sure to include New

York's 13.625 per cent room tax and a $2 to $6 per-night occupancy tax when planning your travel budget. Be warned that many smaller hotels adhere to a strict three-night minimum booking policy.

Pre-booking blocks of rooms allows reservation companies to offer reduced rates. The following agencies are free of charge: **Hotel Reservations Network**, (1-214 369 1264, 1-800 246 8357, www.hotels.com); **Quikbook**, 3rd Floor, 381 Park Avenue South, New York, NY 10016 (1-212 779 7666, 1-800 789 9887, www.quikbook.com).

If you can afford to splash out, you've come to the right town. There are so many stylish hotels opening, it's hard to keep up. The most recent among them is Night Hotel (p179), where the chic interiors are strictly black and white. Also, look for actor Robert De Niro's Downtown Hotel in Tribeca, which is sure to generate plenty of buzz when it finally opens later this year.

Downtown

Abingdon Guest House

13 Eighth Avenue, between Jane & W 12th Streets (1-212 243 5384/www.abingdonguesthouse.com). Subway: A, C, E to 14th Street; L to Eighth Avenue. **$$**.

This charm-saturated guest house is a good option if you want to be near the Meatpacking District but can't afford the Gansevoort. The nine-room townhouse offers European ambience for a reasonable price. The popular Brewbar Coffee doubles as a check-in desk and café, and you can sip your latte in the trellised garden (if you're lucky enough to get the garden room).

Bowery's Whitehouse Hotel of New York

340 Bowery, between 2nd & 3rd Streets (1-212 477 5623/www.whitehousehotelofny.com). Subway:

SHORTLIST

Best new
- Night Hotel (p179)
- Hotel QT (p178)
- Hotel on Rivington (p171)

Best for hipsters
- Chelsea Hotel (p170)
- Hotel 17 (p171)

Glossy mag favourites
- Hotel Gansevoort (p171)
- 60 Thompson (p173)

Most stellar restaurants
- Mercer (p172)
- Four Seasons Hotel (p177)

Best hotel bars
- Dream Hotel (p177)
- Maritime Hotel (p172)
- SoHo Grand Hotel (p173)

Best super-cheap
- Jazz on the Park Hostel (p181)
- Central Park Hostel (p181)
- East Village Bed & Coffee (p171)
- Chelsea Star Hotel (p170)

Cheap for the location
- Gershwin Hotel (p177)
- Hotel Beacon (p181)
- Hotel Pennsylvania (p178)
- Hudson (p179)

Best old New York
- The Waldorf-Astoria (p179)
- The Pierre (p181)
- The Algonquin (p176)
- Washington Square Hotel (p175)

Cosy comfort
- Inn on 23rd Street (p172)
- Abingdon Guest House (p169)

Best for theatre buffs
- 414 Hotel (p177)
- Big Apple Hostel (p176)
- Broadway Inn (p176)
- Hotel Edison (p177)

Chelsea Hotel

B, D, F, V to Broadway-Lafayette Street; 6 to Bleecker Street .$.

Although the Bowery progressively looks more sleek than seedy, with pricey restaurants and flashy clubs popping up in recent years, the unapologetically second-rate Whitehouse Hotel remains steadfastly basic. The no-frills hostel offers semi-private cubicles (ceilings are an open latticework, so be warned that snorers or sleep talkers may interrupt your slumber) at unbelievably low rates. Towels and linens are provided.

Chelsea Hotel

222 W 23rd Street, between Seventh & Eighth Avenues (1-212 243 3700/ www.hotelchelsea.com). Subway: C, E, 1 to 23rd Street. **$$**.

Built in 1884, the Chelsea has a long (and infamous) past: Nancy Spungen was murdered in Room 100 by her boyfriend, Sex Pistol Sid Vicious. This funky hotel has seen an endless parade of noteworthy guests: in 1912, *Titanic* survivors stayed here, and celebrated former residents include Mark Twain, Thomas Wolfe and Madonna. Rooms are generally large with high ceilings, but some of the amenities – such as

flatscreen TVs, washer-dryers and marble fireplaces – vary. The lobby doubles as an art gallery.

Chelsea Lodge

318 W 20th Street, between Eighth & Ninth Avenues (1-212 243 4499/ www.chelsealodge.com). Subway: C, E to 23rd Street. **$$**.

If Martha Stewart decorated a log cabin, it would look not unlike this 22-room inn, housed in a landmark brownstone. All rooms have new beds, televisions, showers and air-conditioners. Although most are fairly small, the rooms are so aggressively charming that reservations fill up quickly.

Chelsea Star Hotel

300 W 30th Street, at Eighth Avenue (1-212 244 7827/1-877 827 6969/ www.starhotelny.com). Subway: A, C, E to 34th Street-Penn Station. **$**.

To keep costs down, opt for one of the 16 themed rooms – but be warned, they're on the small side and lavatories are shared. Ultra-cheap, shared hostel-style dorm rooms are also available. A recent renovation more than doubled the hotel's size – there are now 18

ESSENTIALS

superior rooms and deluxe suites with custom mahogany furnishings, flatscreen TVs and private baths.

Cosmopolitan

95 West Broadway, at Chambers Street (1-212 566 1900/1-888 895 9400 /www.cosmohotel.com). Subway: A, C, 1, 2, 3 to Chambers Street. **$$**.
Despite the name, you won't find any trendy pink cocktails at this well-maintained hotel (or indeed even a bar to drink them in). That's because the Cosmopolitan is geared towards budget travellers with little need for luxury. Open continuously since the 1850s, it remains a tourist favourite for its Tribeca address and affordable rates. Mini-lofts – multilevel rooms with sleeping lofts – start at $119.

East Village Bed & Coffee

110 Avenue C, between 7th & 8th Streets (1-212 533 4175/www.bed andcoffee.com). Subway: F, V to Lower East Side-Second Avenue; L to First Avenue. **$**.
Popular with European travellers, this unassuming East Village B&B (minus the full breakfast as the name makes clear) is a great place in which to immerse yourself in downtown culture without dropping the cash. The nine guest rooms come with eclectic furnishings and quirky themes. Shared areas include three separate loft-like living rooms, bathrooms and fully equipped kitchens.

Hotel Gansevoort

18 Ninth Avenue, at 13th Street (1-212 206 6700/1-877 726 7386/ www.hotelgansevoort.com). Subway: A, C, E to 14th Street; L to Eighth Avenue. **$$$$**.
It's hard to miss this soaring, 14-floor contemporary structure set against the cobblestone streets and warehouse storefronts of the Meatpacking District. Opened in early 2004, this full-service luxury hotel gets strong marks for style. The private roof garden features a glassed-in heated pool complete with underwater music and 360-degree

Inn on 23rd Street p172

views of the city. The latest addition to the hotel is the G Spa & Lounge (see box p175).

Hotel on Rivington

NEW *107 Rivington Street, between Essex & Ludlow Streets (1-212 475 2600/www.hotelonrivington.com). Subway: F to Delancey Street; J, M, Z to Delancey-Essex Streets.* **$$$**.
Hotel on Rivington has a high cool factor. Floor-to-ceiling windows are a theme throughout: the second-floor lobby overlooks Rivington Street, and every room has an unobstructed city view. Super-hip restaurant Thor (p78) recently opened here.

Hotel 17

225 E 17th Street, between Second & Third Avenues (1-212 475 2845/ www.hotel17ny.com). Subway: L to Third Avenue; N, Q, R, W, 4, 5, 6 to 14th Street-Union Square. **$-$$**.
Equivalent to a good dive bar, Hotel 17 has a grungy cachet that draws you in. Except for a recent sprucing up of the lobby, the place remains a little rough and funky. The hotel has been used for numerous films shoots. Labyrinthine

ESSENTIALS

Maritime Hotel

corridors lead to tiny high-ceilinged rooms filled with discarded dressers and mismatched 1950s wallpaper. Expect to share the hallway bathroom with other guests.

Inn on 23rd Street

131 W 23rd Street, between Sixth & Seventh Avenues (1-212 463 0330/ www.innon23rd.com). Subway: A, C, E to 14th Street; L to Eighth Avenue. $$$.

This real-deal B&B in the heart of Chelsea gives you a warm and fuzzy feeling from the moment you enter. Owners and innkeepers Annette and Barry Fisherman renovated a 19th-century townhouse into this homey hostelry with 14 themed rooms (all accessible by elevator and each with its own private bathroom).

Maritime Hotel

363 W 16th Street, between Eighth & Ninth Avenues (1-212 242 4300/ www.themaritimehotel.com). Subway: A, C, E to 14th Street; L to Eighth Avenue. $$$.

In 2002 this nautical-themed building was spun into the high-gloss Maritime Hotel; the decor blends the look of a luxury yacht with a chic 1960s airport lounge. Modelled after ship cabins, each room features one large porthole window and lots of glossy teak panelling. The hotel offers four food and drink spaces: Matsuri, a gorgeous Japanese restaurant; La Bottega, an Italian trattoria with a lantern-festooned patio; Cabana, an airy rooftop bar; and Hiro, a basement lounge that draws a buzzing crowd.

Mercer

147 Mercer Street, at Prince Street (1-212 966 6060/1-888 918 6060/ www.mercerhotel.com). Subway: N, R, W to Prince Street. $$$$.

Almost a decade on, Soho's first luxury boutique hotel is still a notch above nearby competitors. Rooms are large by New York standards and feature furniture by Christian Liagre, spacious washrooms with tubs for two and Face Stockholm products. The lobby, with oversized white sofas and book-lined shelves, acts as a bar, library and lounge – open exclusively to guests. The restaurant, Mercer Kitchen, serves Jean-Georges Vongerichten's stylish version of casual American cuisine.

Pioneer of SoHotel

341 Broome Street, between Elizabeth Street & Bowery (1-212 226 1482/ www.sohotel-ny.com). Subway: 6 to Spring Street; J, M, Z to Bowery. **$$**.
Newly renovated, the Pioneer lives up to its name: it's the only hotel in Nolita, known for its boutiques and cafés. Rooms are small and basic, but have decorative paintings and hardwood floors; most have private baths. Larger rooms have charming stucco walls and vaulted ceilings. Complimentary morning coffee is served in the lobby.

St Marks Hotel

2 St Marks Place, at Third Avenue (1-212 674 0100/www.stmarkshotel.qpg.com). Subway: 6 to Astor Place. **$$**.
Positioned among all the tattoo parlours and piercing shops of St Mark's Place, this small hotel is unexpectedly bright, clean and understated. The basic rooms have double beds with their own private baths. St Mark's biggest asset is its location – it's perfectly situated for immersing yourself in the East Village's historic punk-rock culture and new-found restaurant scene. Note that the hotel is in a pre-war walk-up building (no elevators).

60 Thompson

60 Thompson Street, between Broome & Spring Streets (1-212 431 0400/1-877 431 0400/www.60thompson.com). Subway: C, E to Spring Street. **$$$$**.
Don't be surprised if you have to walk through a fashion shoot when you enter this stylish hotel – it's a favoured location for fashionistas. A60, the exclusive guests-only rooftop bar, offers commanding city views. The modern rooms are dotted with pampering details like pure down duvets and pillows, and a 'shag bag' filled with fun items to get you in the mood. The highly acclaimed restaurant Kittichai serves creative Thai cuisine beside a pool filled with floating orchids.

SoHo Grand Hotel

310 West Broadway, between Canal & Grand Streets (1-212 965 3000/ 1-800 965 3000/www.sohogrand.com). Subway: A, C, E, 1 to Canal Street. **$$$**.
Regarded by many as Soho's living room, the Grand makes good use of industrial materials such as poured concrete, cast iron and bottle glass. Built in 1996, Soho's first high-end hotel features Bill Sofield-designed

60 Thompson

ESSENTIALS

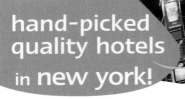

rooms in a restrained palette of greys and beiges, and sport photos from local galleries. Sip cocktails in the Grand Bar and Lounge, or dine on haute macaroni and cheese in the Gallery.

Wall Street District Hotel

15 Gold Street, at Platt Street (1-212 232 7700/www.wallstreetdistricthotel. com). Subway: A, C to Broadway-Nassau Street; J, M, Z, 2, 3, 4, 5 to Fulton Street. $$$.
This small, tech-savvy hotel might be the best value for business travellers, fusing comfort with amenities like automated check-in kiosks. The hotel's San Marino Ristorante, serves casual Italian cuisine.

Wall Street Inn

9 South William Street, at Broad Street (1-212 747 1500/www.thewallstreet inn.com). Subway: 2, 3 to Wall Street; 4, 5 to Bowling Green. $$.
The area surrounding this boutique hotel in the financial district has seen a reincarnation in recent years, sprouting new pâtisseries, bars and restaurants along its cobblestone streets. To lure travellers beyond financiers, the hotel offers hefty discounts at weekends. There's no restaurant or room service, but breakfast is included.

Washington Square Hotel

103 Waverly Place, between MacDougal Street & Sixth Avenue (1-212 777 9515/1-800 222 0418/www.washington squarehotel.com). Subway: A, B, C, D, E, F, V to W 4th Street. $$.
Bob Dylan and Joan Baez both lived here back when they sang for change in nearby Washington Square Park. Today the century-old hotel remains popular with travellers aiming to soak up Village life. Recently, the deluxe rooms were expanded into larger chambers decked out with art deco furnishings and leather headboards. Rates include a complimentary continental breakfast – or you can splurge on the Sunday jazz brunch at North Square (1-212 254 1200), the hotel's restaurant.

Inn-dulge

Check in, and check out these recently opened hotel spas.

The only spot in New York where a boozer can undo the damage where the damage was done, **G Spa & Lounge** at Hotel Gansevoort (p171) is an inviting subterranean refuge by day that converts into a slick bar at night. The full-service salon features hydrotherapy and customised massage but, come 10pm, the venue undergoes a Jekyll and Hyde transformation: the three treatment rooms morph into nocturnal VIP lounges and the juice bar becomes a scenesters' watering hole.

Massages and facials at Deepak Chopra's wellness sanctuary, **Chopra Center & Spa** at Dream Hotel (p177), are as much about healing as pampering. Unwind at daily yoga and meditation classes or at one of the frequent health seminars. Looking for good old-fashioned coddling? The light, detoxifying abhyanga massage will have you soaked from head to toe in fragrant oil.

When Manhattan spa darling Bliss teamed up with the wildly successful W Hotels empire, the duo began a process of 'blissintegration' – flooding guest rooms with Bliss products. **Bliss49** (W Hotel, 541 Lexington Avenue at 49th Street) is the spa's largest endeavour to date: a 23,000-square-foot full-service retreat on the fourth floor. Here you can indulge in the trademark oxygen facials and rubdowns such as the 'rubber neck' and 'super blissage'.

ESSENTIALS

Time Out Shortlist | **New York 2007** **175**

The Algonquin

59 W 44th Street between Fifth & Sixth Avenues (1-212-840-6800/1-800-555-8000/www.thealgonquin.net). Subway: B, D, F, V to 42nd Street-Bryant Park; 7 to Fifth Avenue. **$$$**.

This landmark hotel with a strong literary past (greats like Alexander Woollcott and Dorothy Parker gathered in the infamous Round Table Room to gossip) is beautifully appointed with upholstered chairs, old lamps and large paintings of important figures of the Jazz Age. In 2004 the entire hotel underwent renovations but it retains its character; hallways are covered with *New Yorker*-cartoon wallpaper to commemorate Harold Ross, who secured funding for the magazine over long meetings at the Round Table. Quarters are on the small side and the decor is a bit dated, but the feel is still classic New York. Catch readings by local authors on some Mondays; cabaret performers take over in the Oak Room from Tuesday to Saturday.

Americana Inn

69 W 38th Street, at Sixth Avenue (1-212 840 6700/www.newyorkhotel.com). Subway: B, D, F, N, Q, R, V, W to 34th Street-Herald Square; B, D, F, V to 42nd Street. **$$**.

This budget hotel, situated close to Times Square, has a speakeasy feel: the signage is very discreet, and you'll have to ring the doorbell to enter through the second-floor lobby. What the Americana might lack in ambience (with its linoleum floors and fluorescent lighting), it makes up for in location (a rhinestone's throw from the major Broadway shows) and reasonable prices (rooms start at just under $100). Although all bathrooms are shared, rooms come with a mini-sink and large walk-in closets.

Big Apple Hostel

119 W 45th Street, between Sixth & Seventh Avenues (1-212 302 2603/www.bigapplehostel.com). Subway: B, D,

F, V to 42nd Street; N, Q, R, S, W, 1, 2, 3, 7 to Times Square-42nd Street. **$**.

This basic hostel is lacking in frills, but the rooms are spotless and as cheap as they come. The Big Apple puts you just steps from the Theater District and the bright lights of Times Square. Beware if you're travelling in August: dorm rooms have no air-conditioning.

Broadway Inn

264 W 46th Street, at Eighth Avenue (1-212 997 9200/1-800 826 6300/www.broadwayinn.com). Subway: A, C, E to 42nd Street-Port Authority. **$$**.

Theatre junkies should take note: this endearing little hotel can arrange a 35 to 40% discount on tickets; it also offers several Broadway dinner-and-show combinations. The warm lobby has exposed-brick walls, ceiling fans and shelves that are loaded with bedtime reading material. The fairly priced basic guest rooms and suites get lots of natural light. On the downside, there are no elevators, and the hotel is strict about its three-night-minimum policy on weekends and holidays.

Carlton Arms Hotel

160 E 25th Street, at Third Avenue (1-212 679 0680/www.carltonarms.com). Subway: 6 to 23rd Street. **$**.

A bohemian hotel boasting themed spaces (check out the 'English cottage' room). Discounts are offered for students, overseas guests and patrons on weekly stays. Most guests share baths; tack on an extra $15 for a private lavatory. Rooms are usually booked early, so reserve in advance.

Casablanca Hotel

147 W 43rd Street, between Sixth Avenue & Broadway (1-212 869 1212/1-800 922 7225/www.casablancahotel.com). Subway: B, D, F, V to 42nd Street-Bryant Park; N, Q, R, W, 42nd Street S, 1, 2, 3, 9, 7 to 42nd Street-Times Square. **$$**.

This 48-room boutique hotel has a cheerful Moroccan theme. The lobby is an oasis in the middle of Times Square: walls are adorned with blue and gold Mediterranean tiles, and giant bamboo shoots stand in tall vases. The theme is diluted in the basic rooms, but wicker furniture, wooden shutters and new carpets and sofas warm up the space.

Dream Hotel

210 W 55th Street, between Broadway & Seventh Avenue (1-212 247 2000/ 1-866 437 3266/www.dreamny.com). Subway: N, Q, R, W to 57th Street. **$$$**.

In 2004 hotelier Vikram Chatwal enlisted boldfaced names to turn the old Majestic Hotel into a luxury lodge with a trippy slumberland theme. David Rockwell dressed up the restaurant, an outpost of Serafina; Deepak Chopra conceived the ayurvedic spa. The lobby sums up the resulting aesthetic – walls are cloaked in Paul Smith-style stripes and a crystal boat dangles from the ceiling. Rooms are more streamlined, with white walls, satin headboards and an ethereal blue backlight that glows under the bed. Rooftop bar Ava has panoramic views.

414 Hotel

414 W 46th Street, between Ninth & Tenth Avenues (1-212 399 0006/ www.414hotel.com). Subway: A, C, E to 42nd Street-Port Authority. **$$**.

This small hotel's shockingly affordable rates and reclusive location (tucked away on the Theater District's Restaurant Row) make it feel like a secret you've been lucky to stumble upon. Immaculate rooms are tastefully appointed with suede headboards, vases full of colourful roses and framed black-and-white photos of the city. There's a glowing fireplace and computer available to guests in the lobby, and a leafy courtyard outside.

Four Seasons Hotel

57 E 57th Street, between Madison & Park Avenues (1-212 758 5700/ 1-800 332 3442/www.fourseasons. com). Subway: N, R, W to Lexington Avenue-59th Street; 4, 5, 6 to 59th Street. **$$$$**.

New York's quintessential hotel hasn't slipped a notch from its heyday. Everybody who's anybody – from music-industry executives to political figures – continues to drop in for a dose of New York luxury. Renowned architect IM Pei's sharp geometric design (in neutral cream and honey tones) is sleek and modern, and rooms are among the largest in the city. The hotel is known for catering to a guest's every need; your 4am hot-fudge sundae is only a room-service call away.

Gershwin Hotel

7 E 27th Street, between Fifth & Madison Avenues (1-212 545 8000/www.gershwinhotel.com). Subway: N, R, W, 6 to 28th Street. **$**.

Rates are extremely reasonable for a location just off Fifth Avenue. All rooms received a facelift in 2005, which brought in new chairs and upholstery. If you can afford a suite, book the Lindfors, which has screen-printed walls and a sitting room. Just off the lobby, but unaffiliated, is Gallery at the Gershwin, a bar and lounge with glowing countertops and mod Lucite orbs.

Hotel Chandler

12 E 31st Street, between Fifth & Madison Avenues (1-212 889 6363/ www.hotelchandler.com). Subway: 6 to 33rd Street. **$$$**.

Rooms at this delightful hotel are style-conscious, with checked carpeting, black-and-white photographs of New York streetscapes on the walls, and Frette robes and Aveda products in the bathroom. The in-house 12:31 bar offers cocktails and light nibbles.

Hotel Edison

228 W 47th Street, at Broadway (1-212 840 5000/1-800 637 7070/ www.edisonhotelnyc.com). Subway: N, R, W to 49th Street; 1 to 50th Street. **$$**.

Theatre lovers flock to this newly renovated art deco hotel for its affordable rates and convenient location. Rooms are standard sized, but decidedly spruced up. Café Edison, a classic diner just off the lobby, is a long-time favourite of Broadway actors and their fans – Neil Simon was so smitten that he put it in one of his plays.

ESSENTIALS

Hotel QT

Hotel 41

*206 W 41st Street, between Seventh
& Eighth Avenues (1-212 703 8600/
www.hotel41.com). Subway: N, Q, R,
W, 42nd Street S, 1, 2, 3, 7 to 42nd
Street-Times Square.* **$$**.
Although its looks are cool, this tiny
boutique hotel feels comfy-warm: read-
ing lamps extend from the dark-wood
headboards, and triple-paned windows
effectively filter out the cacophony
from the streets below. The penthouse
suite has a large private terrace with
potted trees and views of Times
Square. Bar 41 serves breakfast, lunch
and dinner.

Hotel Metro

*45 W 35th Street, between Fifth
& Sixth Avenues (1-212 947 2500/
1-800 356 3870/www.hotelmetro
nyc.com). Subway: B, D, F, N, Q,
R, V, W to 34th Street-Herald
Square.* **$$**.
It may not be not posh, but the Metro
offers its guests good service and a
retro vibe. Black-and-white portraits
of Hollywood legends adorn the
lobby, and the tiny rooms are clean.
You can take in views of the Empire
State Building from the rooftop bar of
the Metro Grill.

Hotel Pennsylvania

*401 Seventh Avenue, between 32nd
& 33rd Streets (1-212 736 5000/
1-800 223 8585/www.hotelpenn.com).
Subway: A, C, E, 1, 2, 3 to 34th Street-
Penn Station.* **$$**.
The Pennsylvania is one of the city's
largest hotels. Its reasonable rates and
convenient location (directly opposite
Madison Square Garden and Penn
Station) make it a popular choice with
tourists. Rooms are fairly basic but
pleasant. Jazz fans take note: the hotel's
Café Rouge Ballroom once hosted such
greats as Duke Ellington and the Glenn
Miller Orchestra.

Hotel QT

NEW *125 West 45th Street, between
Sixth & Seventh Avenues (1-212 354
2323/www.hotelqt.com). Subway: N, Q,
R, W, 42nd Street S, 1, 2, 3, 7 to 42nd
Street-Times Square.* **$$**.
Celebrity hotelier André Balazs has
taken a stab at a youth hostel – well,
one that's kitted out with Egyptian
cotton sheets, flatscreen TVs and a
lobby pool with underwater music.
This stylish new hotel, with rooms for
under $200 a night, is the last thing
you'd expect to find in the middle of
Times Square. That and the trippy

corridors, which get smaller as you get to your room. Rooms are also likely to be narrow, but with furnishings well adapted to the space.

Hotel Thirty Thirty

30 E 30th Street, between Madison Avenue & Park Avenue South (1-212 689 1900/1-800 497 6028/www. thirtythirty-nyc.com). Subway: 6 to 28th Street. **$$**.
Ambient music sets the tone in the spare, fashionable, block-long lobby. Rooms are small but sleek and complemented by clean lines and textured fabrics. Executive-floor rooms are slightly larger, with nifty workspaces and slate bathrooms. The hotel's restaurant, Zanna, serves Mediterranean fare.

Hudson

356 W 58th Street, between Eighth & Ninth Avenues (1-212 554 6000/www. hudsonhotel.com). Subway: A, B, C, D, 1 to 59th Street-Columbus Circle. **$$**.
Outside of its teeny bedrooms the Hudson has lots to offer. A lush courtyard is shaded with enormous potted trees, a rooftop terrace overlooks the Hudson River, and a glass-ceilinged lobby with imported English ivy is crawling with beautiful people.

Murray Hill Inn

143 E 30th Street, between Lexington & Third Avenues (1-212 683 6900/ 1-888 996 6376/www.nyinns.com). Subway: 6 to 28th Street. **$**.
A recent renovation added hardwood floors and new bathrooms – most of which are private – to this affordable inn. Discounted weekly and monthly rates are available. It's advisable to book well in advance.

Night Hotel

NEW *132 W 45th Street, between Sixth & Seventh Avenues (1-212 835 9600) Subway: N, Q, R, W, 42nd Street S, 1, 2, 3, 7 to 42nd Street-Times Square.* **$$$**.
At Midtown's Night Hotel, the new 72-room boutique property from Vikram Chatwal (of Dream and Time fame), out-of-town guests will see the city through the romantic lens

of 21st-century 'gothic Gotham'. The hotel's stylish black-and-white motif extends beyond the loungey lobby to the handsome rooms.

Park South Hotel

122 E 28th Street, between Park Avenue South & Lexington Avenue (1-212 448 0888/1-800 315 4642/ www.parksouthhotel.com). Subway: 6 to 28th Street. **$$$**.
Everything about this quaint boutique hotel says 'I love New York'. The mezzanine library is crammed with books on historic Gotham, and the walls are covered with images from the New York Historical Society. Rooms are appointed in warm amber and brown tones, and some have dazzling views of the Chrysler Building. The hotel's bar-restaurant, Black Duck (1-212 204 5240), serves live jazz with brunch.

Pickwick Arms

230 E 51st Street, between Second & Third Avenues (1-212 355 0300/1-800 742 5945/www.pickwickarms.com). Subway: E, V to Lexington Avenue-53rd Street; 6 to 51st Street. **$**.
Rooms at this no-frills hotel are clean and bright, and many have baths. (Some share an adjoining facility; otherwise, the lavatories are down the hall.) There are two on-site restaurants and a rooftop garden.

Roosevelt Hotel

45 E 45th Street, at Madison Avenue (1-212 661 9600/1-888 833 3969/ www.theroosevelthotel.com). Subway: 42nd Street S, 4, 5, 6, 7 to 42nd Street-Grand Central. **$$**.
Several films have been shot here, including *Wall Street*, *The French Connection* and *Maid in Manhattan*. Built in 1924, the enormous hotel was once a haven for celebs and socialites, and a certain nostalgic grandeur lives on in the lobby.

The Waldorf-Astoria

301 Park Avenue at 50th Street (1-212 355 3000/1-800 924 3673/ www.waldorf.com). Subway: E, V to Lexington Avenue-53rd Street; 6 to 51st Street. **$$$**.

Plaza sweet

An apartment at the Plaza

It has a reputation as one of the world's best-loved grand hotels, but the struggling Plaza is turning most of its rooms into luxury condominiums. Slated for completion in spring 2007, the $350 million renovation will see the iconic French Renaissance-style building, on Central Park South at 57th Street, converted into 182 luxury residences, costing from $2-$32 million, and 282 hotel rooms – plus posh retail outlets and upscale restaurants.

'The Plaza is an elite landmark and we're building on that legacy,' says Miki Naftali, president of Elad Properties, the hotel's new owner. 'We're making extraordinary apartments and the great public spaces will be thoughtfully restored.' In fact, eight of those public spaces – including the Oak Room, Palm Court and Grand Ballroom – are so great they've been designated as landmarks. Features such as the Palm Court's stained-glass ceiling are being recreated in the neo-classical style that architect Henry Hardenburgh

intended (the original was painted over in the 1940s). 'When the conversion was announced there was a huge public outcry, so we stepped in,' says Robert Tierney, chairman of the Landmarks Preservation Commission.

The Plaza certainly has star qualities. Since it opened in 1907, it has featured in books (*The Great Gatsby, Eloise*) and movies (*North by Northwest, The Way We Were*) and hosted swank society events (such as Truman Capote's Black and White Ball in 1966). Besides providing city pieds-à-terre to such diverse personalities as Alfred Hitchcock and Frank Lloyd Wright, it's hosted thousands of events for ordinary families looking to celebrate in grand style. Perhaps that's why the recent auction of fixtures and furniture raked in $1.8 million (more than double the original valuation) as sentimental guests scrambled for souvenirs. 'The Plaza resonates in so many people's memories,' Tierney says. 'It's everyone's romantic dream of New York City.'

First built in 1893, the Waldorf-Astoria was the city's largest hotel, but it was demolished to make way for the Empire State Building. The current art deco Waldorf opened in 1931 and has protected status as a historic hotel. It still caters to the high and mighty (guests have included Princess Grace, Sophia Loren and many US presidents). Check your attire before entering – you won't be allowed in if you're wearing a baseball cap, T-shirt or ripped jeans.

W New York-Times Square

1567 Broadway, at 47th Street (1-212 930 7400/1-877 976 8357/www. whotels.com). Subway: N, R, W to 49th Street; 1 to 50th Street. **$$$**.
NYC's fifth and flashiest W has a street-level vestibule with a waterfall (reception is on the seventh floor). To your right, the Living Room is a massive sprawl of white leather seating. Every private room features a floating-glass desk and a sleek bathroom stocked with Bliss spa products, but it's the bed-to-ceiling headboard mirror and sexy room-service menu that get the mind racing. Steve Hanson's Blue Fin (p116) serves stellar sushi and cocktails. The second hotel bar, Living Room Bar, is on the seventh floor.

Uptown

Central Park Hostel

19 W 103rd Street, at Central Park West (1-212 678 0491/www.central parkhostel.com). Subway: B, C to 103rd Street. **$**.
Housed in a recently renovated brownstone, this tidy hostel offers dorm-style rooms that sleep four, six or eight people; private chambers with two beds are also available. All baths are shared.

Hostelling International New York

891 Amsterdam Avenue, at 103rd Street (1-212 932 2300/www.hinew york.org). Subway: 1 to 103rd Street. **$**.
This budget lodging is NYC's only real hostel (ie, non-profit accommodation belonging to the International Youth Hostel Federation). It's also one of the most architecturally stunning – the Gothic-inspired building spans a city block. The immaculate rooms are spare but air-conditioned. There is a shared kitchen and a large backyard.

Hotel Beacon

2130 Broadway, between 74th and 75th Streets (1-212 787 1100/1-800 572 4969/www.beaconhotel.com). Subway: 1, 2, 3 to 72nd Street. **$$**.
The Hotel Beacon offers good value in a desirable residential neighbourhood just a short walk from Central and Riverside Parks. Rooms are clean and spacious and include marble baths.

Hotel Belleclaire

250 W 77th Street, at Broadway (1-212 362 7700/www.hotelbelleclaire. com). Subway: 1 to 79th Street. **$$**.
Housed in a landmark building near Lincoln Center and Central Park, the sleek Belleclaire is a steal for savvy budget travellers. Rooms feature goose-down comforters, sleek padded headboards and mod lighting fixtures.

Jazz on the Park Hostel

36 W 106th Street, between Central Park West & Manhattan Avenue (1-212 932 1600/www.jazzhostel.com). Subway: B, C to 103rd Street. **$**.
Jazz on the Park might be the trendiest hostel in the city – the lounge is outfitted like a space-age techno club and sports a piano and pool table. Make sure to double-check your room type and check-in date before you arrive.

The Pierre

2 E 61st Street at Fifth Avenue (1-212 838 8000/1-800 743 7734/www.four seasons.com/pierre). Subway: N, R, W to Fifth Avenue-59th Street. **$$$$$**.
A landmark of New York glamour, the Pierre marked its 75th birthday in 2005. A black-and-white chequered pavement leads up to the gleaming gold lobby. Front rooms overlook Central Park, and wares from fancy neighbouring stores are on display in the lobby. There are three restaurants, including the opulent Café Pierre.

Getting Around

Arriving & leaving

By air

For a list of transport services between New York City and its major airports, call 1-800 247 7433. Public transport is the cheapest method, but it can be both frustrating and time-consuming. None of the airports is particularly close or convenient. Private bus or van services (a selection is listed below) are usually the best bargains. Medallion (city-licensed) yellow cabs, which can be flagged on the street or picked up at designated locations at airports, are more expensive but take you all the way to your destination for a fixed, zoned price, with any tolls on top. (Not so in reverse.)

New York Airport Service *1-212 875 8200/www.nyairport service.com*
Olympia Trails *1-212 964 6233/ 1-877 894 9155/www.olympiabus.com*
SuperShuttle *1-212 209 7000/www.supershuttle.com*

Airports

Three major airports service the New York City area, plus the smaller MacArthur airport on Long Island, served by domestic flights only.

John F Kennedy International Airport

1-718 244 4444/www.panynj.gov
At $2, the bus and subway link from JFK is dirt cheap but it can take up to two hours to get to Manhattan. At the airport, look for the yellow shuttle bus to the Howard Beach station (free), then take the A train to Manhattan. Thankfully, JFK's AirTrain now offers faster service between all eight airport terminals

and the A, E, J and Z subway lines, as well as the Long Island Rail Road, for $5. Visit www.airtrainjfk.com for more information. Private bus and van services are a good compromise between value and convenience (see above). A medallion yellow cab from JFK to Manhattan will charge a flat $45 fare, plus toll (varies by route, but usually $4) and tip (if service is fine, give at least $5). Although metered (not a flat fee), the fare to JFK from Manhattan will be about the same cost. Check out www.nyc.gov/taxi for the latest cab rates.

La Guardia Airport

1-718 533 300/www.panynj.gov.
Seasoned New Yorkers take the M60 bus ($2), which runs between the airport and 106th Street at Broadway. The ride takes 40 minutes to an hour (depending on traffic) and runs from 4.30am to 1.30am daily. The route crosses Manhattan at 125th Street in Harlem. Get off at Lexington Avenue for the 4, 5 and 6 trains; at Malcolm X Boulevard (Lenox Avenue) for the 2 and 3; or at St Nicholas Avenue for the A, B, C and D trains. You can also disembark on Broadway at 116th or 110th Street for the 1 and 9 trains. Less time-consuming options: private bus services cost around $14; taxis and car services charge about $25, plus toll and tip.

Newark Liberty International Airport

1-973 961 6000/www.newark airport.com
Although it's in next-door New Jersey, Newark has good public transport links to NYC. The best bet is a 40-minute, $11.55 trip by the New Jersey Transit to or from Penn Station. The airport's monorail, AirTrain Newark (www.airtrain newark.com), is now linked to the NJ Transit and Amtrak train systems.

For inexpensive buses, see the bus services below. A car service will run about $40 and a taxi around $45, plus toll and tip.

By bus

Buses are an inexpensive means of getting to and from New York City, though the ride takes longer and is sometimes uncomfortable. Buses are particularly useful if you want to leave in a hurry; many don't require reservations. Most out-of-town buses come and go from the Port Authority Bus Terminal.

Port Authority Bus Terminal
625 Eighth Avenue, between 40th & 42nd Streets (1-212 564 8484/ www.panynj.gov). Subway: A, C, E to 42nd Street-Port Authority.
This somewhat unlovely terminus is the hub for many transportation companies offering commuter and long-distance bus services to and from New York City. If you have an early departure, bring your own breakfast, as the concessions don't open until around 7am. As with any transport terminal, watch out for petty criminals, especially late at night.

Long-distance bus lines

Greyhound Trailways
1-800 229 9424/www.greyhound.com
Greyhound offers long-distance bus travel to destinations across North America.

New Jersey Transit
1-973 762 5100/1-800 772 2222/ www.njtransit.com
NJT provides bus service to nearly everywhere in the Garden State and some destinations in New York State; most buses run around the clock.

Peter Pan
1-800 343 9999/www.peterpanbus.com
Peter Pan runs extensive service to cities across the North-east; its tickets are also valid on Greyhound.

By car

If you drive to the city, you may encounter delays at bridge and tunnel crossings (it's a good idea to check www.nyc.gov and www.panynj.gov before driving in). Tune your car radio to WINS (1010 on the AM dial) for up-to-the-minute traffic reports. Delays can last anywhere from 15 minutes to two hours – plenty of time to get your money out for the toll ($4 is average). It makes sense, of course, to time your arrival and departure against the commuter flow. For parking garages, see p185.

By train

America's national rail service is run by Amtrak. Nationwide routes are slow, infrequent and unreliable (if characterful), but there are some good fast services linking the eastern seaboard cities. For information about commuter rail services serving New York and New Jersey, see p184.

Grand Central Terminal
From 42nd to 44th Streets, between Vanderbilt & Lexington Avenues. Subway: 42nd Street S, 4, 5, 6, 7 to 42nd Street-Grand Central.
Grand Central is home to Metro North, which runs trains to more than 100 stations throughout New York State and Connecticut. Schedules are available at the terminal. As well as one of New York's loveliest buildings, it's a big retail centre with some excellent eating and drinking venues, including the famous Oyster Bar.

Penn Station
31st to 33rd Streets, between Seventh & Eighth Avenues. Subway: A, C, E, 1, 2, 3 to 34th Street-Penn Station.
Amtrak, Long Island Rail Road and New Jersey Transit trains depart from this terminal, which has printed schedules available.

In the city

Manhattan is divided into three major sections: Downtown, which includes all neighbourhoods south of 14th Street; Midtown, roughly the area between 14th and 59th Streets; and Uptown, north of 59th Street. Generally, avenues run north-south along the length of Manhattan. They are parallel to one another and are logically numbered, with a few exceptions, such as Broadway, Columbus and Lexington Avenues. Manhattan's centre is Fifth Avenue, so all buildings located east of it will have 'East' addresses, with numbers getting higher towards the East River, and those west of it will have 'West' numbers that get higher towards the Hudson River. Streets are also parallel to one another, but they run east to west, or crosstown, and are numbered, from 1st Street up to 220th Street.

The neighbourhoods of lower Manhattan – including the Financial District, Tribeca, Chinatown and Greenwich Village – were settled prior to urban planning and can be confusing to walk through. Their charming lack of logic makes frequent reference to a map essential.

Public transport

Metropolitan Transportation Authority (MTA)

Travel info 1-718 330 1234/updates 1-718 243 7777/www.mta.info
The MTA runs the subway and bus lines, as well as a number of alternative commuter services to points outside Manhattan. You can get news of service interruptions and download the most current MTA maps from the website. Schedule changes can occur at the last minute, so look out for posters in stations.

City buses

These are white and blue and display a digital destination sign on the front, along with a route number preceded by a letter (M for Manhattan). The $2 fare is payable with a **MetroCard** (*see below*) or exact change (coins only; no pennies).

Subway

The fare is $2 per ride. Trains run around the clock, but with sparse service and fewer riders at night, it's advisable (and usually quicker) to take a cab after 10pm.

To enter the subway system, you need a **MetroCard** (it also works on buses), which you can buy from a booth inside the station entrance or from one of the brightly coloured MetroCard vending machines, which accept cash, debit and credit cards and can usually give change when available. Free transfers between buses and subways are available only with a MetroCard.

Trains are identified by letters or numbers and are colour-coded according to the line on which they run. Stations are most often named after the street on which they're located. Entrances are marked with a green globe (open 24 hours) or a red globe (limited hours). Many stations have separate entrances for the Uptown and Downtown platforms – look before you pay. Local trains stop at every station on the line; express trains make major-station stops only.

Train services

The following commuter services ply NY's hinterland.

Long Island Rail Road

1-718 217 5477/www.lirr.org
LIRR provides rail service from Penn Station, Brooklyn and Queens.

Metro-North

1-212 532 4900/1-800 638 7646/
www.mnr.org
Commuter trains service towns north
of Manhattan and leave from Grand
Central Terminal.

New Jersey Transit

1-973 762 5100/1-800 772 2222/
www.njtransit.com
Service from Penn Station reaches
most of New Jersey, some points in
New York State and Philadelphia.

PATH Trains

1 800 234 7284/www.pathrail.com.
PATH (Port Authority Trans-Hudson)
trains run from six stations in
Manhattan to various places across
the Hudson River in New Jersey,
including Hoboken, Jersey City and
Newark. The system is automated,
and entry costs $1.50; you need
change or crisp bills for the ticket
machines. Trains run 24 hours a day.
Manhattan PATH stations are marked
on the subway map (see back flap).

Taxis & car services

Taxis carry up to four people for
the same price: $2.50 plus 40¢ per
fifth of a mile, with an extra 50¢
charge from 8pm to 6am and a
$1 surcharge during rush hour
(weekdays from 4 to 8pm). The
average fare for a three-mile ride
is $9-$11, depending on the time of
day and on traffic (the meter adds
another 20¢ per minute while the
car is idling). Below is a selection
of call-out car services.
Carmel *1-212 666 6666*
Dial 7 *1-212 777 7777*
Tri-State Limousine *1-212 777
7171/1-212 410 7600*

Car rental

Avis *US: 1-800 230 4898/www.
avis.com; UK: 0870 606 0100/
www.avis.co.uk*
Budget *US: 1-800 527 0700/
www.budget.com; UK: 0870 153 170/
www.budget.co.uk*

Enterprise *US: 1-800 261 7331/
www.enterprise.com; UK: 0870 350
3000/www.enterprise.com/uk*
Hertz *US: 1-800 654 3131/www.
hertz.com; UK: 0870 844 8844/
www.hertz.co.uk*
National *US: 1-800 227 7368;
UK: 0116 217 3884. Both:
www.nationalcar.com*
Thrifty *US: 1-800 847 4389/
www.thrifty.com; UK: 01494
51600/www.thrifty.co.uk*

Parking

Parking on the street is problematic
and car theft not unheard of.
Garages are plentiful but
expensive. If you want to park for
less than $15 a day, try a garage
outside Manhattan and take public
transport into the city. Listed below
are Manhattan's better deals. For
other options, see the *Yellow Pages*.

Central Kinney System

www.centralparking.com. **Open** 24hrs
daily, most locations.
One of the city's largest parking
companies, Kinney is accessible and
reliable, though not the cheapest in
town. Rates vary, so call for prices.

GMC Park Plaza

1-212 888 7400. **Open** 24hrs daily,
most locations.
GMC has more than 70 locations in
the city. At $23 overnight, including
tax, the one at 407 E 61st Street,
between First and York Avenues
(1-212 838 4158), is the cheapest.

Icon Parking

1-877 727 5464/www.iconparking.com.
Open 24hrs daily, most locations.
Choose from more than 160 locations
via the website to guarantee a spot
and price ahead of time.

Mayor Parking

*Pier 40, West Street, at W Houston
Street (1-800 494 7007).* **Open**
24hrs daily.
Mayor Parking, another large chain,
offers indoor and outdoor parking.
Call for details of other locations.

ESSENTIALS

Resources A-Z

Accident & emergency

For ambulance, fire brigade or police in the event of a serious emergency, dial **911**. The hospitals listed below have 24-hour Accident & Emergency departments.

Cabrini Medical Center

227 E 19th Street, between Second & Third Avenues (1-212 995 6000). Subway: L to Third Avenue; N, Q, R, W, 4, 5, 6 to 14th Street-Union Square.

Mount Sinai Hospital

Madison Avenue, at 100th Street (1-212 241 7171). Subway: 6 to 103rd Street.

New York – Presbyterian Hospital/Weill Cornell Medical Center

525 E 68th Street, at York Avenue (1-212 746 5454). Subway: 6 to 68th Street.

St Luke's – Roosevelt Hospital

1000 Tenth Avenue, at 59th Street (1-212 523 6800). Subway: A, B, C, D, 1 to 59th Street-Columbus Circle.

St Vincent's Hospital

153 W 11th Street, at Seventh Avenue (1-212 604 7998). Subway: F, V, 1, 2, 3 to 14th Street; L to Sixth Avenue.

Age restrictions

In NYC, you must be 18 to buy tobacco products and 21 to buy or to be served alcohol. Some bars and clubs admit patrons between 18 and 21, but you will be ejected if you're caught drinking alcohol in the venue. Always carry photo ID as even those who are well over 21 can be asked to show proof of age and identity.

Credit card loss

American Express
1-800 528 2122

Diners Club
1-800 234 6377

Discover
1-800 347 2683

MasterCard/Maestro
1-800 826 2181

Visa/Cirrus
1-800 336 8472

Customs

For allowances, see US Customs (www.customs.gov).

Disabled travellers

New York can be challenging for a disabled visitor. *Access for All* is a useful guide to the city's cultural institutions published by Hospital Audiences Inc (1-212 575 7660, www.hospaud.org). The database is also on its website.

All Broadway theatres are equipped with devices for the hearing-impaired; call **Sound Associates** (1-212 582 7678, 1-888 772 7686) for more information. There are a number of other stage-related resources for the disabled. **Telecharge** (1-212 239 6200) reserves tickets for wheelchair seating in Broadway and Off Broadway venues, while Theatre Development Fund's **Theatre Access Project** (1-212 221 1103, www.tdf.org) arranges sign-language interpretation and captioning in American Sign Language for Broadway and Off Broadway shows.

Electricity

The US uses 110-120V, 60-cycle
alternating current rather than
the 220-240V, 50-cycle AC used
in Europe and elsewhere. The
transformers that power or
recharge many newer electronic
devices such as laptop computers
are designed to handle either
current and may need nothing more
than an adaptor for the wall outlet.

Embassies & consulates

Check the phone book for a full list.

Australia
1-212 351 6500

Canada
1-212 596 1628

Great Britain
1-212 745 0200

Ireland
1-212 319 2555

New Zealand
1-212 832 4038

Insurance

If you are not an American citizen,
it is advisable to take out
comprehensive insurance before
you travel, as insurance for
foreigners is almost impossible
to arrange once you are in the
US. Make sure your insurance
includes adequate health coverage
as medical costs are high.

Internet

Cyber Café
*250 W 49th Street, between Broadway
& Eighth Avenue (1-212 333 4109).
Subway: C, E, 1, 9 to 50th Street;
N, R, W to 49th Street.* **Open** 8am-
11pm Mon-Fri; 11am-11pm Sat, Sun.
Cost $6.40 per half hour; 50¢ per
printed page.
This is a standard internet-access
café that also happens to serve great
coffee and snacks.

FedEx Kinko's
1-800 463 3339/www.kinkos.com
Outposts of this ubiquitous and very
efficient computer and copy centre can
be found throughout the city.

NYCWireless
www.nycwireless.net
This group has established 113 nodes
in the city for free wireless access.
(For example, most parks below 59th
Street are covered.) Visit the website
for more information.

Starbucks
www.starbucks.com
Many branches offer wireless access
through T-Mobile (10¢ per minute).

Money

All denominations except for the
$1 bill have recently been updated
by the US Treasury. One dollar ($)
equals 100 cents (¢). Coins include
copper pennies (1¢) and silver-
coloured nickels (5¢), dimes (10¢)
and quarters (25¢). Half-dollar
coins (50¢) and the gold-coloured
dollar coins are less commonly
seen, except as change from
vending machines. All paper
money is the same size. It comes
in denominations of $1, $2, $5,
$10, $20, $50 and $100.

ATMs

Automated teller machines (ATMs)
are located throughout the city in
bank branches, delis and many
small shops. Most accept American
Express, MasterCard, Visa and
major bank cards, if they have
been registered with a personal
identification number (PIN).
Commonly, there is a usage fee
of between $1.50 and $2.

ESSENTIALS

Banks & currency exchange

Banks are generally open from 9am to 3pm Monday to Friday; some stay open later and on Saturdays. Many banks will not exchange foreign currency, and the bureaux de change, limited to tourist-trap areas, close between 6pm and 7pm.

People's Foreign Exchange

3rd Floor, 575 Fifth Avenue, at 47th Street (1-212 883 0550). Subway: E, V to Fifth Avenue-53rd Street; 7 to Fifth Avenue. **Open** *9am-6pm Mon-Fri; 10am-3pm Sat, Sun.*

Travelex

29 Broadway, at Morris Street (1-212 363 6206). Subway: 4, 5 to Bowling Green. **Open** *9am-5pm Mon-Fri.*

Travellers' cheques

Travellers' cheques are routinely accepted at stores and restaurants. You will usually need to show a photo ID such as your driver's licence or passport. If cheques are lost or stolen, contact:

American Express
1-800 221 7282

Thomas Cook
1-800 223 7373

Visa
1-800 336 8472

Pharmacies

Be aware that pharmacies will not repeat foreign prescriptions.

Duane Reade

224 W 57th Street, at Broadway (1-212 541 9708/www.duanereade. com). Subway: N, Q, R, W to 57th Street. **Open** *24hrs daily.*
This chain operates all over the city, and some stores are open 24 hours. Check website for additional branches.

Post

For a complete list of NYC post offices visit www.usps.com.

General Post Office

421 Eighth Avenue, between 31st & 33rd Streets (24-hour information 1-800 275 8777/www.usps.com). Subway: A, C, E to 34th Street-Penn Station. **Open** *24hrs daily.*

Smoking

New Yorkers live under some of the strictest anti-smoking laws on the planet. The 1995 NYC Smoke-Free Air Act makes it illegal to smoke in virtually all indoor public places, including the subway and cinemas. Recent legislation went even further, banning smoking in nearly all restaurants and bars; for a list of exceptions, see p17.

Tax & tipping

In restaurants, it is customary to tip at least 15 per cent, and since NYC tax is 8.625 per cent, a quick method for calculating the tip is to double the tax. In many restaurants, when you are with a group of six or more, the tip will be included in the bill. In taxis, tipping ten per cent is typical.

Telephones

Dialling & codes

■ As a rule, you must dial 1 + the area code before a number, even if the place you are calling in is the same area code. The area codes for Manhattan are 212 and 646; Brooklyn, Queens, Staten Island and the Bronx are 718 and 347; 917 is reserved mostly for mobile phones and pagers.
■ Numbers preceded by 800, 877 and 888 are free of charge when dialled from anywhere in the US.

■ For international calls, dial 011 + country code (Australia 61; New Zealand 64; UK 44) and the number.

Directory assistance

Dial 411 or 1 + area code + 555 1212. For a directory of toll-free numbers, dial 1-800 555 1212.

Operator services

To reverse the charges (make a collect call) or pay by credit card, dial 0 followed by the number, or dial AT&T's 1-800 225 5288, MCI's 1-800 265 5328 or Sprint's 1-800 663 3463.

Public phones

Payphones take any combination of silver coins: local calls usually cost 25¢ for three minutes; a few require 50¢ but allow unlimited time on the call. The best way to make long-distance calls is with a phonecard, available from post offices, delis and newspaper kiosks.

Tickets

With the exception of the major cultural institutions, which have in-house box offices, most venues subcontract their ticket sales out to agencies. To find out which one, see the venue's website. Between them, **Ticketmaster** (1-212 307 4100, www.ticketmaster.com) and **Ticket Central** (1-212 279 4200, www.ticketcentral.org) represent most venues, for a fee (to you).

Time

New York is on Eastern Standard Time, which extends from the Atlantic coast to the eastern shore of Lake Michigan and south to the Gulf of Mexico. This is five hours behind Greenwich Mean Time. In 2007, clocks are set forward one

hour on 11 March for Daylight Saving Time and back one hour on 4 November. Going from east to west, Eastern Time is one hour ahead of Central Time, two hours ahead of Mountain Time and three hours ahead of Pacific Time.

Tourist information

NYC & Company

810 Seventh Avenue, between 52nd & 53rd Streets (1-800 NYC VISIT/ www.nycvisit.com). Subway: B, D, E to Seventh Avenue. **Open** 8.30am-6pm Mon-Fri; 9am-5pm Sat, Sun.
This is the city's official visitors' and information centre.

Visas

Some 27 countries participate in the **Visa Waiver Program** (VWP). Citizens of Andorra, Australia, Austria, Belgium, Brunei, Denmark, Finland, France, Germany, Iceland, Ireland, Italy, Japan, Liechtenstein, Luxembourg, Monaco, the Netherlands, New Zealand, Norway, Portugal, San Marino, Singapore, Slovenia, Spain, Sweden, Switzerland and the UK do not need a visa for stays in the US shorter than 90 days as long as they have a machine-readable passport valid for the full 90-day period and a return ticket. If you do not qualify for entry under the VWP, you will need a visa; check before travelling.

What's on

Several free listings magazines are distributed around town, but the weekly *Time Out New York* ($2.99), which hits newsstands on Wednesdays and contains listings for Thursday to Wednesday, is the essential arts and entertainment guide. For gay listings, look out for *HX* magazine in venues.

ESSENTIALS

Index

ESSENTIALS

Index

ESSENTIALS

THE BROOKLYN TOURISM & VISITORS CENTER

Historic Brooklyn Borough Hall, Ground Floor
209 Joralemon St. (btw Court/Adams), Brooklyn, NY 11201
Tel: (718) 802-3846
Subway: M R 2 3 4 5 A C F
Open Monday-Friday 10am-6pm
Visit our Gift Shop for authentic Brooklyn apparel,
books, postcards, and other souvenirs

www.visitbrooklyn.org

Brooklyn Tourism is an initiative of
Borough President Marty Markowitz
& Best of Brooklyn, Inc.
All profits to
Best of Brooklyn, Inc., a 501(c)(3)